ONE DRY SEASON

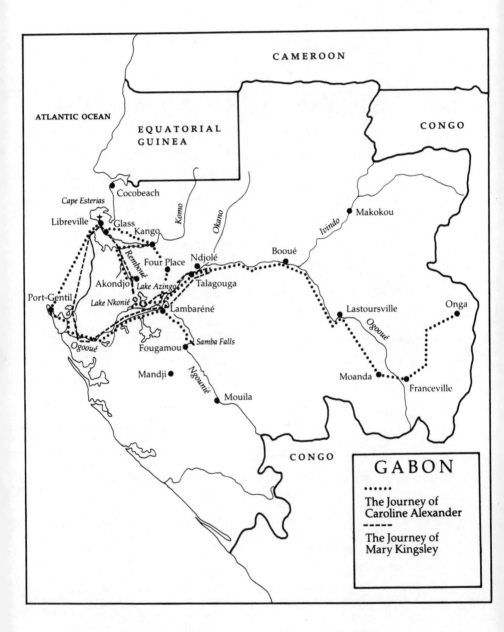

CAMEROON

ATLANTIC OCEAN

EQUATORIAL
GUINEA

CONGO

Cape Esterias

Cocobeach

Libreville

Komo

Okano

Makokou

Glass

Kango

Ivindo

Four Place

Ndjolé

Booué

Remboué

Akondjo

Lake Azingo

Talagouga

Lake Nkonié

Port-Gentil

Lambaréné

Lastoursville

Onga

Ogooué

Ogooué

Fougamou

Samba Falls

Mandji

Ngounié

Moanda

Mouila

Franceville

CONGO

GABON

••••••
The Journey of
Caroline Alexander

The Journey of
Mary Kingsley

ONE
DRY
SEASON

In the Footsteps of Mary Kingsley

CAROLINE ALEXANDER

ALFRED A. KNOPF NEW YORK 1990

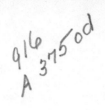

916
A 375 od

IN MEMORIAM

Eric Mitchell

What were your wares that they sold out so quickly?
—AKAN TRADITIONAL DIRGE

"What are you going to call your book?" one of the little boys in the village asked me.

I had not even thought of this, but realized that I needed to come up with a title quickly if I expected to be taken the least bit seriously. "I shall call it *One Dry Season,*" I replied, saying the first thing that came into my head.

The little boy nodded. "That is good," he said gravely. "You are writing a book about our country, but you have only been here one dry season."

CONTENTS

ONE DRY SEASON

LIBREVILLE

I FIRST HEARD of Gabon when I was camping near the North Rukuru river, which flows in the foothills of the Nyika Plateau, in central southeast Africa. The camp had been made by my two friends Pete, who was a geologist, and Spaña, who was an archaeologist. The tents and thatched shelters stood at the top of a low hill that sloped down to a narrow river, where birds swooped and dove among the rushes.

"This is nothing—nothing," said Pete. "You should have seen some of my other camps." They were both old hands, but I was new to Africa.

Pete's job, as far as I could make out, was to establish cozy, self-contained camps in the most remote and beautiful places in the world, under pretext of mapping the area. His present assignment was nearing its end, and he and Spaña were discussing where he might next be stationed.

"There's a possibility of Gabon," said Spaña, adding, "that would be lovely." I had never heard of the country.

"Gabon? It's in West Africa, right on the equator. It's nearly all forest, and still quite wild. And yet very French along the coast—lots of cafés in Libreville." And I had wondered if the camp in Gabon would be on one of those legendary sites, which so surpassed the present setting.

In fact, Pete was next sent to Nottingham. When, much later, I reminded them of this conversation, I found that they had all but forgotten it; but I had remembered.

More than eighty percent jungle; its interior drained by the great Ogooué river; its population of under one million divided into forty different tribes, each with its own culture and language; gorillas, elephants, the rare bongo; the Fang people, who practice cannibalism; charted by one of the greatest of African explorers, Count de Brazza—over the years, from time to time, from one place and another, I garnered a haphazard collection of facts, a collection made without any conviction that Gabon was a place to which I would ever really go.

On a cold December evening, some years later, when I was roaming the top floor of my local library, I came upon a weighty book entitled *Travels in West Africa.* Leafing through the biographical introduction, my interest was at once aroused on learning that in the summer of 1893, the author, Mary Henrietta Kingsley, had "decided to spend her respite from domesticity in West Africa, a region notorious for its deadly climate and diseases, its alarming wildlife, and its cannibals." Turning to the frontispiece map, which indicated the route of Miss Kingsley's travels, I was startled to see names I recognized—Libreville, the Ogowé river— and I realized that Miss Kingsley's travels had been in Gabon.

Following the map, I traced Miss Kingsley's route: a neat dashed line indicated her purposeful path southward along the coast from the capital city, Libreville, to the entrance of the Ogowé (as the Ogooué was then spelled). From here, the line leisurely followed the river's course some distance into the interior, where, at a point above a place called Njole, its path was barred by a slash across the river, indicating rapids. The arrows and dashes then made an abrupt about-face back down the Ogowé as far as Lambaréné, where instead of following the main river channel, they diverged into a northern artery and then abruptly left the river altogether and continued overland. At this point something seemed to have gone terribly awry, for a question mark appeared beside the dashes and arrows, and the broken line seemed to falter as it threaded its way past unspecified lakes northward to the Rembwé river, which it reached at a place marked "Agonjo." From this point, the line made more confident progress, zipping downstream to the river mouth and continuing triumphantly across the Gaboon estuary to Glass, situated on the coast only a few miles south of its starting point, at Libreville.

Turning to the text, I discovered that while the opening chapters of the *Travels* briefly characterized Miss Kingsley's ports of call along the West African coast—at Sierra Leone, the Gold Coast, the Spanish island of Fernando Po, and Calabar—and the concluding chapters described her exploits in Cameroon, the bulk of the book's nearly seven hundred pages was concerned with her extensive travels in what was then the Gaboon territory of the French Congo, by her own account the "wildest and most dangerous part of the West African regions."

Transfixed by my discovery, I settled down among the stacks to investigate the book on the spot and found that it contained an odd mixture of personal travel narrative, history, and hefty doses of African religion and customs. But the greatest revelation was the style in which the book was written, of which selected examples can give but a mere taste. Describing her arrival in Libreville, for example, Miss Kingsley relates how French customs officials demanded that she pay fifteen shillings for a license for her pistol. "This seems a heavy sum," she muses, "so I ask . . . what I may be allowed to shoot if I pay this? . . . May I daily shoot governors, heads of departments, and *sous officiers?*"

Or the following conversation at Lambaréné: "I availed myself of the offer of a gentleman to paddle me back in his canoe. He introduced himself as Samuel, and volunteered the statement that he was 'a very good man.' . . . Mrs. Samuel was a powerful, pretty lady, and a conscientious and continuous paddler. Mr. S. was none of these things, but an ex-Bible reader, with an amazing knowledge of English, which he spoke in a quaint, falsetto, far-away sort of voice, and that man's besetting sin was curiosity. . . . 'Where be your husband, ma?' was the . . . conversational bomb he hurled at me. 'I no got one,' I answer. 'No got,' says Samuel, paralysed with astonishment . . . 'No got one, ma?' 'No,' says I furiously. 'Do you get much rubber round here?' "

Or an incident on the Remboué river: "I received a considerable shock by hearing a well-modulated evidently educated voice saying in most perfect English: 'Most diverting spectacle, madam, is it not?'

"Now you do not expect to hear things called 'diverting spectacles' on the Rembwé; so I turned round and saw standing on the bank against which our canoe was moored, what appeared to me to be an English gentleman who had from some misfortune gone black all over and lost his trousers and been compelled to replace them with a highly ornamental table-cloth. . . ."

Breezy, ironic, bantering, the passages of brilliant hilarity mixed with informative discussion and descriptive beauty—the author's voice sparkled from the pages. Having thumbed to the end of the book, I turned back to the beginning and read Miss Kingsley's Preface to the Reader, where, after begging pardon for her "heinous literary crime," she concludes as follows: "I have endeavoured to give you an honest account of the general state and manner of life in Lower Guinea and some description of the various types of country there. In reading this section you must make allowances for my love of this sort of country, with its great forests and rivers and its animistic-minded inhabitants, and for my ability to be more comfortable there than in England. Your superior culture-instincts may militate against your enjoying West Africa, but if you go there you will find things as I have said."

". . . If you go there you will find things as I have said." Although I had lived and traveled in East Africa, I had never been to the western coast. It was several years since I had begun to harbor an interest in Gabon; now I had a reason for going. Even before I checked her book out of the library, let alone read it, I had made up my mind to take Miss Kingsley up on her offer.

•/•/•

AT THE TIME of Mary Kingsley's visit, the Gaboon was an administrative district within the Congo Français, the French colony that straddled the equator from the Atlantic to the north bank of the Congo river. The first French territory had been acquired in 1839, when King Denis, one of the four Mpongwé chiefs who controlled the Gaboon estuary, was persuaded to cede to France a strip of land near his village in exchange for twenty pieces of cloth, two hundred and fifty pounds of gunpowder, twenty guns, two sacks of tobacco, a barrel of *eau-de-vie*, and ten white hats. Over the years, similar treaties with the other chiefs were to follow until the French had established government posts in strategic places throughout the region.

European exploration of the Gaboon had been conducted by a sometimes motley crew of amateur explorers, missionaries, traders, and a succession of Frenchmen, who were usually employed in some capacity—as doctors or naturalists for example—by the French Navy. The most important—and professional—explorations were led between 1875 and 1885 by Count Pierre Savorgnan de Brazza, an Italian by birth but an officer in the French Navy, who in the course of three separate expeditions to the Congo explored the Ogooué river to its source. In 1885, the Congress of Berlin recognized French rights over the territory between the coast and the right bank of the Congo, which Brazza had also claimed for France, and the following year the Congo Français was established, with the Gaboon as an autonomous region. Four years later, in 1890, the Gaboon was formally annexed to the French Congo.

In 1910, Gabon was one of four territories, along with Chad, the Central African Republic, and Congo, organized to form the federation of French Equatorial Africa. When the federation was dissolved in 1958, Gabon became an autonomous republic within the French Community. Independence was formally declared on August 17, 1960, and the territory of just over one hundred thousand square miles—bordered to the north by

Equatorial Guinea and Cameroon, and to the south and east by the Congo—became the modern republic of Gabon.

The French had not been the only European residents of the region. As early as 1842, American Protestant missionaries had founded a mission and school in Glass, a settlement just south of what was to become Libreville, and were soon engaged in a proselytizing contest with the Roman Catholics, who came from France only a few years after them. By the time of Mary Kingsley's visit, Protestant and Catholic missions had been established in the interior, especially on the Ogooué river. Although the French had official control of the region, it was the British traders who held economic sway, having trading houses, or "factories," in Libreville and points along the Ogooué, as well as a network of subfactories throughout the more remote interior.

These three groups—French officials, missionaries, and traders—constituted the Gaboon's small European population when Mary Kingsley made her journey. A somewhat irregular steamer service operated between Libreville and the French post at Ndjolé, two hundred and twenty miles up the Ogooué river, but missionaries and traders still relied on the native pirogues for local transport on the crocodile- and hippopotamus-infested rivers. The hinterland was covered with dense equatorial forest, which, to judge from the reports of the early explorers and missionaries, teemed with a variety of dangerous beasts and cannibal savages. Perhaps the most dreadful threat of all came from the "West-Coast fever," or malaria, which was at the time so little understood as to be believed to be contracted by "malarial microbes" thought to swarm in the water and evening air.

·/·/·

TAKEN AS I WAS with my new project, I could not help wondering what had prompted Mary Kingsley to embark upon an extended journey in the first place, let alone what had led her to this specific region of the earth. Her ostensible reason for first going abroad is given, with characteristic breeziness, in her own introduction to the *Travels*, as follows: "It was in 1893 that, for the first time in my life, I found myself in possession of five or six months that were not heavily forestalled, and feeling like a boy with a new half-crown, I lay about in my mind, as Mr. Bunyan would say, as to what to do with them. 'Go and learn your tropics,' said Science. . . ." She narrowed her choice of tropical regions to two, South America and West Africa—Malaysia she deemed to be too expensive—before eventually deciding in favor of the latter.

Mary Kingsley left no written account of this first adventure but evidently enjoyed it, for on her return to England in early 1894, she immediately began to plan a second trip. On December 23, 1894, she set out for Africa again, and it was this journey that she described in the *Travels.*

In the course of the first, unrecorded, African adventure, Kingsley had made small collections of fish and insects that had been well received by the British Museum of Natural History on her return to London. For her second journey she made advance arrangements with the museum regarding further collections, particularly of fish. She had also become an eager student of African "fetish," or religious beliefs and practices, and African law. Kingsley's motives for making her journeys, then, on the surface seem straightforward—she had set out on her first trip simply to explore the tropics and, having discovered that Africa was a place where she felt particularly "comfortable," set out on her second to collect fish and study fetish.

Even a superficial glance at Kingsley's biography, however, reveals a more complicated situation. Mary Kingsley was born on October 13, 1862, less than one week after the marriage of her parents, George Kingsley (the brother of Canon Charles Kingsley, the author and social reformer) and Mary Bailey, an innkeeper's daughter, who had previously been employed by her husband in some form of domestic service. George Kingsley was a doctor and spent most of his working life traveling in the private employ of one wandering aristocrat or another, usually spending no more than two to three months a year at home with his wife and children, whom he kept somewhat abreast of his adventures with infrequent letters from places as exotic as

Tahiti, Fiji, Australia, North America, and Mexico. Mary's childhood and youth were absorbed in caring for her reclusive and chronically ill and depressed mother, and for Charles, her "delicate" and ineffectual younger brother. Her free time seems to have been spent in her father's library, which was well stocked with books on travel and exploration, as well as ethnology and natural history, of which he was an amateur student. In 1884, the family moved to Cambridge, where her brother was to attend university. During this period George Kingsley, now in his sixties, retired from his travels and consequently could not altogether avoid spending time at home. He began to apply himself more seriously to his ethnological studies, and in particular to do research on sacrificial rites. Mary Kingsley became his willing assistant in this task, collecting accounts of sacrificial practices reported by travelers. Some years earlier, her father had arranged for her to be tutored in German so as to be able to read the important literature in that language, and these German lessons constituted Mary Kingsley's only formal education. Everything else that she mastered or dabbled in—natural science, Latin, Sanskrit, ethnology, and even chemistry—Mary Kingsley taught herself from the often outdated books available to her in her father's library. When her travels and her own book had made her famous, she was widely regarded as an erudite authority on all things African, but one senses that to the end of her life her perception of herself was in some degree of an untrained and undereducated woman.

In 1890, her mother suffered a stroke and her father contracted rheumatic fever, and Mary Kingsley was forced to spend most of her time at her parents' bedsides. In February 1892, her father died in his sleep, and less than three months later her mother followed him. Mary Kingsley found herself, to quote the biographical introduction to her book, "not only desolate with grief but bereft of purpose."

Although it was largely due to George Kingsley's almost sublime selfishness that she had been forced to lead a life of extreme seclusion, deprived of even the rudiments of education normally awarded a daughter of an upper-middle-class family, Mary

Kingsley worshipped her father, whom she regarded as a brilliant, learned, dashing adventurer. As early as the time of her first African voyage, she had been eager to publish a collection of his travel writings—and it is entirely characteristic that virtually everything we know about the early years of her own life is gleaned incidentally from the biographical chapters she wrote about her father for this memorial book. In these same chapters, too, she speaks of her father's passionate love of "the Tropics," adding that the "sunlight, the colour, and the magnificent exuberance of the life in the Torrid Zone absolutely called across the latitudes to every member of the Kingsley family of the same generation." It becomes clear, then, that Kingsley's own impulse to go to "the Tropics" after her parents' deaths was not solely in the cause of Science, but because it was what her father would have done. Similarly, her desire to study African "fetish" probably arose as much from a desire to "complete" the ethnographical studies her father had so inauspiciously begun as from an innate fascination with the subject.

·/·/·

AS IT WAS my intent to see if I would "find things as Kingsley had said," my immediate interest lay in those features of Gabon that had remained the most unchanged since the time of her journey. In addition to virtually the entire land area still being covered with dense equatorial forest, I found that the tribal names are much the same as those I had encountered in Kingsley's *Travels,* although their populations and importance have changed significantly. The Mpongwé and the Orungu, for example, formerly two extremely powerful tribes who once controlled all coastal trade by virtue of their strategic positions in the estuary and the Ogooué delta respectively, were already in decline at the time of Kingsley's travels and have fallen into relative insignificance, although inhabiting more or less the same region today. The Eshira, who inhabit the southern shore of the lower and middle Ogooué, are today the second most populous tribal group, although they receive scant mention in Kingsley's *Travels.* But by far the most dramatic change is reflected in the fact that the Fang (also referred to as Fan, Fanwe, and Pahouin) are now the single most important tribe in Gabon, while in Kingsley's time they were still migrating into the region, lured toward the coast by reports of the arrival of wealthy European traders. The arrival of the Fang, who were known to be belligerent and cannibal, had been met with alarm by both Africans and Europeans. Entering from the north in the nineteenth century, they had made steady progress toward the Ogooué basin, eventually moving westward along the river and displacing other panic-stricken tribes as they advanced. Although the Fang are today widely dispersed throughout the country, the north of Gabon, where the descendants of the earliest migrating wave have retained intact much of their traditional culture, is said to be "pure Fang"; and in the spirit of the project I had undertaken, I supposed that I was glad that they were still rumored to be cannibals.

As much as sixty percent of the "animistic-minded" people with whom Mary Kingsley had felt so comfortable are now estimated to be Christian, mostly Roman Catholic. The rest of the population, however, with the exception of a small number of Muslims, still follows traditional African tribal religions. While Gabon boasts the highest per capita income in sub-Saharan Africa ($3,900 per annum), most of its active labor force practices traditional subsistence agriculture.

In short, though much had changed since the time of Mary Kingsley's travels, much appeared to have remained the same. Above all, I was encouraged by finding most of the place names in the *Travels* on modern maps, if with glossier francophone spellings—Libreville, Glass, the Ogooué, Lambaréné, Ndjolé, Akondjo, the Remboué.

Determined to parallel Kingsley's journey as closely as possible, I planned, like her, to stay in missions and villages during the course of my travels. I set my departure date for late May so as to arrive, as she had, at the beginning of the long dry season, which extends from June until the October rains. I was not so great a purist, however, that I felt obliged to mirror her journey in every respect: having suffered past unhappy experiences at sea, I thought I could probably forgo the lengthy boat trip, and so whereas Kingsley had arrived in the Gaboon five months after leaving Liverpool, I took the midnight plane from Paris.

•/•/•

MARY KINGSLEY landed in the Gaboon on May 20, 1895, disembarking at the wharf of Hatton and Cookson's factory in Glass, the suburb of Libreville where many of the trading houses had their headquarters. Libreville was named to commemorate the settlement of a group of freed slaves who had been rescued from a slave runner and established near the first French government post. "Glass" was formerly the territory of the Mpongwé king Rendambou, nicknamed "Will Glass," who had most strenuously resisted the French attempts to "buy" his land. Both settlements had been established on the estuary just before the mid-nineteenth century, in the belief that it was the outlet of a major river; in fact, the "estuary" turned out to be only a deeply recessed bay. Although she passed several weeks in Libreville and Glass at both ends of her journey, Mary Kingsley does not give a detailed description of either, and the contemporary account of an American missionary offers a better picture: a good road, paralleling the sea and shaded with coconut palms, connected Libreville and Glass and was traversed by three iron bridges that spanned streamlets coming down from the hills. The Old Road, shaded with mango trees, led away from the sea from the Long Bridge, past the Botanical Gardens. An avenue of coconut palms lay to the right of the gardens, "with cosy little homes on either side nestling amid a wealth of shrubbery; occasionally a larger house occupied by some French official, or used as a shop or café, stood out in an open space." The trading factories of the English, French, German, and Portuguese were strung out along the seafront boulevard. Most of the town's buildings were white, with painted white iron or red-tiled roofs. There were many trees, but few flowers, apart from those that grew on vines in a profusion of scarlet, purple, and lavender.

I arrived at the Libreville airport in the early hours of the morning, when it was too dark to make out what kind of country I had stepped into; but by the time I was heading into town by taxi the dawn had broken, and it was light enough for me to see that I would be negotiating a very different kind of city. Modern Libreville appeared as an unattractive complex of large drab buildings painted dirty white or jaundiced yellow, all of which seemed to have been built in exactly the same year and then left to fend for themselves against the humid salt sea air, the dust, and the unrelenting rainy seasons. The majority of buildings seen from the busy road that parallels the sea, including even the grandiose Presidential Palace, appeared to have been built of cinder blocks and therefore were architecturally limited to the flattest of surface planes, the most banal of outlines. The occasional balcony rails and upstairs shutters gamely painted in pink and turquoise did not succeed in alleviating the despondent drabness that—in spite of the natural beauty of its setting—the city emanated. Trees showing their heads randomly among the rooftops seemed to have sprung up between the buildings like the long tufts of weedy grass that thrust themselves between the pavement cracks. On the roadsides, in the car lots, the vegetation threatened to break free, giving the impression that this city, for all its bricks and mortar, sat only loosely on the soil that had previously nurtured jungle.

The Customs House, the factories and administrative buildings that Kingsley visited, have all gone. The grassy hill country that she tells us she wandered—and got lost in—is now built up. Glass today is less a suburb of Libreville than an outlying quarter of the city, with a Volkswagen repair shop and a Sheraton Hotel. But there was a surprise: Kingsley spent much of her time in Glass in or around the American Protestant Mission, called Baraka—and I now discovered that a Baraka mission, in the *quartier* of Glass, was still indicated on modern maps of Libreville.

Turning off the main coastal boulevard, my taxi rocked slowly past the shop stalls, houses, and garages that crowded either side of the uneven road leading to the mission hill. The tiny wooden, steepled church lay to the left of the wide compoundlike clearing of the summit, and opposite, on somewhat lower ground, a row of flat cement houses stood amid scattered patches of grass and a few palms. Higher up the hill, and a little beyond the church, the mission house was set among some trees.

From the high verandah of the house, an old man who had watched my arrival beckoned me to him. He was slight but not frail, with gray hair and a stern manner—unmistakably a personage to be reckoned with. I explained the purpose of my visit, and he introduced himself as the Pastor Wora. Holding open the verandah's wrought-iron gate, he invited me inside.

Church pews with carved wooden sidings stood in rows to one side of the verandah, which was almost as deep as the house itself. "For the choir," said the Pastor as we passed. The heavy wooden entrance doors of the house had been folded back out of sight, and the living room seemed to be a more deeply recessed extension of the verandah. The room was simply but colorfully decorated; a sofa was strategically placed against the back wall opposite the wide entrance so as to look out over the street. Printed curtains screened the interior doorways, and a red and gold paisley rug covered the smooth, blond wooden floors. The walls were painted alternately in pink and pale blue and were hung with religious pictures—the Stations of the Cross, the Last Supper—and awe-inspiring inscriptions: *"Hôte invisible present à chaque repas. Auditeur silencieux de chaque conversation."* The only exception to the obvious religious character of the pictures was a poster of a rhinoceros, the photograph apparently taken from somewhere around the animal's knees so that its horn stood like a battlement against the sunset sky; I could only assume it was in some way symbolic.

"Sit down, Madame." The Pastor guided me to the sofa, moving slowly, less because he was aged than because his every action was made with great deliberation. "Marie Kingsley," he said thoughtfully, when he was settled in his chair. His face was that of a respected elder, but his eyes were wide and boyish, and he seemed to watch the air in front of him, as if his own thoughts had become embodied and he could follow their performance.

"Marie Kingsley," he repeated. He shook his head. "I don't know her."

Titi, the Pastor's wife, came in with a tray of tea. She was somewhat younger than the Pastor and exuded an air of smiling contentment. Sitting comfortably in her chair, her arms folded across her chest and her head turned to look out over the verandah, she smiled and nodded in agreement as her husband spoke. She and the Pastor were both Fang, and their marriage had been arranged by their parents.

"My parents were Christian," said the Pastor, "but my father drank a lot." His parents had known Dr. Robert Nassau, the American missionary who was in charge of Baraka at the time of Mary Kingsley's visit and whom she refers to throughout the *Travels*. The last person to have known Nassau personally, he said, died in 1969, and she had spoken English, as Nassau had taught her.

"Our education was French," said the Pastor, and with a twinkle he began to recite an old history lesson: " 'Our ancestors, the Gauls . . .' " He had been to mission school in Lambaréné, before deciding to enter the ministry. "Latin I can read a bit—it is a strong, curt language, Latin. Martin Luther said, 'Drink from the source,' and so I tried to learn Hebrew, but in those days there were no such teachers.

"We have a Jewish woman living in the rooms beneath us," he continued, apropos perhaps of Hebrew. *"Une femme abandonnée.* She had no money, nowhere to go, and a little child. Her husband is a Gabonese; I think she met him in Paris, but I don't know—*ce n'est pas poli de demander.* There are few Jews in Gabon."

Saying that she would ask Deborah to come upstairs so that I could meet her, Titi disappeared down the verandah steps, returning minutes later with an attractive raven-haired woman in her early thirties, whom she introduced as Deborah. The Pastor, it turned out, had taken Deborah in because she was a Jew and he was a fervent Zionist. He and Titi had made two trips to Israel with a church group, and for several years he had been holding a prayer session for Jerusalem every Sunday evening in his home. His congregation, as I learned later, was well informed about Jewish history and had been following the Klaus Barbie trial, which was then in progress, with close attention.

The Pastor's favorite topic was his last trip to Israel: "Jerusalem. We stayed outside the Old City, and we had dinner not far from the Sultan's pool. I walked around at Qumran and thought, truly, I am far from Libreville. At the Festival of Booths there were flags of all the nations. We filed into the city, past soldiers, and we Africans said to them, 'Many are against you, but you are not alone. . . .' Where are *you* staying?" the Pastor demanded, turning suddenly to me. I told him that I had taken a room in a Catholic Mission school on the outskirts of town, and he shook his head and insisted that I stay at Baraka.

"There is room with me," said Deborah; and so it was settled.

When I returned in the evening, the distracting lines of the telegraph wires and the houses down the road had been absorbed into the darkness, while the outlines of the little steepled church and the palms closer to the mission house stood out in black relief. After dinner, I joined the Pastor and Titi in the living room, where a continual breeze blew in from the verandah, billowing the curtains in the doorways.

The Pastor knew the mission history well, and in his citation of dates he was not content with merely stating the year in question: "The Americans founded Baraka on June the twenty-second, eighteen hundred and forty-two. . . ." He also insisted that the church was built of wood that had been brought from New Jersey by the early American missionaries. At one time, the mission grounds had extended down the hill to a private beach; today, one can easily overlook the fact that the sea is only a quarter of a mile away, for the buildings that clutter the hill slope almost obscure it from view.

Outside, people had begun to drift in for choir practice and were greeted at the top of the verandah steps by Titi. The women wore long dresses that were a cross between a caftan and the old missionary hubbard, and kerchiefs around their heads, while the men were dressed in safari suits. The choir leader was a man of immense gaunt height, clad entirely in starched white. He set up a blackboard on the verandah facing the rows of benches and began to tap it with a long pointer. Each choir member began to sing in their own key, the voices somehow blending in uncanny harmony.

In the dim recesses of his living room, as the choir's unaccompanied song drifted in from the verandah, the Pastor spoke of the need to pray for the heathens, "those people who believe in magic, in superstitions, the *goyim* in the forest." The persistence of traditional beliefs takes several forms. During the last eclipse, for example, people buried their valuables and money and locked their children inside. More seriously, many tribes still practice ritual murder in order to obtain the genitals and hearts of their victims, which are believed to confer power. The organs of children are considered to be particularly desirable, and in Libreville the ubiquitous posters warning parents to look out for their children after school refer to this as much as to the usual dangers faced by unattended children. Election time is an especially dangerous period as candidates sometimes resort to traditional magic to ensure their successful bids for office. While I was in Libreville the local paper carried a story about a murder that had been discovered when a passerby came upon a body lying in the road in a pool of blood that literally trailed to the door of a prominent man. Inside the gates of the man's walled-in house, a guard was found indiscreetly wiping a blood-stained knife upon his trousers. Discussing the motive of the crime, the article quoted the murderer as saying that he had killed his victim with a view to taking his genitals.

"There are pastors here who preach, who pray to Jesus, but who keep their father's head in a box to worship," said the Pastor. Whenever there is a burial, watch must be kept in the cemetery through the following nights, to ensure that the body is not exhumed and its valuable organs cut out.

When the choir meeting had broken up, I went downstairs to Deborah's tiny apartment, where I was to spend the night. One could cross the largest room in the apartment in six easy strides and the ceiling was little more than a foot above my head. The walls were white, the floors of bare polished cement. The living room had a set of raffia chairs and a sofa with cushions that had been covered with old curtains. A round glass table nearly blocked the front entrance.

In the bedroom, a cot had been laid for me next to the double bed in which Deborah slept with her son, Jean-Louis, leaving three feet or so of space between the ends of the beds and the wall, and no space at all to either side. In the storeroom, Deborah's unpacked suitcases and boxes overflowed with her possessions. Designer clothes lay in stacks on the suitcases and on the shelves of the wardrobe, the room's sole piece of furniture. The boxes contained a bewildering supply of glass, plates, and silverware—*ce n'est pas poli de demander.*

Deborah was in the living room when I arrived, surrounded by a circle of female friends. Her face under her raven hair was stark white, its lines set to reveal no expression at all, as if she had taken a vow that she would never again show emotion. Only her lips phrased each word, each careful syllable, with greater than normal exaggeration, as if she were in an elocution class and had been told that she must enunciate. In what I was to discover was a nightly practice, she was telling the story of her abandonment—continually, loudly, and at great length, almost without complaint, certainly without a plea for aid or justice. The women sitting solidly around her shook their heads or gave little cries of sympathy. Like Job's ministers, each responded to her tale with an interpretation, which, Job-like, Deborah then rejected. Sometimes the response was but a retelling of her story, and then she sat silent, not placated, but in some way momentarily reassured.

"My husband, *il est drogué,*" Deborah said, to put me in the picture. I asked if drugs were a problem here, and everyone said yes. Only slowly did I come to realize that Deborah did not mean that her husband took drugs; she meant that another woman had put magic in his food and had bewitched him.

From time to time Deborah's son, Jean-Louis, came storming in from outside, where he was playing with two little boys from the neighborhood. Jean-Louis was a handsome if sullen child of eight, whose Gabonese and French parentage had combined to bestow on him a wondrous golden color. He rarely spoke but stomped around the house, the compound, the street, scowling and aggrieved. He listened without apparent interest to the discussion of his father's wickedness, his mother's plight. Deborah he regarded generally with a look of blazing contempt: *femme abandonnée.* His two playmates followed behind him like shadows. They were thin, like little stick men, as black as the night, and in marked contrast to Jean-Louis, alight with laughter. They carried javelins made of branches and had been stalking fantasies in the darkness. Their father was good in the hunt, they told me; they had eaten monkey meat many times, but never crocodile. They were bilingual in French and Fang.

Eventually her friends took their departure, entrusting Deborah to God for the night, and Deborah went to the door and called Jean-Louis in from outside, where he and the two brothers were dancing wildly with their shadows in the dusty yard under the yellow streetlight. We barricaded ourselves in the bedroom, locking inside as well as outside doors to trick the thieves. The bedroom was the only room with a window air conditioner, which unfortunately could not be regulated. The icy air was thick with a scent that was to become so familiar that I came to associate it with nighttime in Libreville—the heavy, strangely sweet blend of Deborah's pungent skin freshener and her last cigarette. Jean-Louis lay enfolded in her arms, the only moment of the day when he seemed vulnerable, and we both fell asleep to Deborah murmuring, ". . . and we will have a house, and Maman will not have to work, she can stay at home with you, *enfant d'or;* you will stay with Maman?"

In the morning we walked together down to the main road. Deborah never ate breakfast in her house but waited until she was at the small gift shop, which she co-owned and managed. She walked, as always, very erect, her whole being braced in resolution against the new day. And expressionless as always, she told her story; she had owned a prosperous *prêt-à-porter* shop, and had lived in one of the elegant modern beachside apartments in one of Libreville's most chic *quartiers.* She had had a dishwasher, a washing machine, a television. . . . She counted off the lost amenities on her fingers. She had gone to Paris for a holiday and returned to find that her husband was living with another woman, had sold the apartment and taken its contents, emptied her bank account, and taken her jewels; *"Il les a ramassé,"* she said, making a scooping motion with her hands, like a casino croupier. She had sold her successful shop and become part owner of the gift shop. She had met the Pastor through a friend who belonged to a Bible group.

She outlined her plan: "One year, perhaps two. I shall save my money. Then I go to Israel. They pay your way there. Then I get out of here," she said with clenched jaw.

We parted company at the road, Deborah taking a taxi into town, I taking one to the industrial area that lay in the opposite direction. Of all the great trading firms that had once had factories here—Woermann's, of Germany, John Holt, of Liverpool, Laughland and Co., of Glasgow—only Hatton and Cookson remains. This was the firm that received Mary Kingsley when she first arrived and arranged for her to use credit with their remote trading posts to pay her guides and porters; it was, in fact, her acquaintance with Mr. Hudson, then the agent-general for Hatton and Cookson, that had drawn Kingsley specifically to the French Congo. She had met him in the course of her first, ill-documented trip to West Africa in 1893, and felt she could rely on his position of authority to enable her to ascend the Ogooué river. Hatton and Cookson is now a subsidiary of Unilever and no longer deals in cloth, tobacco, and powder but in electrical appliances, engines, and automobiles. I was as hospitably received by M. Biyogo, the general secretary, as Mary Kingsley had been by the agent who first welcomed her. M. Biyogo made it clear that he was to be called upon to help in whatever way he could. I expressed my thanks; "I am—" I was fumbling for the correct French word.

"Touchée?" he suggested and gave a little bow.

At the time of Mary Kingsley's travels, economic conditions in the Gaboon were more favorable than ever—Count de Brazza's extensive explorations had opened up the hinterland, and the Gaboon's formal annexation to the Congo territory had ensured that its economic possibilities would be considered more seriously. I seemed to have arrived at the ebb of its prosperity. Gabon's economy, now largely dependent on its oil (petroleum accounts for over eighty percent of all exports), has been severely affected by the drop in world oil prices. Amoco and Gulf have closed down their operations, and as much as a third of Gabon's expatriate population is rumored to have left between 1986 and 1987. Hatton and Cookson have closed all their branches except those at Port-Gentil and Libreville, and the Port-Gentil branch is soon to go the way of the others. The enormous luxury hotels that had been built to accommodate the conferences, the consultants, the workshops, were closed down or virtually empty. Shopkeepers, taxi drivers, businessmen, residents—everyone told me about *la crise,* everyone told me that things had been busier and brighter before, everywhere figures were cited regarding the filtering away of the expatriate community.

My time in Libreville was mostly spent in libraries, forestry offices, government bureaus, mission headquarters, and the Peace Corps office, getting what information I could before setting out for the interior. Between appointments and in the long lunch hours when shops and offices close down, I passed the time in one or another of the city's many cafés, which—as Spaña had known—are the most immediately striking indication that, in spite of independence, the French presence in Gabon is still strong. Mary Kingsley, one gathers, spent most of her time in Libreville shell hunting in the bay and taking walks to and around the mission: but I wondered if she passed the hours between her desultory excursions in the cafés mentioned in the missionary's description of the early town.

Throughout all this time of preparation, I had the uneasy feeling of being at a loose end: the character of Libreville has changed so drastically since Kingsley's visit that there were few points at which I could make meaningful comparisons. So far, I had found nothing at all remotely reminiscent of the land of forests and rivers that I had come to explore; I had encountered neither the past nor the present in which I was specifically interested. It was with relief, therefore, that I returned to Baraka every evening, where at least in the Pastor's stern keeping, the weight of history hung so heavy.

On Sunday, I was woken at dawn by the deep rumbling of the Pastor's organ, which he thundered on intermittently from half past six until just before the service at ten; the only other sounds to be heard at that hour were the squawks of chickens behind the house. When I went outside after breakfast, a little naked boy was returning from the local bakery, struggling up the hill with a long, unwieldy loaf of bread.

The church was already full when I entered for the service, but a member of the choir stepped forward and gently guided me to the front, where a chair had been set aside for me next to people I took to be local dignitaries. It was our unhappy prerogative to sit facing the congregation, and this distinction, combined with the fact that I alone of the congregants was white, placed me in an unenviably conspicuous position. It was the first time I had been inside the church. A table stood in lieu of the altar, and a lectern to one side served as a pulpit. The walls were plainly whitewashed, but the window woodwork was shiny green, and the windows themselves adorned with palm fronds. With only a narrow center aisle left clear, the church was filled from wall to wall by the congregation, the women in pastel-colored dresses, the men in white or beige suits.

The old iron bell on the front porch rang out, and from the side door the Pastor entered, transformed from the stern but approachable man I had passed so much time with into a formidable, foreboding vessel of God's wrath. The choir began to sing with tender solemnity, as if already chastised and repentant, then slowly gathered courage, and soon the congregation was swaying together. All movement ceased, however, when the Pastor stood, and with a face on which the omniscient judgment of God had been carved, approached the pulpit. Never losing his characteristic carefulness, never significantly raising his voice, he delivered a smoldering sermon against these evil times, and with almost sardonic resignation prophesied the purging winds and blasts of fire from heaven that would be the inevitable—indeed desirable—result of human wickedness. A woman of voluptuous size was then baptized, an act that the Pastor performed after carefully spreading a towel on the ground before the altar to absorb the beaker of water that he poured upon her head.

One, two, nearly three hours passed. Staring the congregation squarely in the face, I tried to sit in the same position as those who seemed most comfortable. When the Pastor prayed that the offering of our hearts be accepted as a living sacrifice and called the congregation to partake of the flesh and blood of divinity, my mind wandered uneasily to the article I had read about the probable ritual murder, and I wondered if the language of sacrifice had helped the early missionaries make conversions.

At half past one, the Pastor grimly closed his book and left the church through the same door he had entered. Shortly afterward when I met him outside, he was all smiles: "Just a little sermon, nothing special," he said, with uncharacteristic pride.

In the evening he held his prayer service for Israel, which was well attended. Sitting comfortably in his chair, he read from a book about the history of the Jews, interjecting his own comments from time to time. "Are you tired?" he asked suddenly, looking up innocently an hour and a half later, to which we replied as one that we absolutely were not. The night wind as usual billowed in from the verandah. Outside, children could be seen prancing in the streetlight shadows. Hymns were sung, and the session became more conversational. I asked the Pastor if the church bell was a legacy of the missionaries, and he looked almost shy: "That bell was my father's. He rang it to call people to the compound—it was not a church bell."

He reverted again to his favorite theme, his trips to Israel. "In Israel, one hears Hebrew in the streets," he said; then suddenly turning on the congregation, who had by now split into small groups, he demanded angrily, "Where is *your* language? Where is your Fang tongue? Over three thousand years and the Jews still speak the same language as their fathers. And you"—waving impatiently at his congregation—"you, how long have the French been here? Pah! Less than two hundred years. My son, I tell you," he said, looking hard into space and somehow including every individual in his gaze, "my son, who works in the bureau in Paris, writes to me in our language, in Fang."

So at last I understood something of the nature of his ardent Zionism. I left the session early and went below to Deborah's apartment to do some ironing and to pack my bag, as I was to leave Libreville the next morning. I heard Christine, the over-sized daughter of Deborah's closest neighbor, moving heavily in the kitchen. For a small sum, she regularly came to wash or clean for Deborah. Now I found that she had anticipated me, and all my clothes, including socks, lay ironed and neatly folded on my bed. Her movements were slow and somewhat clumsy, and her speech was slurred.

"No, no, Madame," she said when I came to say thank you and to pay. She flapped her enormous hands in a gesture of dismissal. "It was a gift."

LAMBARÉNÉ

"I SHALL AWAIT you as always," said my friendly Cameroon taxi driver, and he settled back for a snooze in his car, which he had parked under the shade of an acacia tree. I was in search of a ticket for the hydrofoil that went three times a week down the coast from Libreville to Port-Gentil. The tickets, as I was told at each encounter, could be purchased in advance in the big hotels, but each hotel seemed to be temporarily out of stock. At the Hotel Dialogue, the desk clerk, looking strangely harassed in the utterly vacant and desolate foyer, informed me that here, indeed, there were tickets to be had.

"But unfortunately, the office is closed; or rather it is open, but not inhabited. You must return."

I asked when would be a good time. He smiled pleasantly.

"Later."

Mary Kingsley departed from Libreville to begin her travels on the Ogooué River on June 5, 1895. At the time of her journey, one entered the Ogooué by Nazareth Bay, a major channel in the delta of waterways at the river mouth, from which point it was another two days upriver to Lambaréné, her first important port of call.

Today, the most direct route from Libreville to Lambaréné is by land, a distance of only one hundred and fifty miles, but on the torturous half-finished or half-destroyed roads, a journey of up to five hours. If one is perverse enough to wish to go by boat, the journey must be divided into two stages, from Libreville to Port-Gentil by hydrofoil, thence up the river to Lambaréné by the ponderous double-decked barges that make the journey once a week to Lambaréné, and to Ndjolé beyond.

I turned up at the harbor on the morning of departure and at last purchased my ticket. Uniformed stewardesses waited smartly by the doors to conduct passengers to their seats in a cabin that was similar to the first-class section of an airplane. Shortly after the hydrofoil had pulled away from the dock, a video screen on the front wall came to life and began a nonstop series of Tom and Jerry cartoons, which played throughout the trip. Carts of French bread and coffee were wheeled by. I reread Mary Kingsley's description of this leg of her journey on the wood-stoked *Mové*. "... At my feet, the engine-room stoke-hole, lit with the rose-coloured glow from its furnace, showing by the great wood fire the two nearly naked Krumen stokers, shining like polished bronze in their perspiration. . . ." Through the spray-spattered windows, I caught only occasional and indistinct glimpses of forest-fringed beach. Two hours later, we disembarked at Port-Gentil.

Port-Gentil is situated roughly a third of the way down Gabon's coastline, on a spit of land that is virtually an island, cut off as it is by the Ogooué's channels, which fan out into the surrounding coastal marshlands. As early as 1850, missionaries had attempted to found a station at Cape Lopez, the modern suburb port of Port-Gentil located at the extreme northern tip of the spit, but had been thwarted by the Orungu, the tribe that controlled the southern coast and rightly feared that a missionary presence would interfere with, among other things, their lucrative slave trade. In 1862, after persistent efforts, the French at last succeeded in signing a treaty with the Orungu. The treaty was important, for it gave the French a legal claim to the delta region of the Ogooué River, which was belatedly discovered to be the interior highway first assumed to have existed in the Gaboon, and by the time of Mary Kingsley's visit the center of trade had shifted south from the "estuary" to Cape Lopez. Nonetheless, up until the end of the First World War, Port-Gentil consisted of little more than a circle of villages around the post, and a Catholic Mission.

Today, Port-Gentil–Cape Lopez is the center of Gabon's petroleum industry. Here Elf-Gabon and Shell Oil have their offshore refineries and loading facilities for the oil that is brought in by pipeline from deposits in the northwest and Mandji Island. The European personnel of these foreign corporations constitute a high percentage of Port-Gentil's population of one hundred and twenty thousand.

In spite of the late date of its foundation, Port-Gentil itself, with its coconut- and palm-lined streets and wooden, verandahed houses, has an old-fashioned colonial air. A market extends along the shore, selling overpriced fruit and vegetables and fish that are brought in by the fleets of pirogues, the shallow local craft. Moored in the harbor was a dilapidated and rust-eaten blue and white boat bearing the word *Ekwata* on her stern; it was this vessel that was to make the trip to Lambaréné.

A crowd was already waiting at the water's edge. At around one o'clock, the *Ekwata* began to move laboriously toward us. *"Attention,"* warned the man standing beside me, "a friend of mine had his foot cut off by the boat when it ran ashore." The *Ekwata* drew nearer, its metal gangway down, plowing surf and sand before it like a bulldozer, and headed steadily for the crowd, many of whom were by now ankle deep in the water. When it became apparent that the boat was going to run aground, people began to shout and scatter, clearing a space for it in the nick of time. The *Ekwata* ground neatly to a halt on the beach and was swiftly boarded by a dangerously jostling swell of people eager to claim places on board. Two small vans were driven onto the open bow, stuffed with the drivers' possessions and extensive family, who remained inside the van cabins for the duration of the trip; there was in fact nowhere else for them to go, as the bow was already packed with mattresses, fans, refrigerators, buckets, barrels, and passengers.

The lower, shaded deck was also well filled by small family settlements by the time I fought my way on board, and so I went to the upper deck and settled by the wall of the rear cabin. The floor space around me was soon taken up, and part of the continuing stream of embarking passengers was diverted to the cabin roof, which was reached by way of the metal rungs just behind my head. By two o'clock everyone was more or less wedged into the position he would have to maintain for the next twenty-five hours. The *Ekwata* floundered out some distance from the shore but then became quiet again, and we remained at anchor just outside the harbor for the next two and one half hours.

The *commandant,* wading through the people and goods that filled every inch of deck space on the side passageways, made his way toward the stern, where I sat. He had come from his glass-fronted cabin at the bow, where he was to stand at the wheel throughout the afternoon, night, and following day, stripped down to a pair of shorts and mass of gold chains. He was a large, burly man, as one expects all good skippers to be, with wide, slightly protruding eyes that became more prominent and red-streaked as the hours wore on. He had come to the stern to see that all was well with the *femme blanche,* the white woman who had conspicuously boarded his vessel.

He found me propped up between my bags and introduced himself as the captain. "You are safe on my ship," he assured me. A tall man stood behind him carrying something tucked under his arm, for which the captain now gestured. "For the night, Madame," he said as he produced a folded camp bed. He opened the door of the little stern cabin, which contained two tiny rooms: a galley, with a sink and hot plate, and an empty room where I guessed his second-in-command usually slept, but which he indicated was to be my cabin for this trip.

The heat was already oppressive. I had been waiting impatiently for us to get under way, looking forward to the breezes of the moving boat. When, at half past four, the *Ekwata* finally pulled out, however, I realized how ill-chosen my spot had been; all cool breezes were blocked by the height of the stern cabin, and the engines were roaring from somewhere under my seat. On the other hand, I was in the best of company, my neighbors being mostly small families and older women, who although traveling singly, had quickly formed a sociable group. To my left, on the other side of the cabin door, barricaded by his neatly piled possessions, an old man sat primly in the middle of a straw mat, his legs straight out before him and his hat on his knees, pursing his lips in obvious disapproval of the noisy activity around him. Young children and teenage boys crowded the side and stern railings, looking intently at the water churning under the boat.

The first hour of our slow progress revealed nothing except the flat, watered-silk blue of the sea, Port-Gentil and its palms getting smaller behind us, and nothing but the horizon line appearing ahead. Then, peering around the cabin door, I saw at last the two green arms of forest that marked the entrance to the Ogooué.

The Ogooué River, as Mary Kingsley notes with feeling, is the greatest strictly equatorial river in the world, and its basin contains virtually all Gabon's interior. The Ogooué rises beyond the present-day Congo border and is fed by two major tributaries to the north and south. From the Congo plateau, it flows some seven hundred miles through forest and savannah to its marshy delta on the Atlantic Ocean. This river was the backbone of Mary Kingsley's travels. For the early missionaries it had been a River of Lost Souls, the great inroad into the darkness of brutality and godlessness that awaited their salvation. From the 1860s, European trading firms had established their depots of ivory, ebony, and rubber along its shores, and ferried their clutter of calico, guns, powder, beads, fishhooks, rum, and diseases up and down these waters. This had been the highway that had carried Brazza's flotillas of great war canoes in and out of the interior; and on these waters, too, for centuries before, the inland tribes had plied their own trade.

I, then, was already already predisposed to be captured by the glamour of this great river, the largest in West Africa between the Niger and the incomparable Congo. And, above all, I had been prepared to sit as Mary Kingsley had done and watch the water part and flow as my little steamer made its picturesque way upriver between banks of towering forest that held so many collective memories.

The disparity of our respective vantage points may account in part for our very different memories of this trip. "She is a fine little vessel," writes Mary Kingsley of the *Mové,* "far finer than I expected. The accommodation I am getting is excellent. A long, narrow cabin, with one bunk in it and pretty nearly everything one can wish for. . . ." By this time, the traffic leading to the roof by way of the rungs at my head had thinned somewhat, due to the simple fact that not just anyone was welcome on the rooftop. An exclusive bar of sorts seemed to have been established, and the people that came up and down were soon showing different degrees of intoxication. Several women who attempted the ascent into this rarefied realm were angrily shouted down by the men who had claimed places. A tiny hunchbacked man with a badly withered leg limped along the starboard passageway and, on seeing a sturdy woman win her way to the upper roof, gave a bark of delight, and with his tongue flickering out of his mouth, cupped his hands before him in a pantomime of breasts. Lurching his way toward the ladder by my head, he disappeared over the top. A strolling soldier or gendarme—his role was never clear to me, but he was dressed in blue and black camouflage fatigues—stopped to sway his hips before me, his hand upon the knife he wore ostentatiously at his belt.

"Food is excellent," Kingsley continues, "society charming . . ."

It was early dusk when we came beneath the trees, and in the dim light the forest appeared as a high, dark facade, with only its most obtrusive details visible, most often the stark bleached limbs of some doomed tree shining white against its relentlessly thriving brother greenery. Many living trees were hung with ghostly lianas, which seemed to have been lassoed about them like guy-ropes, as if it were someone's intention to drag these giants down. The sun set promptly at half past six. By seven o'clock it was already dark, and many people had begun to curl themselves into sleeping positions. A splash of water was heard only occasionally above the deep, vibrating hum of engines. People spoke drowsily, and the louder voices floating down from the rooftop tavern made little impression on the sense of stillness. The *Ekwata* veered toward something shining in the darkness on the left bank. Like the great coils of a metallic serpent, a mass of gleaming blue pipes rose out of the black water, surreally lit by floodlights, as if this creation of sleek modernity were the most noteworthy, not-to-be missed feature of our journey through primeval forest. The captain and his assistant began to shout at the passengers and were then echoed more aggressively by the soldier in fatigues.

"Descends, descends . . ." The passengers, sleepily but obediently, began to file off the boat. The soldier appeared suddenly, his face only inches from mine, his hands held out before him.

"Alors, Mademoiselle . . ."

Ignoring him, I went directly to the captain, who told me that I did not have to disembark: "But no, Madame, it is merely a ticket check—some people have not paid."

I did not ask why the check was to be made here, some three hours upriver, in the dark, on the muddy banks, and not at the beginning of the trip, when it could have controlled in part the mad dash for places to sit. Many people were making use of this opportunity to wash, and with rolled-up trousers or tucked-up skirts, stooped and squatted in the river, deftly scooping water over their necks and faces with practiced gestures that bespoke of frequent river bathing. Some way up shore, a yellow light shone above the doorway of a little hut, presumably the power station office. From somewhere out of the night, two statuesque women in high-heeled shoes and tight skirts stepped into its circle of dingy light and began to prowl through the crowd like a pair of cheetahs stalking in a herd of game. A station worker, balanced precariously on a platform by the pipes, obligingly showed one of the passengers how a pump worked, and a jet of white spray shot out of the inky water.

We waited. I gathered that the ticket checkers had to be sent for, perhaps from a nearby village. The passengers settled down to wait dutifully, uncomplainingly, for however long they might be asked. It was while watching this scene, half-shadowed and half-revealed by the incidental light of the floodlights, that I experienced the only real fear I was to have on my entire trip: this was where *it* could happen. The images of horror offered by the modern world could not have been guessed at by the traveler of Kingsley's day—the brutal pulling out of the patient line, the interrogation in the yellow light, the detention witnessed only by the black river and indifferent forest.

At last, from somewhere behind us on the river, a small boat chugged up to the station. Slowly the passengers were cleared, and slowly they reboarded. We resumed our trip, having been at this nameless spot for an hour and a half. People returned to their places and again settled down to sleep. I entered the cabin to discover the soldier lying on the cot the captain had given to me. Politely, I explained that the cot was already taken. The soldier responded by shifting to one side and indicating that there was room for two. He was too drunk to argue with, and so I set out again to find the captain, walking carefully along the rails, as the floor was completely covered with people. The captain and his second-in-command expressed immediate, and gratifying, rage and stormed off toward the cabin. Following in their wake, I arrived to witness them heaving the cot into the air and spilling the soldier onto the ground.

"You are drunk," said the captain, and the soldier nodded happily. "Madame, your cabin," said the captain with a flourish once the soldier had been shooed out, and I suspected from the zeal of his attack that this had been a welcome exercise.

The cabin itself was unnervingly hot. Assuming that this was because its iron, boxlike walls still retained the heat of the day, I fell asleep expecting to wake later in the night and find it cool. Instead, I awoke with an oppressive headache to discover that

I was lying in alarmingly deep pools of my own sweat that had collected in the sagging canvas of the cot. There seemed to be a furnace beneath me, and when I at last summoned strength to touch the floor, I found it red-hot. A half-acknowledged thought stirring in the depths of my mind registered that I was, of course, directly above the engines. The night passed strangely for me; the disorienting heat and the uneasy feelings aroused by the nocturnal ticket check—the stage set for what could happen—grew stronger. In my half dreams, I saw detention halls, I thought of the terrible middle passage, of fever victims incapable of action but lucid enough to know of their predicament, borne down a river such as this to some distant hospital station. No radio, no emergency airlift—no short cut, no way out.

The *Ekwata* stopped at a number of villages in the night. I heard neither the new passengers board nor the old depart. I listened only for the sound of the engine backwatering, pausing, and then humming forward, and lay in dread that each halt might mean that we had hit a hidden sandbar: two days aground was not unheard of in the dry season. At one halt, I leaned my head back to see the almost-full moon peering in the cabin doorway.

The dawn revealed scenery so different from that of the day before that one might wonder if the *Ekwata* had strayed in the night down a side channel that had tipped it over the edge of the world onto another continent. Broad expanses of tall, wide-bladed saw grass, like fields of cornless maize, stretched away from either river shore. Arising from the grass were occasional thin scatterings of trees that looked in the distance less like remnants of the forest we had passed through than poplars lining a Dutch canal. Gray herons and egrets sailed out of the marsh, not bothering to lift their lazy flight above the grass tops. From the water level up through and just above where the herons glided, the air was a delicate mauve-gray, becoming paler and more indistinct as one looked higher, as if the morning had only been half-colored.

People began to stir and rearrange their clothes and possessions. The old man beside the cabin door was smoothing his mat and reshaping his hat, which he had slept in. The old women, in charge of setting the day's routine in motion here as in the village, began to untie their bundles and bring out rolls of manioc wrapped in banana leaves. The older women took a kindly interest in me. Even collectively, they spoke little French, and conversation, although not necessarily communication, was difficult. They seemed most intrigued by my not being French and therefore truly foreign.

By nine o'clock, the rising sun had managed to turn the morning dewiness into a thick stew and had seared away all subtle pastel shadings. The colors of the world now appeared hard and immutable, as if baked into the sky and grass and river. People lolled listlessly against the railings and one another. On the roof above, all seemed very quiet, although cases of beer continued to be lifted from some hidden, inexhaustible source. By the starboard rail, a young couple was curled up together with their new baby. The woman dozed or gazed with superior amusement at her husband, who passed the hours examining in wonderment his baby's every toe and finger. Another young mother brought her baby into the cabin, where, unmindful of the paralyzing heat, she conscientiously wrapped him in careful layers of cloth before putting him to rest on the cot, where he lay darkly shining, his brow beaded with sweat and his little fists clenched in the air. Around his chubby wrists was twined a bracelet of string as a charm against evil.

We drifted again into forest, which to me appeared far less intriguing in the bold light of day than it had when blended with the rising dusk. In the long season of heavy rain, which falls between February and the end of May, the Ogooué rises above its banks and rampages through the outskirts of the forest; now the low, dry-season water level exposed what one felt should be kept decently buried—the forest roots, desiccated and bone white, which like great, long-fingered skeletal hands arched above the water, the fingertips seeming reluctantly, fastidiously to skim the water surface. From the height of the forest coronal, birds launched themselves in perilous and startling swoops and then fell or floated out beyond the forest with no perceptible movement of their wings. An egret, in a welcome flash of white, shot low, like a sniper's bullet, across the water grasses.

Mary Kingsley's description of the Ogooué forest scenery was much admired by her contemporaries. It was quoted at length by the missionary Dr. Robert Nassau when he came to write about his own experience of some twenty-five years in the Ogooué basin: "It is thus splendidly described by Miss Mary Kingsley," and there follows her extravagant and exotic vision of the flower-bedecked Ogooué forest, likened to a gaudy Cleopatra, "as full of life and beauty and passion as any symphony Beethoven ever wrote." To me, however, the forest manifested not passion so much as an inscrutable front, jealously screening what it felt alien eyes had no business seeing. Again, our different perspectives might have arisen as much from our respective circumstances as from our different temperaments. I was still suffering from the effects of the night spent in the ferocious heat above the engine room, and while I duly noted all the forest features Mary Kingsley sang of, the temperature and my splitting headache from dehydration impressed themselves more vividly upon me. The heat of the sun alone would have made the trip memorably uncomfortable, and I began to marvel at Kingsley's endurance, particularly as I, who had grown up in the Florida tropics, was dressed in loose cotton clothing, while Kingsley, who had lived virtually all of her life in England, had traveled in a thick wool skirt and boots. Since not a word about the discomfort of the heat intrudes upon her narrative at this point, I had to conclude that unless her memory had been highly selective, she was certainly made of sterner stuff than I.

A clearing in the forest or the glossy green of a banana plantation marked a village. Sometimes, usually on a high bank, the row of huts could be seen from the river; more often one saw only a white, sandy trail leading off to somewhere in the forest. The *Ekwata* did not stop at every village, but there was great activity on board whenever she did. It had been discovered early in the trip that it was easy to catch fish from the boat rail, and consequently whenever we approached a village, virtually every able-bodied male on board—those on the roof excluded—had a fishing line over the railing. The young husband was particularly skillful and quickly filled a basket with fish, as if eager to prove to his young wife that he was a capable provider.

The new mother in the cabin was joined by other women, who, with their solid legs placed wide apart, sat on the cot or chairs, their arms hanging slackly in their laps so as to allow the sweat to run off them freely. They had gutted and scaled a mass of fish and soon had a pan boiling on the galley hot plate. The old man on the mat watched these messy operations with horror and elaborately pulled back from the women as they went in and out of the galley, his lips more primly pursed than ever. Watching the pile of gutted entrails on the deck steadily grow and quiver in the heat, I found I shared his distaste and decided to go forward to the bow to see how the people in the vans were faring. In their cramped quarters, they were going about the business of daily life, more or less as in a village. Babies were being fed, food was being cooked, and a group of women, barebreasted or stripped down to their bras, were taking sponge baths.

The captain summoned me from his glass-fronted cabin to ask me how I was enjoying the trip. I replied I was enjoying it very much and had slept well on his cot.

"You have nothing like this where you come from?" he asked, and looked pleased when I said, indeed, we did not. He pointed ahead. "We have nearly arrived. One half hour and we will be in Lambaréné. We are"—he broke off to consult his watch—"an hour late. Forgive us, Madame, we were late in starting. But don't remember that." He also insisted with some fierceness that I was on no account to leave the boat without assistance.

From the captain's cockpit, I watched as more huts and then square cement buildings began to appear high up on the increasingly deforested shores. The afternoon light had lost the unrelenting hardness of the earlier day and was scattered and golden. The spits and wedges of beige sand standing out of the water revealed how low the river had already fallen. Ahead of us, the thin pencil line of a bridge span came into view, connecting the mainland with Lambaréné island. The harbor, which consisted of a dock and a medium-size shed, was nestled on the shore to our left at the bottom of a high bank of bald red clay, just before the bridge. The *Ekwata* sounded her whistle to give notice of her arrival, although a crowd of people was already waiting.

Mayhem broke loose once we touched the dock. The vans in the bow were revved up before the gangway was lowered, and the passageways and stairwells were immediately blocked with people and their unwieldy bundles. Everyone was shouting, and from the shore came the strident voices of the drivers of the communal taxis and minibuses that were lined up in the dusty road at the top of the bank. When the gangway was lowered and the wave of departing passengers met the embarking passengers head on, the volume of shouting rose even higher. The haziness of the late afternoon light became accentuated by the rising clouds of red dust that were stirred up once people had clambered up to the road, where they were instantly accosted by the enterprising drivers. At the captain's insistence I remained on board until the two crowds had more or less exchanged places, and when at last he deemed it safe to let me go, he commanded one of his assistants to escort me and carry my bags.

Once on the dock, I found a boatman to take me to the Catholic Mission and followed him down to the water's edge, where he had moored his motorized pirogue. We backed out of the harbor while behind us other pirogues, like streamlined waterbirds, darted out from either side of the river. We had gone no distance at all before we turned toward the left shore, where we ran up onto the beach near a trail that led up to the main road through rushes, banana trees, and bush. The boatman accompanied me, carrying my bags. The red dust of the road puffed up around our feet and clung to the hem of my skirt and the sweat on my legs. Ahead of us on the high side of the road was a long wall covered with yellow trumpet flowers and tendrils of tiny blossoms that resembled pink lily of the valley. The upper story of a tall brick building overlooked it, and a small, plump chapel of whitewashed bricks stood just to the right of its wrought-iron gates.

I stepped inside, and I found myself in a garden cloister. Behind the chapel was a two-story building of pink-orange brick, with glossy green shutters and doors. The loggia of the adjacent building was painted in purple and pink. Salmon, red, and yellow hibiscus grew along the short gravel driveway, and everywhere one looked—on the covered walkways, on the balcony railings above—were pots and tubs of flowers. I settled with the boatman and then turned back to the cloister to see that a small figure dressed in white was slowly coming toward me from the shadows of the broad-leafed tree that dominated the sandy courtyard.

The figure was a nun, dressed in a white uniform and wearing a headpiece of crisp white linen, such as nurses wore in the First World War. She was slim and dark and, in spite of her warm smile, very shy. I explained that I was seeking accommodation.

"Yes, of c-c-c-c-course," she said and introduced herself as Sister Carmen, and little by little—green door by green door— she initiated me into the tranquil world of the Sisters of the Immaculate Conception. The doors at the back of the purple and pink loggia led to generous bedrooms, with slow-turning ceiling fans and sinks demurely screened by curtains of faded floral print. Another building of the attractive rosy brick was immediately adjacent, linked by a covered walkway. Down here, Sister Carmen said, was the laundry room. Its heavy green door swung back with difficulty, and the spacious room within was dark and cool. Old-fashioned country kitchen tables had been carefully covered with blankets and old sheets in lieu of ironing boards, and along the walls were dark wood cabinets containing neat stacks of towels and bedding. A portrait of the pope beamed down from above the ironing tables.

"The k-k-k-kitchen," said Sister Carmen with her shy stammer, leading the way back down the corridor to another green door; the kitchen also served as a cafeteria for the kindergarten that the Sisters ran in term time, and rows of tables and wooden benches had been marshaled into the middle of the room. Sister Carmen led me to the right wall, where there was a hot plate attached to a canister of gas and cabinets full of china and silverware. "And if you need light," she said, putting down the pile

of sheets and towels she was taking to my room, "you c-c-c-c-
can open the window," and she flung back the green shutters of
the far wall. Only a heartbeat away from the mission's walls
loomed the jungle, its enormous rich tangle of ferns and vines
and trees filling the window like an intricate screen.

Back and forth across the courtyard the tour continued: the
cold bottled water in the refrigerator in the Sisters' own kitchen,
the hot-water switch and showers, the deep porcelain sinks and
bars of laundry soap for washing clothes. The Sisters themselves
lived in the handsome two-story brick building that I had seen
from the road. Downstairs, the open doors allowed one to look
into their living room, furnished with curved raffia chairs, and
the dining room, with its long communal table. Under the upstairs balcony, trim wood-slatted doors marked the entrance to
each Sister's private bedroom, and a tall yellow and green grand-
father clock looked gravely down upon the little cloister. On the
other side of the upper balcony, facing the road and outer world,
stood a statue of the Virgin, painted in her classic blues and
pinks and golds.

It was dark when I returned from the showers. Through the
lighted windows of the chapel I saw that the Sisters were at
prayer. Someone had spread a faded tablecloth on the small
wooden loggia table in front of my bedroom door; I suspected
Sister Carmen. I made tea and settled down to dinner. The Sisters
filed out of the chapel and made their way to the dining room,
from where I continued to hear their voices and laughter. A full
moon rose out of the black gulf that I knew was the Ogooué. It
occurred to me—really for the first time—that this was a lovely
country.

Lambaréné is situated on a large island approximately one
hundred and thirty miles upriver from the coast, where the
Ogooué bifurcates into its northern and southern branches, and
a few miles below the mouth of the Ngounié river, its southern
tributary. At the time of Mary Kingsley's visit, "Lambaréné"
referred to both the island and the surrounding mainland settlements; today the name is properly applied to Lambaréné town,
situated on the northeast tip of the island.

Squarely set within the mesh of interconnecting lakes and waterways that riddle the region, Lambaréné is strategically placed for trade. From historical times it was occupied by three principal tribes: the Galoa, who originally came from the south near Fernan Vaz to the Middle Ogooué at about the time of the arrival of the Portuguese and Dutch traders in the sixteenth and seventeenth centuries, and who inhabited the northern mainland opposite Lambaréné island; the Enenga, who descended from the upper Ogooué in the mid-sixteenth century and claimed the area around Lake Zilo, upriver from Lambaréné on the southern shore—they had been the principal traders in this region prior to the arrival of the Europeans; and the Bakélé, a warlike people who supplied the coastal slavers and whose settlements were spread along the Ogooué's northern banks above Lambaréné. The Galoa and Enenga were both celebrated for their skill as navigators and boatmen, and the European expeditions recruited their guides and piroguers from these tribes. By the time of Mary Kingsley's visit, the Fang migrations from the north had already displaced some of the Galoa and Bakélé villages from their choice riverine locations.

The first European factories had been established on the northern mainland at Adolinanongo ("looking out over the people"), a little above Lambaréné island and at the time under the firm control of the Galoa "Sun King" Nkombè, with whom the trading firms had to negotiate for the right of settlement. According to tradition, it was Nkombè who gave Lambaréné its name: in the 1870s the Europeans decided to relocate their factories from Adolinanongo to the island because the dry season sandbars prohibited the use of a steamboat at the present site. When Bruce Walker, the founder and director of the Hatton and Cookson factory, informed Nkombè of this decision, the king is said to have mockingly replied, *"Lembaréni!"*—"Try it then!"—and the name stuck.

Mary Kingsley arrived here on June 7, at more or less the same time in the late afternoon as I had done; I wondered if the same low gold light had filled the scene when she first saw it. "At 5:15," she writes, "without evident cause to the uninitiated, the

Mové took to whistling like a liner. A few minutes later a factory shows up on the hilly north bank." For her, then, there were no scattered huts and houses, bare, plucked hills, or roads to give warning that Lambaréné lay ahead; she came from stark jungle and was there. She disembarked on the island and was escorted to Hatton and Cookson's factory—a long two-story, thatch-roofed building with a deep verandah that ran its entire length—where she was entertained by representatives of the firm. She spent most of her time in the Lambaréné area, however, both on her first visit and when she later returned from a trip farther upriver, at the Protestant Mission station at Andèndé, on the mainland facing the opposite side of the island.

The Kangwe Mission, so called because of its location on Kangwe Hill, had been established in 1874 by the same Dr. Nassau who was in charge of the Baraka Mission at the time of Mary Kingsley's visit. In 1893, the Americans had been forced to surrender Kangwe, along with another Ogooué station, being unable to comply with the French government's decree that all instruction in the mission schools be given in French. The missions were taken over by the French Protestant Société Mission Evangélique, with whom the Jacots, Mary Kingsley's hosts, were associated. In spite of the transfer of authority, the memory of the first founders died hard among the local people, and Pastor Wora told me that even in his time Kangwe Hill had been called "The Hill of the Americans."

I visited Andèndé on several occasions, following the road around to the other side of the island, where a bridge crossed the Ogooué's northern arm to the mainland. The view of Andèndé from the middle of the bridge, with the roads and houses of Lambaréné island behind, and the bridge itself no longer in the panorama before me, was probably, I thought, of all views in Lambaréné, least changed from when Mary Kingsley visited. Although the mission's deserted church, with its single fairy-tale spire, was after Kingsley's time, dating from the 1930s, and the square, wing-eaved colonial-style house on the hill slope was built of cement and roofed with corrugated iron, from the distance they seemed "authentic." Kangwe Hill itself, the surrounding forest, the river at the tiny settlement's feet, the triangular wedge of sand that Madame Jacot had said she welcomed because it relieved the terrible monotony of river and forest, and the isolated air that still pervades the place, in spite of its being only minutes by car from Lambaréné town, are all unchanged since Kingsley's time.

On the other side of the bridge, I scrambled down the steep clay banks that drop away from the roadside, into a strikingly neat and well-swept village below, where the inhabitants greeted me courteously from the steps of their huts as I passed by. The path wound out of the village, along the white river sand, then back into thick bush. The church, looking splintered and forlorn up close, rose somewhat shakily out of a wilderness of waist-high grass. Its wooden shingles were blue-gray, a rope still hung from its belfry, and its roof, as I saw when I climbed the hill above it, was tiled with diamonds of red, turquoise, and green, like the scales of an exotic fish. It was a perfect little European toy church, left all alone in Africa. It was dark inside, in part because the high grass did not allow much light to enter the unshuttered windows. Behind the pulpit were stacks of mimeographed song sheets for a service.

On the same hill, above the church, stand the burned-out remains of a house on iron piles. The floor struts and some of the wall supports remain, and it is possible to trace the different rooms. A balcony once ran around the house on all four sides. This, as an obscure plaque on the wall commemorates, was once the house of Albert Schweitzer; for it was here, of course, at Lambaréné, that he established his famous hospital.

A life as extraordinary as Schweitzer's belies tidy synopsis, and his own works best tell his story. He was born in 1875, in Alsace, into a deeply religious family; his father was a Lutheran pastor, his mother the daughter of a pastor. While still a young man, Schweitzer formed the belief that he could fully realize the ethical imperatives of Christianity only by directly ministering to humanity. At the age of twenty-one, Schweitzer vowed to allow himself ten years to indulge in the study of art and science before dedicating himself to medicine. Within this allotted period, he became distinguished in the fields of philosophy, theology, and music, and obtained doctorates in each subject.

In the autumn of 1904, he came upon an article entitled "The Needs of the Congo Mission" in the Paris Missionary Society's monthly journal and took the author's appeal for help in this neglected part of the world as a personal directive: a few months later, he wrote, "I resolved to realize my plan of direct human service in Equatorial Africa."

In 1912, he married Hélène Bresslau, and in February of 1913, he completed his medical training and prepared to go to Africa. This was not to be as easy as he had assumed: Schweitzer's religious beliefs were unorthodox and well known and now presented him with grave difficulties in securing a position with the Paris Missionary Society. He and his wife, therefore, proposed to go at their own expense as a doctor and nurse to the centrally placed Andèndé station, still in the hands of the Paris mission. Schweitzer further vowed to be "as mute as a fish" on sensitive religious issues and stressed that he was going to Africa as a doctor, not as a preacher. He and Hélène raised the money from fees at Schweitzer's organ recitals and lectures and from donations of a circle of generous friends. Finally, in April 1913, nearly nine years after reading the missionary article, Schweitzer and Hélène disembarked at Lambaréné.

Like Mary Kingsley, they arrived by steamer and then continued upriver by canoe to Andèndé. Once at the mission, they were led by a procession of singing children to their house, which had been decorated with flowers and palm fronds. Their belongings, in seventy packing cases, and Schweitzer's piano, equipped with organ pedals, were delivered later over a period of two days by relays of canoes. "The station," wrote Schweitzer, "is about 650 yards long and 110 to 120 yards across. We measure it again and again in every direction in our evening and Sunday constitutionals." The forest, which at that time pressed much closer around Andèndé than it does today, made the air as heavy and stagnant as a prison's: "If we could only cut down a corner of the forest which shuts in the lower end of the station we should get a little of the breeze in the river valley." In the dry season, the mission dwellers took their constitutional strolls on the sandbars, where they were exposed to the river breezes.

The doctor's first clinic was set up in the mission's deserted fowl house. The mission itself proved to be supportive, and its council voted to help fund a new hospital building, which had to be built from scratch. Within months of his arrival, Schweitzer was invited to preach, which allowed him to break his pledge of silence on theological issues.

Schweitzer and his wife had been in Lambaréné only a short time before war broke out, and on the evening of August 5, 1914, French government officials arrived in canoes from Lambaréné island at the three hills of Andèndé, that tiny clearing of 650 by 120 yards in the expanse of forest and river, walked up the beaten trail, and told the doctor that he and his wife were now prisoners of war and would be kept under house arrest. This place was, after all, French territory, and the doctor was a German. Guards were stationed at the Schweitzer residence to ensure that the doctor and his wife could neither leave nor practice medicine. This image, which confounds one's rational senses, is reminiscent of Conrad's description in *Heart of Darkness* of a French gunboat off the African West Coast: "In the empty immensity of earth, sky, and water, there she was, incomprehensible, firing into a continent."

In the fall of 1917, Schweitzer and his wife returned to Europe, where he gave more recitals and "popular" lectures to pay off hospital debts. Ill health and the lack of means prohibited his returning until April 1924, this time without Hélène. An outbreak of dysentery in 1925 impressed upon him the urgent need for larger hospital facilities, and although it entailed the daunting prospect of building again from scratch, he made the decision to relocate. He chose a place some two miles upstream from Andèndé, at Adolinanongo, the site abandoned years before by the trading factories, and it is here that his legacy, the present Schweitzer Hospital, still stands. Schweitzer was awarded the Nobel Peace Prize in 1952. He died in Lambaréné in 1965.

Extraordinary as Schweitzer's venture was, he stood at the end of a long tradition, and his undertaking differed from that of the earlier missionaries in degree but not in kind. Schweitzer uniquely had attained a measure of success and fame before his departure to Africa, and this contributed in no small part to the subsequent legend, although it is fair to say that most of the missionary pioneers similarly sacrificed other, more comfortable and lucrative careers for their sense of mission. In general it is possible to draw many close parallels between Schweitzer and the earlier, virtually nameless missionaries who "labored" here and in other parts of West Africa, and it is astonishing that Schweitzer became an international personality, while the world knows little at all of his predecessors. The establishment of the early mission stations had required the missionaries to embark on extensive exploration, clear jungle, construct buildings with only the help of local laborers who were often dealing with a white man for the first time, all the while trying to avoid inter-tribal warfare, combat tribal hostilities, and fend off diseases that were at the time very imperfectly understood. Formidable as Schweitzer's task was, by the time he arrived at Andèndé, the most difficult work had already been done.

Schweitzer's was a markedly personal enterprise; he did not work closely with any outside organization, and the funds for the hospital were largely from his own resources. He had considered several charitable options before the catalytic article in the missionary journal. "I naturally thought first of some [charitable] activity in Europe," he wrote in *Out of My Life and Thought* and went on to remark that all his attempts to serve as a volunteer to various organizations were unsuccessful. When the Strasbourg Orphanage was burned down, for example, he offered to take in a few boys; his offer was dismissed, and Schweitzer, somewhat peevish at the memory even after so many years, recalled that "the superintendent did not even allow me to finish what I had to say." He continued to search for worthy causes but eventually came to the conclusion that "what I wanted was an absolutely personal and independent activity."

If one delves into the annals and letters of the men who

preceded Schweitzer, one soon comes to realize that one of the greatest difficulties about being a missionary was working with one's fellow missionaries, and that the craving for an independent operation was not unusual. Dr. Nassau, disgusted with the gossip and politics of the Baraka station, wrote to his sister, saying that he had decided to leave his missionary board's service and seek "employment of some wealthy individual or Body" to sponsor his work. "I would either live and board at a factory, or build myself a little house—probably at Gaboon—and would spend my time in writing the books I have so often planned." Schweitzer's independence, therefore, should perhaps not be seen as an additional burden; it was something many missionaries desired. The key to Schweitzer's successful realization of his dream may have lain in the fact that no one before him had undertaken his task with such intense self-consciousness.

Schweitzer's unorthodox conception of Christianity may have played a part in shaping this self-consciousness. His most important early theological work was *The Quest of the Historical Jesus,* a work that attempted to understand Jesus in the context of his contemporary Jewish eschatological thought. Schweitzer claimed that Jesus' erroneous belief that the end of the world was at hand had led to his radical conception of a new ethical order. Schweitzer's Jesus, therefore, was a great ethical leader, but a fallible man, and tempered, as are all men, by the thought of his times. This has interesting implications in terms of understanding Schweitzer himself. Whereas other missionaries had come to spread the word of God incarnate, Schweitzer came to offer religious service by, in a sense, living *in imitatione Christi,* a goal that was perhaps, given his conception of the historical Jesus, not wholly impossible.

After the hospital had been relocated to its new site, Schweitzer was answerable to no one and was free to preach as often as he liked. One cannot help wondering what impression a sermon about a good man who walked with God and cured the sick would have made when preached to a heathen assembly by the doctor: did Schweitzer inevitably appear to be preaching about the example of his own life? When he became an international figure, he was visited by an inordinate number of generally unskilled western women, who came to find fulfillment by serving in the Schweitzer establishment. An objective, if somewhat ruthless, analysis of this phenomenon invites comparison with modern cult figures (the Bhagwan Shree Rajneesh, for example), who have attracted a remarkably similar type of female disciple.

For the early missionaries, an African's conversion to Christianity entailed his adoption of "civilized" dress, manners, and even speech. Schweitzer resisted this trend strenuously, and from the beginning his guiding philosophy had been that his hospital must be a place to which villagers who were unfamiliar with western customs and medicine would want to come. Modernization, he maintained, would banish comfortable village features: extended families would no longer be able to camp out behind the wards and prepare food for their sick relatives, for example. Goats, pigs, dogs, and chickens would no longer be able to roam at large throughout the hospital compound—and African patients might be less likely to come for treatment as a result. But it was rumored by his critics that Schweitzer shunned modernization for other reasons; the arrival of other doctors with up-to-date training would have shown his own knowledge to be outdated and he would have had to yield at times to the newcomers' judgments on matters of medicine and perhaps eventually hospital policy. Above all, he might have found himself compelled to work within a system and so lose forever the "absolutely personal and independent activity" that had been the dream that led him to Africa so many years before. Perhaps, then, it was not only the Africans who needed the comfort of a village atmosphere; in a more progressive, western environment Schweitzer might have become merely a doctor, not *le Grand Docteur,* a man with a mission in Darkest Africa.

The world changed drastically in the course of Schweitzer's long life, and a great part of the fascination he holds for us lies in his closeness to that "other" age of the earliest explorers, missionaries, and traders; Schweitzer corresponded with Dr.

Nassau, who had hosted Mary Kingsley and Count de Brazza, and yet he died in recent memory. The sun topee, the old-fashioned clothing—Schweitzer himself was acutely aware that he was seen as straddling two eras. His deliberate anachronisms of both dress and hospital management are perhaps precisely what won him such wide attention, and whereas the early missionaries could present only a picture of earnest toil, the image of Schweitzer that was beamed out from Lambaréné served the modern world as a touchstone with a more glamorous past.

The present Schweitzer Hospital is one of the best hospitals in its part of the world. It is a modern establishment, equipped for out-patient, surgical, and dental treatment, with beds for three hundred people. When the hospital was threatened with closure in 1975, President Bongo pledged the support of the Gabonese government, which today contributes approximately a quarter of the hospital budget. Patients are charged a minimal fee, but the hospital is largely financed, in addition to government support, by various Schweitzer Fellowship organizations around the world and by private donations. Volunteer doctors and nurses from Europe, America, and other parts of Africa come to work for periods ranging from three months to two years. Ironically, there are no Gabonese doctors at the Schweitzer establishment, as they are attracted to the state hospitals, which pay higher salaries. Gabon's medical infrastructure is as a whole one of the best in West Africa.

At the sandy cove directly across from the hospital, I waited while the piroguer who had spotted me from the opposite mainland paddled slowly and somewhat unsteadily across the channel. The red roofs of the hospital buildings showed picturesquely among the palm crowns, exactly as they do in the old photographs of the early Schweitzer Hospital. The sound of a radio playing loud music carried clearly from the other shore; I wondered if this was a modern element in the village atmosphere Schweitzer had sought to foster. The piroguer was an old man, with sad, watchful eyes. "Schweitzer?" he asked as I got in. A wooden crutch lay beside him, and I saw that he was crippled. The boat rhythmically lurched forward and drifted, in unison with the quiet plops of the paddle, whose blade seemed too small for the volume of water it needed to move. A little girl appeared on the mainland bank as we drew near: "One hundred francs! Give him one hundred francs only, Madame!" she shouted, running alongside our pirogue as it briefly paralleled the shore. "He will ask you for a thousand, but the Gabonese pay only"—deep breath—"ONE HUNDRED FRANCS!"

Other pirogues lay with water-logged tree trunks on the hospital beach, where women were doing their washing. The path to the hospital complex led up past a cemetery, where a crude wooden cross marks Schweitzer's grave, and a pen where antelope are kept—the doctor himself had many pets. The new medical facilities and the *marché* lie some distance farther up the hill, but it is to the old hospital, where Schweitzer himself lived and worked, that most visitors come to pay tribute. Its wooden buildings stand above the ground on low piles and have walls of open latticework, in deference to the climate. They comprise the living quarters of some of the staff, the kitchen and dining room, and the Schweitzer Museum. The latter preserves Schweitzer's study and bedroom, containing his oversize, worn books, printed in Gothic German lettering, his glasses, various little tins, bed linen, his sun topee—the mundane bric-a-brac of a human life, both ludicrous and eloquent in their abstraction from the individual person. Far more compelling was the deserted clinic, whose modest size, cellar dankness, and remaining crude medical equipment convey something of the Herculean task the *Grand Docteur* had set himself.

•/•/•

IT IS POSSIBLE for visitors to stay at the hospital, but I was by now cozily established at the mission, which in spite of its size had only four sisters in residence. Sister Agnes was the only Gabonese nun, and the garden seemed to be her special province. She had an exceedingly upright bearing, walking as if a board had been strapped to her back. Her French inflection was slightly "off" and lent even her friendliest comments a certain tartness. Sister Carmen worked primarily in the kitchen and also "visited the poor." Her ability to derive pleasure from simple objects can only be described as Proustian; watching her handle tomatoes from the garden, one sensed her delight in their satiny weight, in their deep color in the light, in their fat shapes clustered together on the kitchen table. Sister Yves Marie had an air of concerned competence; events did not exactly cause her anxiety, but she seemed always aware that things could go wrong. If for some reason it ever became necessary to abandon the mission to the hands of a single person, then one would entrust it to Sister Yves Marie and return even ten years later to find it faithfully well run and guarded. Mother Jacques Marie was the Mother Superior. At some early point in her life the Almighty must have swept her up to heaven to view the human comedy from a divine perspective and allowed her to return to earth with secret insight into the way things *really* were; she now regarded life's apparent joys or hardships alike with superior bemusement—she who had looked behind the veil, *she* knew better. Her offhand cheerfulness was therefore comforting, and induced one to feel that there was reason to be optimistic about the eventual outcome of this ephemeral existence.

Each morning, I had my breakfast of coffee and croissants at the verandah table, looking out over the quiet mission courtyard. At seven o'clock, the Sisters emerged from their green doors for matins in the chapel. It was still school term time, during the early part of my stay, and after breakfast a minibus used to draw up outside the wrought-iron gates and empty a stream of children into the courtyard. They were met by the Sisters and assembled on the benches under the broad-leafed tree, where they sat twittering and laughing like a flock of little birds. Later, they were led into the classroom beside the kitchen, and I would hear them solemnly chanting their alphabet.

The mission's height gave it a view over the red road below, the bananas and palms at the water's edge, and the Ogooué river, which now, from the comfort of solid land, appeared green and peaceful. In the dry season, a perpetual cloud of dust arises from the unpaved road that runs beside the river into Lambaréné town, about three-quarters of a mile from the mission. On the way into town, one passes the harbor and several restaurants run by West Africans, who sit outside their premises, dressed in the voluminous opulence of their caftans. The communal taxis and minibuses congregate at the town center, near the market and shops, which all carry an identical stock of tinned food, toiletries, lengths of batik-patterned fabric, and poor-quality metal cooking pots. The exception is the supermarket, Hollando, run by a European couple, which has a small *charcuterie* and carries wine, cheese, and croissants and sweet rolls kept under a heated glass cover. From the town center, the road continues for roughly another three-quarters of a mile, flanked on its water side by piles of rubble, debris, scrawny grass, and the occasional tree, and on the other by more shops, the Place de l'Indépendance, the chemist, and the bank.

The Peace Corps office in Libreville had given me the names of two volunteers working in the Lambaréné area, whom I could contact for information about the best way of getting to the nearby lakes. Of the two, the easier to get hold of was a Professor Goodfriend, who taught mathematics at the Lycée d'Etat, on the top of the hill. Near the turnoff that led eventually to his house, I passed a group of women bathing naked in the muddy water by a pile of stones that jutted out into the river like a rough jetty, and which seemed to be the public laundry. Two old women shuffled toward town, bent double under the loads of wood that hung heavily across their backs from woven headbands. They had been foraging, perhaps in the forest beyond the hills.

The police station lay some little distance up the road, and the gendarmes were lolling on the porch, watchful for passing drivers whom they could stop and cajole for cigarettes or petty cash. Farther along was the old post office, a classic colonial building, now abandoned and boarded up. In the road lay a newly killed, immensely fat snake, with dirty brown and jaundiced-yellow diamond patterning.

The road climbed steeply, edged by walls covered with bougainvillea, hibiscus, and morning glory. On a bright morning, such as this was, Lambaréné was shown to great advantage. It seemed full of flowers, of yellow acacia and orange flame trees, of pretty houses in muted colors set in walled gardens. On closer inspection, and in duller light, one saw that lush foliage was in part overgrown grass and weeds, that buildings perhaps once had been brightly colored but were now filthy, that everything—roads, houses, trees, gardens, stray animals—was left to fend for itself. Most houses were not privately owned, but belonged to firms which rent them to their employees, and neither landlord nor tenant seemed anxious to shoulder the responsibility of their upkeep.

Professor Goodfriend's house was situated some distance behind the Lycée, and had a staggering overview of the forest extending to the west. Different intensities of light hung trapped in the different levels of foliage below, and the result was a scene of strangely hazy indistinctness. Somehow, as always, the glossy banana trees managed to stand out from even the densest and most varied greenery. No one was around, but a message board hung on the porch. After much thought, I wrote that I was retracing the journey of Mary Kingsley, a Victorian traveler, and had been told by the Peace Corps office in Libreville that Professor Goodfriend might have information about how to get to the many lakes around Lambaréné; I was acutely aware that this would be a somewhat strange message to come home to.

Back at the mission, I sat down to study some maps at the table outside my room. A noise at the verandah gate made me look up to see a young man with an unmistakably American face, who was wearing a baseball hat back to front. This turned out to be Professor Goodfriend; he had not yet been home to see his message board but had been told by a friendly passing taxi driver that a stranger had been looking for him. He himself was leaving Gabon for good in a few days and as a farewell trip he was accompanying Brent, the other Lambaréné volunteer, to a village on the shores of one of the lakes the next day, and he suggested that we try to find him. Peace Corps volunteers in Gabon are generally either high school teachers, like Kurt Goodfriend, or construction workers, like Brent Friedrich, who build schools in usually remote villages. Brent's base in Lambaréné, which he used when he returned from his village site to organize transport of materials and equipment, was on the other side of the island, facing Andèndé.

After lunch, when the heat of the afternoon sun was beating up off the dusty road, Kurt and I set out in the opposite direction to town. The Church of Saint-François-Xavier, the original Catholic Mission that is the fraternal counterpart of the Sisters' order, lay only a couple of hundred yards away. The Brothers' dormitory, built of the ubiquitous orange-rose brick, was more imposing than the Sisters' sanctuary but was not secluded by a garden and stood openly on a hilltop amid parched and scanty grass—at the time of Mary Kingsley's visit, the area around the church had been settled with Galoa villages. The church itself, situated up a steep incline to the left of the road, was of a handsome type recognizable from black and white photographs of similar churches throughout the colonial world, and which one would expect to approach by an avenue of palms. Inside was a hideous and distorted wooden statue, carved by an American—a white man's vision of the African conception of Christ. "Me, I didn't bring it here," said one of the Fathers with disgust.

Beyond the church, several square, cinder-block houses, half-painted and half-built like so many houses in Gabon, faced a marshy expanse of beach across the road. An enormous sandbank formed an island in the river channel; I was told that it had appeared months earlier than usual this year. "Better" houses lay around the corner of the island's northern tip; they were larger, with two stories, and with gardens, but had the usual ill-kempt and untended air. The roadside grass was higher than our heads and filled with the sound of singing birds. Indeed, it seemed to me that Lambaréné was always singing; at night it rang with frogs, in the day with birds. Brent's "boutique," a shed that was part storeroom and part living quarters, stood on the riverside not far from the bridge that led to the mainland and to Andèndé. I was told by several Europeans that the Gabonese do not like to use the bridge at night because "they do not like to be over the water in the dark"; but no Gabonese ever told me this.

Brent was inside, busy getting things together for his trip the next day. He was moustached, tall and stringy, made lean, one imagined, from untiring, perpetual activity. He was from Iowa and spoke French with a distinctive twang: "Murcy bowcoop," he would say by way of thanks.

"So you're the traveling lady. I saw your note at Kurt's and left a message of my own, asking if you wanted to come with us to the lakes." Peace Corps hospitality was to play an important part in my trip. I recalled an incident in Mary Kingsley's *Travels;* on the boat trip from Lambaréné to Ndjolé, she shared the company of a French official who was on his way to Franceville. He was, she tells us, "a tremendously lively person" and "excellent company." At Ndjolé, seeing the encampment of Adouma boatmen and the convoy of shallow pirogues that would take her companion on the rest of his journey, she wistfully remarks on what a "blessing he will be to Franceville when he gets there." How delightful—how easy—it would have been if the French official had turned to her and said, "Miss Kingsley, would you like to come along with me for the ride?" But in her day, such an invitation would have been very difficult to extend, let alone to accept. In this respect, I was far more fortunate, and when two total strangers asked me to join in their excursion, I was able, unreservedly, to say yes.

I found the mission gates snugly shut when I got back, so I had to scramble over them; I was to climb several gates that summer. The night watchman, who sat wrapped in an old raincoat deep in the shadows by the kitchen door, watched impassively as his two German shepherds bounded over to confront me. The dogs were the bane of visitors to the mission and used to trail me across the courtyard at night, grinning maliciously and nipping my heels with great precision.

"Ah, Al-ex-an-der," Sister Carmen greeted me the next morning, drawing out my name. Her tone seemed ironic; did she know I'd climbed the mission gates? She was pleased to hear that I was going to the lakes and nodded approvingly when Brent arrived in his Peace Corps truck: "You will be p-p-protected then."

We drove back to town, then crossed to the southern main-

land, where there is a large palm oil factory and a cluster of shop
stalls, which Kurt and I looked over, ambling along in the dust
while Brent went off to do errands. Trays containing stones and
lumps of earth were laid out between pink plastic shoes and
batteries. "These are for pregnant women," a proprietor told me,
pointing to something that looked like chalk; but when I asked
about the other stones, he smiled and shrugged, indicating that
he either could not or would not say.

A new restaurant, a shedlike building with shiny red oilskin
tablecloths and paper napkins folded carefully in plastic tum-
blers, lay at the end of the road. The sign outside gave the price
of crocodile, monkey, porcupine, gazelle, and pangolin with rice.
We stopped for a drink at Claude's, which was run by a bitter-
looking German with thinning black hair and a lean, contemptu-
ous face. His bar was made of split bamboo with an elaborately
patterned roof of woven palm fronds. Kurt opened one of the
shutters next to where we sat in near darkness. "Don't touch
what isn't yours," Claude snarled from his corner. The only
other customer was a piroguer who had seen me the day I arrived
in Lambaréné and now began to berate me for not having taken
his boat. A woman entered from the back of the bar with bread
and butter, which is traditionally served to guests by way of
hospitality. "They didn't order that," Claude snapped and took
the sandwich himself, devouring it while he watched us closely,
like a prisoner who fears his food will be snatched away. Claude
had come to Gabon several years ago to work for a European firm
but soon tossed this over, took up with a Gabonese woman, and
began his own business. Two years ago his wife came out from
Germany and lived one year in Lambaréné—a constant despair-
ing presence—before taking her own life. Claude lived on, as if
now trapped in a way of life he had perhaps not meant to
maintain forever.

Brent's village, Alonha, was situated on the shores of Lake
Ezanga, which lies due south of Lambaréné. Elias, Brent's assistant, was going ahead by boat, while we were to drive the truck,
taking the rough and partly overgrown forestry trail that turned
off to Alonha from the main road. There are less than four

hundred miles of bituminized roads in Gabon, and even these, with the exception of those in the immediate vicinity of Libreville and Franceville, are appalling: they are in the first place only wide enough to accommodate two cars, assuming that both are traveling in a straight line on the correct side of the road, an event beyond the pale of probability. The tremendous craters and the jagged erosion of the shoulders account in part for the eccentric, weaving course most vehicles make; other factors are less easily ascertained.

Secondary forest growth borders the road, the glorified weeds that spring up wherever the ancient, real forest has been uprooted. This has a bland homogeneity, dominated by the cupola-shaped crowns of umbrella trees. Variation, no matter how rich, would in any case be disguised by the cloud of dry-season dust that billows up from the road when traffic passes and that settles like dull, red powder on every branch and leaf. The highwater mark of this dustline can be up to twenty feet, and from a hill one sees that the red swath cuts back deep into the forest. To travel down this red corridor is dismally monotonous, except in the low light of morning or late afternoon, when the foliage appears to have been gilded with cheap bronze, and the trees, ferns, and nameless weeds seem transformed into extravagantly wrought metal objects. The huts and houses by the roadside have tightly shuttered windows, but to no avail; the dust filters through wood and stone as through vegetation, soiling clothes, burning eyes, choking lungs, enveloping a village in a red simoon, like an eleventh plague from heaven.

We came to what we took to be the Alonha turnoff, indicated by a barely discernible dent in the roadside bush. The trail looked freshly cut, with fine, severed roots standing up like stray hairs from the slick, newly sliced clay. This puzzled Brent, who had only driven to the village once before but definitely remembered it as an overgrown, indistinct trail. A teenage boy was standing beside a small plantation lying just off the road, and we asked him if this was the way to Alonha. "Yes," the boy replied, pointing along the road with a sapling branch he had been twiddling.

"They're reclearing it, I guess," said Brent as we bounced along. Felled trees lay haphazardly around, and the earth, stripped of its undergrowth, showed red and raw. Lumber is Gabon's second most important export commodity (up until the 1960s, it accounted for seventy-five percent of all exports), the most valuable wood being okoumé, which is used for plywood. It is impossible to stay abreast of the changes in Gabon's road system, for the forestry industry is continually cutting new roads, and old ones are swiftly reclaimed by the waiting forest. A massive okoumé tree lying directly in our path now brought us to a halt; its trunk was wider than I was high, and its cut end had the fleshy look of sliced ham. We backed up and returned the way we had come. The teenage boy was unperturbed to see us again; yes, he repeated, this was a road to Alonha. We had not asked if it was finished.

The villages we passed on the main road are Fang. They are arranged as Mary Kingsley saw them, set out in lines parallel to a road. The houses are no longer made of bamboo and thatch, however, but of wood (and occasionally bamboo) and corrugated iron, usually set in sandy compounds. The iron roofs trap and hold the heat, but are nonetheless a godsend in the rainy season. By government decree, all major villages must be situated by the roads, ostensibly for the convenience of supplying them and for census taking, but also no doubt because it is easier to keep an eye on them. In an effort to combat tribalism and to foster a "Gabonese" identity, villages of different tribes are often forcibly combined and relocated so as to form one new village. Although this system now seems to be working, it was predictably unpopular when first implemented. Stories abound about unsubtle means of government pressure, such as the fire bombing of entire villages in the 1960s to force people to move out. In each case, one man known for his strength of character is chosen to be the *chef de regroupement* of the new hybrid settlement.

Not far from the Alonha turnoff was a *boutique* where we stopped for a drink before continuing. These *boutiques*, which serve as both shop and bar, are large sheds with child-size benches and tables at either end, and a wooden counter running the length of the back wall, opposite an open doorway. Stacked behind the counter are the familiar essentials—dust-covered tins of sardines and milk, cigarettes and soap, lanterns and Nescafé. Other objects for sale are often displayed on overturned oil drums by the roadside, usually fruit, game, or a milky-green bottle of *vin de palme.* Here, the blackened object on the oil drum turned out to be a charred monkey, its eyes shut and mouth open in a death scream and its lower extremities burned off to a stump. Its paws were still tied behind its back, and this detail alone removed the creature from the strictly animal realm. Not all tribes will eat monkey, and even fewer will eat chimpanzee or gorilla. "No, they are like us, in how they look, in all they do," a Malian once said to me, "but these Fang—ah, they eat everything." The Fang too acknowledge the resemblance to humans, even referring to monkeys as "our cousins"; but the Fang are historically cannibal.

The Alonha road was overgrown, as Brent had remembered. High grass blurred the trail, and sharp branches pronged us through the windows. At times the road was sunk low between banks that rose above the truck cabin, and that were all but obscured by a thick mat of greenery. The day was not uncomfortably hot; the sky had taken on the bleached-out colorlessness characteristic of the dry season, and yet the forest leaves were shining, as if they received their light from some source other than the washed-out sky. We crossed occasional streams by way of bridges so fragile that Kurt and I would get out of the truck to lessen its load. There were, according to Brent's memory, eighteen bridges to be crossed between the turnoff and Alonha; on the fifteenth bridge, the planks broke beneath us.

The truck's right front wheel was dangling well below the level of the bridge and its weight was resting on the front distributor pumpkin. We labored for the next two hours, trying, inches at a time, to jack the truck off the distributor, and to wedge a kind of multipart ramp, composed of pieces of stray bridge wood, under the distressed wheel. We were more or less working with only one hand each, employing the other to swat away various stinging insects, including a swarm of bees that had wafted up from under the bridge. Nonetheless, we were optimistic up to the moment of truth when Brent started the engine and the truck, instead of lurching up our cleverly placed ramp, spattered the bits of wood behind it like ball bearings. We regrouped; it was six o'clock, and, as all the geography books will tell you, dusk falls swiftly on the equator. Something large crashed in the trees to one side of us. Brent said that we were not far from the edge of the forest and the beginning of open plateau, and that the plateau was not at all far from Alonha. If we started walking, we would surely be met by Elias leading a posse of concerned villagers searching for us. None of us was too happy about spending a night in the forest, even with the truck on more secure ground and without the bees, and so we decided to cut our losses and try to get to the plateau before dark.

Given our collective credentials—two Peace Corps workers with two full years in the bush of equatorial Africa, and a seasoned traveler who had come to Gabon expressly to make treks of this kind—it may be instructive to list the equipment that our group took with us on its dramatic march. Brent, typically, took not one personal effect but carried a machete, a sack of French bread, and a plastic pail containing two raw, plucked chickens; Kurt took his knapsack, a cumbersome, handleless container of water, and rocket flares; I took my sleeping bag, a sack of biscuits, and my small knapsack, which contained among other things a compass and mosquito coils. No one had matches, a fact that rendered the mosquito coils, rocket flares, and even raw plucked chickens useless, at least for their ordinary purposes. We did not take the conveniently packaged sandwich meats and cheese, nor the smaller, easily carried extra water flasks. I was also forced to leave behind Mary Kingsley's *Travels.* Reflecting on this incident later, I can only conclude that our conviction that we would reach Alonha that night must have been stronger than I now remember it to have been.

The trail, rough in any case, became less clear as it grew darker. The dusk itself seemed to exude from the earth, from the grass roots up, a darkening process disassociated from the slow massing of shadows in the canopy overhead. In the light of the still-undimmed middle ether, I made out blue, pink, and yellow flowers embedded in the foliage, too discreet to have been seen from our fast-moving truck; the truck had obscured too the rustling silence through which we now walked—incredible to think that it had been there all those hours, spread through the trees, as characteristic of the forest as any of the vegetation, and that we had simply missed it.

The plateau, which we reached just after dark, marked a decisive change not only of terrain but of cosmic order; one would not bring the same sacrifices to the deities of the shaggy forest as to those of the open plains. The line between the two was decisively drawn, and the trees seemed to throng an unseen threshold. Looking back, it was no longer possible to make out the entrance to the forest; like a walled city after curfew, it showed us only a black, impenetrable front.

We were walking on a road of white sand, through high plateau grass, also white, but of a stark, brittle intensity, as if lit by stage light. A low, full moon cast a curiously flat light, by which it was difficult to judge depths of field, distances, even the depth of indentations in the sand. Bosses of woodland were studded at a careful distance from one another, like sentry posts; below one, Brent recognized a deserted shed, which had once been a chantier. We walked on, shifting our ungainly baggage from hand to hand, or shoulder to shoulder. The white silica of the road stretched imposingly before us over the land's slow undulation. Other roads began to crisscross our own. We took a turn, then thought better of it, and were startled to discover that it was not easy to regain our earlier route; the flattening light did not pick out footprints, and we had to grope for a while before we found them.

We had been walking for an hour and a half, and our confidence in being on the right path, let alone in reaching Alonha, was all but sapped. Brent wearily put the pail of chicken down and rested his arms, and Kurt and I suggested that he leave it. We again conferred; it was late and we were tired. It seemed best to return to our one sure landmark, the boss with the deserted chantier, and to spend the night there, attempting nothing else until the morning. We turned back, leaving the blue plastic pail and its contents on the roadside, a surreal cairn, or grotesque offering.

On the slope of the hill, we set up camp. Brent had saved the chickens' burlap sack and now used this as the lower part of an improvised sleeping bag, wrapping his upper body in towels that Kurt and I had brought. This was ingenious, but ineffectual, and he spent most of the night sitting up with his arms huddled about him, staring fixedly at the ground. I knew of his suffering firsthand, because I was myself awake throughout the night to witness it, Kurt and I faring no better in a communal sleeping bag. A humming mist of mosquitoes had engulfed us and respite came only when the wind momentarily scattered the fragile swarm; but the slightest breeze also shook loose strange noises from the trees, thumps and occasional crashes, the fluttering of strong wings, and toward dawn the unabashed laughing song of an unseen bird.

The night passed in its slow stages; inch by inch the moon ascended higher in the sky behind an unhurried parade of clouds. The cold increased in careful increments. The noises from the woodland came with cautious deliberateness. All the world seemed to luxuriate in the knowledge that the night would be long and that haste was unnecessary.

A little before six, in a blue-gray dawn, we called quits to our pretense of sleep. We found that in the course of the slow hours, we had each independently formed the resolution to try to free the jeep once more. We marched back over the grassland, gray now in the faint dawn mist and not so ethereal as the night before. The forest was wet and sparkling with dew, more flowers were open in the morning freshness, and but for the elephant dung in the road, and the nearby trees flattened in a clumsy trail, we could have been in a woodland glade.

We found the bees still guarding the jeep and stood well out of their way while we formed our next plan of action; the distributor was clear, and the problem now lay with the fallen wheel. If we took the tire off the wheel, the gap between the wheel rim and the bridge would be crucially lessened, and another ramp could be placed beneath it. Covered with fresh coats of insect repellent, we got to work, and two hours later were ready to try again. The truck whined, its wheels spun, there was a smell of burning wood—and the truck slipped lower between the planks.

Later in the morning, the cool, protective mists having long since burned off, we came again to the plateau, having repeated our walk of the night before. The network of roads was difficult to trace even in daylight; they were deceptively broad, clean, straight tracks of sand, but they ran for only a short distance before becoming lost in the high, wheaten grass, or the dip of a hill. The well-drawn tracks that led to nowhere, the neat bosses of carefully contained forest, the groomed, manicured landscape paradoxically combined with the unmistakable lack of human habitation, gave the impression that this was a place kept specially apart, reserved for a foreordained party—who knows, perhaps for us?

Brent walked anxiously ahead of us, darting off the road from time to time to take his bearings. He had driven to Alonha only once before, in September, a very different season, in which the land had shown a very different face, but he felt full responsibility for our mishap; he seemed incapable of taking food or rest until he had led us safely to the village, and he was becoming leaner by the minute, melting away under his indefatigable energy. Writ large in Kurt's eyes was an awareness that this was his farewell trip to Gabon, that a delay could mean that he would miss his flight to Libreville. I had secretly enjoyed the walk the night before but now felt disoriented; I could not decide if this was a hike or a trek. This plateau might look like the land of Oz, but we were, were we not, in equatorial Africa?

Several times, Kurt and I waited, usually in the shade of a well-chosen tree on the edge of a boss, while Brent went doggedly uphill through the grass for a lookout. Even as we watched him closely, he would vanish from our sight; the grass, the hills, the perspective simply swallowed him up. Once we waited on the road for him to catch us up, but when we next saw him, he was somehow on the hill ahead of us. This was Looking

Glass country, and the roads delivered you not where they appeared to be leading, but wherever they chose to go.

"Did you say there was an airfield?" I asked. We had been walking for nearly five hours and were now coming over the top of another hill. The road we were going to take lay off to the right, but over my left shoulder I had caught sight of a brown triangle below us. Brent began to cheer: "That's it! It's the deserted airstrip. We're nearly there."

Past the airfield, the coarse gold-blond grass gave way to fields of long pale-green blades that looked like river rushes. Farther still were stubble fields that had been recently scorched black. From the ashes, Brent drew forth with his machete an enormous scorpion, perfectly preserved, and all the more evil-looking for its having been burned glossy black. Villages burn their surrounding land every dry season as a means of fertilizing the soil; these blasted fields at least meant that we were near habitation. Soon we came on the boundary marker of a plantation, a wire hung with bits of flattened metal strung through a line of bushes. A red laterite road brought us to our first dwelling, a small wooden hut with a palm thatch roof, standing by itself.

"Kokoko," said Kurt, the equivalent of knocking, and an old man wearing tattered shorts and an unraveling sweater limped toward us on legs and feet so severely swollen that his toes had split open. Yes, this was the way to Alonha, he told us, unflinching as Brent approached with his prize scorpion transfixed to his high-held machete point.

The road continued on past more plantations and cleared ground where new shoots had struggled through the baked soil and ashes. We crossed bridges sixteen, seventeen, and eighteen, the views down their narrow rivulets being more pastoral than along the gloomier forest streams. A low pirogue gently butted the grass bank it was moored to, like a punt on a sunny English river.

A copse of trees set back in an overgrown field showed ahead to our left. "We enter by the tree that looks like an orchard tree," said Brent, leading us on. Half an hour later we were making our way across the marshy beach to the lake's edge. Brent left us here, promising to return with the boat. It was a dismal spot; uninspiring patches of scrub and a few anemic rushes were barely rooted in the gray silty beach, which was strangely pocked with perfectly round craters, as if cartoon dinosaurs had left their footprints on the sand before returning to the black water. Banks of papyrus and some ragged reeds grew in the shallows, and on the opposite shore was the inescapable forest.

An hour later, we heard Brent's boat, and soon it entered the cove, with Elias in the prow to greet us: "Ah! But I could not sleep! We went at night as far as the airfield. If you had not come today, I was going for the Lambaréné patrol." As it turned out, Elias had in fact led a posse of concerned villagers, but they had not come far enough.

Once out of the cove, the lake opened into a small sea, dotted with forest-clad island fragments. The village of Alonha was spread out along a long peninsular arm, with most of its huts appearing on the high banks we sped past. The central part of the village, where the chief lived, was on low ground and not far from the beach where we eventually disembarked. Brent's house stood among palm trees and was built on a foundation of upside-down beer bottles, which glowed green from inside. This is a modern method of preventing ants from eating away the wooden foundations; the early missionaries tried to protect their buildings by painting them with pitch. His house had three rooms—two small back bedrooms with mattresses and mosquito nets, and a large L-shaped front room, which had a bed in the short end and wooden tables and chairs in the long. The fronds of one of the palms outside the house were hung with the nests of a colony of weaverbirds, who jangled the compound with their shrill and incessant song. "We call them 'the gendarmes,' " a villager told me, when he saw me watching them, "because they chatter so much."

Brent's house had been loaned to him by the chief, who lived just across the way, and who came strolling out to greet us. He was a strong, solid-looking man with graying hair, dressed in a khaki suit, who had a somewhat paternal air and seemed gently amused by our trials. There were few other people around when we first arrived, but when Brent, Kurt, and I solemnly processed to the lake to take a bath, more appeared. The high bank to the right of the chief's house, shady with long grass and palms, served as a convenient platform for all interested women and children who wished to observe us as we tried to wash discreetly behind a boat moored in the water. We now discovered the insect damage of the night before, and my shoulders looked raw and covered with red welts.

While Brent slept the sleep of the just, Kurt and I were given a village tour. Past the chief's house stood the old mud brick school, with crumbling walls and a caved-in roof, that Brent had come to replace. As is often the case, the collapsed roof was due to bats nesting between the roof and rafters—it is the weight of their accumulated droppings that eventually brings the rafters down. Farther along was the pharmacy, a tiny building of white-washed mud brick with a clumsy turquoise cross painted on its front. A wide compound area lay beyond this, bordered on the left by a congregation of huts and on the right by the plains we had come through. An old woman, doubled over to the extent that her face was less than a foot from the ground, was scrupulously sweeping away every blade of grass, every stray root, from the sandy compound area with a broom made of bracken. Most of the villages I saw were remarkably clean in this way; sweeping the area around the huts of course keeps insects at bay and makes it easy to see snakes. At the far end of this sandy clearing was a wooden church that had weathered to a delicate gray. The date of its construction, 1960, had been set proudly in cement at the threshold. Inside, the bare benches faced a bare altar, and one felt that a great wind had swept through the huge, low windows from across the plains and scoured the little church of everything that wasn't bolted down. As there was more window than wall space, the view of the blond plains grass outside dominated the interior. I mentioned this to the pastor, who had edged his way through the crowd that had slowly gathered as Kurt and I walked along. The pastor nodded and said that the French Army sometimes did maneuvers here. (The French garrison maintained outside Libreville is yet another indication of the strength of the French presence in Gabon.) "You can see them through the windows. They parachute down. Even on a Sunday," he added darkly. The French Army had cut the road to Alonha and, as was quickly pointed out to us, were therefore responsible for bridge number fifteen.

On our way back to the house, still followed by the crowd, we came on a strange bird—certainly some kind of bird of prey—sitting with an air of insouciance by some bushes on the ground. "Ahh!" the crowd murmured. The bird eyed us coming and then began, oddly, to run, holding its wing to one side like a quarterback running with the ball. An old woman darted from the crowd holding a plank of wood, and the bird, at last taking its cue, rose easily into the air just as the woman slammed the board on the ground behind it.

"Too bad, Madame," said the man next to me, "you would have had a beautiful bird for dinner." *Mais, moi*—I was rooting for the bird.

Back at the house, I took a nap and did not wake until after dark. Oil lanterns had been lit and placed on the ground outside the huts, and they flickered through the trees like the miniature fires of a soldiers' camp. We had been asked to dinner at the chief's house and arrived to find it ablaze with light, every available lantern he possessed apparently having been lit and brought into the dining room. The table had been set with forks and glasses for three places; apart from the table, chairs, and lanterns, there were no other objects in the room. The three of us sat down, and the chief with some ceremony produced and lit an upright Tilley lamp, and after wishing us *bon appétit,* left us in the now-dazzling room to eat in private. It was not unusual for the host to depart when the meal was served; the hostess, who had prepared the meal, needless to say, made no appearance.

Dinner was a cold fried carp that had been cut neatly into three even pieces—the head, the middle, and the tail. Brent valiantly took the head, Kurt the tail, leaving me to enjoy the more appetizing middle bit. The fish was accompanied by a bowl of manioc, a potatolike root vegetable, of which Mary Kingsley had more than her share. It is tasteless, takes much labor to prepare (it must be soaked and beaten before boiling, to extract its poisons), is reputedly of little nutritional value—and is the staple food of most of Africa. But it is filling and therefore at least gives one the impression of having eaten well. Its long, slender leaves can be made into a bitter-tasting salad.

After dinner we joined the chief and Elias around the lantern outside Brent's house. An old woman with a scarf around her head was enjoying her pipe on the doorstep of the hut next door. Other people wandered by with a greeting, fading in and out of the darkness. The chief sat comfortably with his legs apart, swatting himself and those around him with his fly whisk of braided raffia. Elias and the chief were speaking French to each other and now continued a theme that had been begun by the villagers earlier when we were walking back from the church— namely, the strength of the white woman who had made the formidable march. Elias in particular warmed to this: "She is strong! Not like the other women!" and the chief nodded his agreement. It would not have occurred to anyone in the village, male or female, to make a true comparison of my strength with that of the average village woman, who daily cuts wood and carries it many miles, hauls water, and works all day in a plantation. This kind of strength is so taken for granted it is not even noticed.

Another subject that held special fascination for Elias was the fact that Americans use police dogs. "Is it true?" he asked Kurt. "Is it true they use the dogs to find criminals?"

"Nooo," said the chief, looking amused, but skeptical.

"It is true!" retorted Elias, now decisive and defensive. "They have even trained them to drive their cars!"

The lanterns continued to burn outside after we had turned in, and could be seen through cracks in the wood walls. I fell asleep to the noise of the palm's dry fronds rattling against the metal roof, like the patter of heavy rain.

I awoke to the ringing song of the weaverbirds. The house was tightly shuttered and dark, and a lantern was still burning dimly on the table. Outside, the dawn had broken, and the chief and a couple of other men, wearing only wraps of colored cloth

around their waists, were standing easily in the compound talking and looking at the lake, which lay gray and calm in the
morning mist.

"*Bonjour,* Madame," called the chief and his friends as I passed
on my way to the water to bathe. A young woman carrying a
bundle of clothes on her head made her way down to the beach
from one of the huts on the high bank and waded over to a large
smooth stone in the water, where she spread out her laundry and
began lathering it with a bar of soap. On the other side of the
beach, a little boy wearing a white loincloth was intently cleaning fish while his dog watched him curiously from inside a
nearby beached canoe. Behind him, a tawny skein of fishing
nets, hung with coral-colored floats, was stretched neatly between two palms. It was Sunday, and somewhere—not from the
direction of the church—the Lord's Prayer was being chanted.
On the beach again, I saw that the woman had finished pound-
ing her clothes and was rinsing a bright pink cloth by floating
it in the water and pulling it slowly around her in a circle.

The others were awake when I got back, and we had a breakfast of instant coffee and French bread. We were greeted by
everyone who passed as we sat by the open door, and occasionally someone would come inside to sit for a few minutes before
going on their way; the artificial boundaries of walls and doorways count for very little in a village.

Kurt and I shook hands all round when it was time to leave,
while Brent and Elias went down to the boat. The chief handed
me his raffia fly whisk—a sincere present, but handed over with
his ever-so-slight air of amusement. Elias sat again in the prow
of the boat, this time with a rifle that he'd brought along to
Alonha in case he had a chance to hunt. He and Brent were to
return by boat within a few days and, with the help of volunteers from the village, would try to rescue the truck. The forest
road was so little used that it was unlikely the truck would be
disturbed.

The numerous wooded isles we passed stood out from the
open water like highland copses from badly flooded land and
gave the impression that Ezanga might not be a real lake and

perhaps an inundated valley lay below. We turned north into a narrow channel between low banks smothered with saw grass, which in the late dry season can creep from shore to shore and block the channels. Patches of the grass were flattened where hippos had made their heavy way ashore to their night pastures. To my disappointment, I never saw a hippo in Gabon. Their numbers have decreased, but they used to be a requisite feature of travelers' tales. Mary Kingsley encountered them even on the stretch from Libreville to Lambaréné, and early explorer and missionary accounts regale one with details of shattered boats and immense hippo jaws.

The channel widened into darker waters, overlooked by forest. It was a breezy day, and palm fronds shimmered as they were tossed about, like fringed banana leaves. The face of the water changed at every bend, depending upon whether the wind was with it or against it; from a dark and ruffled channel, one would enter waters so smooth that every leaf, particle of wood, or speck of dust on its flawless surface caught the slanting light to shine like a golden bubble.

We entered the Ogooué below Lambaréné and made our way up to the bridge, eventually mooring the boat outside the Tuba, one of the West African restaurants between the Lambaréné harbor and town. It had the standard decor of long tables and benches set on a packed dirt floor under a low-lying roof; one of the tables seemed to be perpetually occupied by a group of children who came to watch cartoons on the television. Tuba himself was a big Senegalese, at turns genial and surly. We ordered a *café complet* each, which consisted of a plate-size omelette, baguettes, and coffee. "Your wife?" inquired Tuba of Kurt, after he had examined me from across the table.

"No—yeah, why not?" said Kurt wearily. "It's easier than trying to explain. Besides, I leave tomorrow," he added with a grin. The whereabouts of my husband was for me, as for Kingsley, the single most-asked question of my trip.

We parted company at the road, and I made my way back to the mission, where I discovered that all was not well. Sister Carmen had been in a bad car accident and had only been saved by her presence of mind: the steering column of the mission jeep had broken while she was driving it back from the post office, and the jeep had bolted over the edge of a high embankment. At the last minute Sister Carmen had snatched the keys from the ignition and somersaulted out of the jeep onto the roadside, where she was found unconscious and still clutching the keys. She had been bruised and had broken an arm, but otherwise, *grâce à Dieu,* she was safe. When I told the Sisters that I would like to visit her, I was invited by Mother Jacques Marie and Sister Agnes to accompany them when they went to the Schweitzer Hospital that evening; Sister Yves Marie was already at the hospital, camping out in Sister Carmen's room to ensure that she was properly taken care of.

Mother Jacques Marie was of course our driver when we went barreling out of the mission gates at dusk. "Oh, the roads are atrocious!" she exclaimed but never slowed to make concessions to the craters and potholes; her secret knowledge had informed her that the worst that could happen would not be so bad. We stopped beside a roadside vendor, and Mother Jacques Marie swung out of the jeep, banging the door briskly behind her.

"How much?" she inquired, casting a connoisseur's eye over the oranges, and when the vendor gave his price she raised an amused eyebrow and said good-bye. "Outrageous," she said when we were under way again. She shook her head—she had known it.

Loud radio music met us in the wards. Sister Carmen's room was easy to distinguish by the crowd of well-wishers gathered in the doorway. We were greeted by Sister Yves Marie, who immediately drew our attention to Sister Carmen's plasma bottle; she pointed out that it was very low and wondered aloud if it would last through the night.

"It will last," said Mother Jacques Marie, with barely a glance. Hands on her hips, she was already surveying Sister Carmen.

Sister Carmen was amazed to see me. "Al-ex-an-der!" she exclaimed, holding out her hand, and at once asked me about my trip.

"Oh, a forest ride, broken bridge, night in the open," said *La*

Mère, answering for me. Sister Carmen was shocked and would not release my hand. An old woman cautiously entered the room; she had just heard about the accident and had walked in from her village. Sister Agnes recited the events and described how Sister Carmen's head had whipped forward, how she had been hurled from the jeep and bruised her side, how her arm had struck the ground and so been broken. . . . The old woman winced as she listened and, in intense identification with Sister Carmen's pain, touched her own head, side, and arm in response to the narration.

"You are going to stay at the mission now?" Sister Carmen asked me hopefully; and when I answered that I had to take another trip, she did not allow me to leave her bedside until I had promised to be careful.

SAMBA FALLS

THE ZAMBESIE, Congo, Shanghai, Zomba, Samba Falls—I number these among the places I would seek out merely for their names. Some seven miles upriver from Lambaréné island, one comes to the confluence of the Ogooué and its southern tributary, the Ngounié, a convergence distinguished by two low-lying islands, named Walker's Islands after the British trader-explorer Robert Bruce Walker. Mary Kingsley writes, "Higher up, [the Ngounié] flows through a mountainous country, and at Samba, its furthest navigable point, there is a wonderfully beautiful waterfall, the whole river coming down over a low cliff, surrounded by an amphitheatre of mountains. It takes the *Éclaireur* two days steaming from the mouth of the Ngounie to Samba, when she can get up. . . ." In fact Mary Kingsley never saw the falls, because the Ngounié's dry-season water level was too low to allow her steamboat to ascend. Her description of the falls was in all likelihood taken from that of their "discoverer," Paul du Chaillu.

Paul du Chaillu was, as Mary Kingsley says, the "inaugurator of geographical knowledge in this region." He was born in

France, and at least one parent, his father, Belloni du Chaillu, was French (his biographer makes no mention of his mother), but he later became a naturalized American citizen, and his expeditions were backed in part by American geographical and natural history societies. As agent for the Parisian firm Oppenheim, his father had managed a factory in the Gaboon. At the age of seventeen, du Chaillu left Paris to join his father in equatorial Africa, at which time he gained, in his own words, his knowledge of the "languages, habits, and peculiarities of the natives." When his father died, du Chaillu, whose closest friends in the Gaboon had been the American missionaries, decided to go to the United States. Possessed of no real means of earning a living, he soon found that his most marketable commodity was his African experience, and at length, in 1855, apparently at a loss for anything better to do, he set out on his first serious expedition, with the object of spending "some years in the exploration of a region of territory lying between lat 2° north and 2° south, and stretching back from the coast to the mountain range called the Sierra del Crystal." This venture lasted four years and was modestly summarized in the preface to his subsequent book, *Explorations and Adventures in Equatorial Africa*, as follows:

> I traveled—always on foot, and unaccompanied by other white men—about 8000 miles. I shot, stuffed, and brought home 2000 birds, of which more than 60 are new species, and I killed upward of 1000 quadrupeds, of which 200 were stuffed and brought home, with more than 80 skeletons. Not less than 20 of these quadrupeds are species hitherto unknown to science. I suffered fifty attacks of the African fever, taking, to cure myself, over fourteen *ounces* [his italics] of quinine. Of famine, long-continued exposures to the heavy tropical rains, and attacks of ferocious ants and venomous flies, it is not worth while to speak.

Du Chaillu was perhaps most proud of his exploits involving the "very remarkable nest-building ape, the *Troglodytes calvus*," or gorilla, about which very little was known at the time. His armed triumphs over the ape are related in heartbreaking detail, and the reader is further educated concerning their appearance by graphic woodcuts, which depict the animal standing upright over a fallen native while bending a rifle with its bare paws or threateningly baring its teeth as it approaches its enemy, which is presumably the Author.

In the course of this first expedition du Chaillu made an abortive attempt to reach Samba Falls, whose existence he had learned of from the Apindji tribe, who inhabited the Ngounié region. He set out down the Ngounié accompanied by a dozen canoes, and as it was the rainy season, swept rapidly downstream through ever more magnificent country until he could "hear the dull boom of the falls in the distance." He spent the night on the riverbank, with the noise of the falls sounding in his ears, and awoke the next morning to a great disappointment: his men refused to go farther, claiming that they would encounter hostile tribes. Du Chaillu had to content himself with marking the position of the falls on his map, and of naming it Eugénie, "in honor of her majesty the Empress of the French."

The initial reaction to his expedition and subsequent book, published in 1861, was highly favorable, and du Chaillu found himself a minor celebrity; but the scientific community quickly became skeptical and questioned the veracity of his accounts. A particularly damaging charge was made by the world-renowned German explorer Dr. Heinrich Barth to the effect that du Chaillu had never ventured more than a few miles from the coast and that his map was entirely imaginary, and eventually his account of the gorilla was similarly dismissed. In fact, the later reports of the explorers and travelers who came after him confirmed that du Chaillu's accounts were true, if prone to exaggeration. ("Perhaps Du Chaillu honestly believed what he wrote," a modern historian has speculated. ". . . The inexperienced and isolated traveler could have been the victim of his own overactive imagination.") Goaded by this skepticism and, one feels, by a growing need to verify his own account for himself, du Chaillu equipped himself with a battery of mapping and photographic equipment and embarked on a second African expedition, in 1863. It was on this second trip that he succeeded in seeing Samba Falls.

According to du Chaillu, what the Apindji called Samba-Nagossi was really a series of three separate falls and rapids. Approaching from the south, he first encountered the Nagossi rapids, the spirit-wife of Samba. The falls proper, some five miles downstream, were actually called Fougamou after a forest spirit, believed to be a forger of iron. The Samba rapids, the third in the series, which du Chaillu in fact never saw, lay a good day's travel farther downstream (the photograph in Mary Kingsley's *Travels* is probably of these latter rapids). One has the impression that du Chaillu was disappointed with the falls: "After a scramble along the rugged hill-side of a mile or so, we came in view of the object I had come so far to see. The stream here was broader (about 150 yards in width), but a rocky island in the middle, covered with trees, breaks the fall of water into two unequal parts. . . . Besides the island several detached islets and masses of rock divided this body of water, so that the cataract did not present one imposing sheet of water, as I had expected."

Du Chaillu's second trip was well received, and an account of it, *A Journey to Ashango-Land,* was published in 1867. After which, as his biographer reports, he made "an irrevocable determination never to go back to Africa."

Like Mary Kingsley, I found that I would not be able to get to Samba by way of the Ngounié, which was too shallow to be ascended by a motorized pirogue, and it is nowadays impossible to find anyone willing to punt a boat for such a distance. I did, however, have the option of going by road. Apart from the excuse that I felt Mary Kingsley *would* have gone to the falls if she had been able, I was determined to see Samba for personal reasons: Samba Falls had captivated me from the time I had first come across its name, not in the work of Mary Kingsley but in that of Trader Horn.

To discover Trader Horn is to have a new planet swim into one's ken. "Trader Horn" is both the author and the title of a book, and this remarkable work must be briefly outlined for the uninitiated. The manner in which the book "happened" is an inextricable part of the book itself; one morning in 1926, Mrs. Ethelreda Lewis, a British writer living in South Africa, had stepped out onto the stoep of her Johannesburg house and discovered an old man peddling wire kitchen goods on the doorstep. The old man's mild voice, his dignified manner, and his "calmly observant" eyes stopped Mrs. Lewis from sending him away. It turned out that he too was English, a Lancashire man, and so they had introduced themselves: "My name's Horn. Aloysius Horn . . ." This exchange of civilities with a compatriot seemed to tap a deep reservoir of memories in the old man. He drew closer: "Ma'am, I could tell you—I've seen—" With an acute sense that she was confronting the "rising pressure of a soul making its last effort to express itself before the walls of age and senility closed in," Mrs. Lewis listened, mesmerized, to her visitor's disjointed recollections:

"Africa, Ma'am. Africa—as Nature meant her to be, the home of the black man and the quiet elephant. Never a sound, Ma'am, in a great landscape at noon. . . . Bound by the rites of Egbo, Ma'am, to be blood brother of cannibals. . . . Why, I was only a lad when I took that other poor lady's body down the river to try and get safe burial for it at Kangwe. Well of course they'd never seen a white woman before, up at Samba Falls. . . ."

Aloysius Horn had come to West Africa in 1871 or so—"in the earlies"—to work as a trader for Hatton and Cookson, a job that had landed him in many adventures. With a writer's instinct, Mrs. Lewis sensed that here was a story that must be told, and it was arranged that "Trader" Horn would come and talk to her for a couple of hours a week. After a few sessions, she hit on the idea of asking him to write up his own story, a strategy that proved to be an instant success, and so for many months Trader Horn came to Mrs. Lewis's house for a weekly meal prepared "in the English tradition," bringing with him his latest chapter, which he had written in the doss house where he was then living. Mrs. Lewis had the forethought to preserve his conversation from each of these sessions, which she appended to the relevant chapter. The result of their partnership was the book

Trader Horn, published the following year, in 1927, and received with instant acclaim.

How to characterize the book? It is a sequence of adventurous, often fanciful episodes in the life of the young trader, from his arrival in the Gaboon to his expeditionary forays into the uncharted forest and onto uncharted rivers in search of better trading routes and treaties from his base at the Hatton and Cookson factory at Adolinanongo. There is a White Goddess who is rescued: "Nina T—her name. But best not to mention that name. I've no wish to betray the tragedies of a noble English family." There is a young missionary woman who dies of fever: "When I heard of it I said 'There goes one more victim to add to their great Josh House called Christianity.'" There is a temple of skulls with a sacred ruby and crystal, an escape and rescue—if pressed, one would have to confess that this is a classic adventure story.

But it is the distinctive and haunting mood of humor, wonderment, and melancholy, told in inimitably archaic language, that ultimately characterizes this work. Trader Horn recalls what few of the other writers who described this part of the world give any evidence of ever having realized, a sense of the freshness of life in as yet unplundered Africa, the wonderment of its beauty and acute consciousness of the uniqueness of his experience. Turning from the self-congratulatory accounts of conquest and deprecating descriptions of African life characteristic of so many other writers, we enter the world of Trader Horn: " 'Twas like the sun pouring colours into them that'd been kept empty," he says of watching the birth of dragonflies. "They stayed for near an hour on my boat and you could see them getting strong and quivering their wings for life's pleasure. Then they flew off on their swift errands. . . . Kingfishers! Above par on that river. Those bonny birds, finer than dream-size. Threading to and fro in front of your canoe like bobbins o' bright silk."

Like du Chaillu, he had collected gorillas' heads and skeletons for museums. "Only once I shot a mother—I think I've mentioned it. When she was dying she lifted her hand and put it on the baby. She—lifted her hand. . . . No man that's not *homo stultus* could stand it. I tried to make amends to outraged Nature."

Trader Horn is valuable not only as a complement to the literature of the missionaries and explorers of this region but also as a manual of sorts for those who wish to explore the relationship between truth and fiction. In spite of the book's obviously romantic cast, it has a backbone of solid fact; the place names and tribal distributions are correct, and the description of the trader's duties and ordeals—if it does tend toward self-praise—is informative and accurate.

Digging deeper into the contemporary literature, one discovers intriguing parallels with even the more improbable features of his story: the Blind King, one of the book's most haunting characters, is modeled on Ranokè, the blind but powerful chief of the Enenga; Griffon du Bellay, a doctor in the French Navy and one of the earliest explorers of the Ogooué, reports that many native idols had European features, while Mary Kingsley refers to the cult of a goddess of albinos, either of which may have been the origin of Trader Horn's White Goddess. Du Chaillu relates how in a village near Cape St. Catherine, on the southern coast, he was taken into a fetish house: "I saw no idol, but only a large chest, on the top of which lay some white and red chalk and some parrot feathers." Were these pieces of chalk the sacred stones of crystal and ruby?

I was happy to discover that my obsession with Trader Horn placed me in good company; no less a personage than Albert Schweitzer had fallen under his spell. In *African Notebook,* one of Schweitzer's less familiar books, an entire chapter is devoted to a discussion of Trader Horn's life, and he was obviously pleased to report that the new Schweitzer Hospital at Adolinanongo stood on the site of Trader Horn's first factory. He attested to the accuracy of Trader Horn's descriptions of the country and its inhabitants and paid tribute to his efforts to establish independent trading settlements farther inland, making it possible to circumvent the coastal middlemen and to barter directly with the interior tribes. Schweitzer's researches yielded the information that Trader Horn's supervisor in Adolinanongo, the unimaginative and unenterprising Mr. Gibson, was still well remembered in the area but that only a few old people could remember his young subordinate agent: "What they still remember is that he was very young, that he wanted to trade according to his own ideas and on his own account and was therefore constantly at variance with Mr. Gibson, that he was very irritable and that he had a liking for rum and good brandy."

Schweitzer disapproved of the fictive romance of Nina and her rescue, claiming that "it disfigures the book." One can, however, read it otherwise: whereas the ostensibly objective accounts of explorers like du Chaillu (whose book was—ironically—dismissed as a fiction), and of Schweitzer himself for that matter, and the more judgmental accounts of the missionaries all betray a sense of the "otherness" of the world in which they have come to sojourn, Trader Horn's fiction is, I believe, an indication of his remarkable empathy for the people and land that is evidenced throughout the book, conveying as it does his sense of his own participation in the region's story.

It is not always clear to what extent Trader Horn himself was conscious of tipping the balance in favor of fiction: the conversations appended to each chapter often reveal that his art was self-conscious in the extreme, but other incidents are more ambiguous: "It sure gave me a strange feeling to see those eyes looking out from a great mask at me," he says to Mrs. Lewis, of the first time that he saw the White Goddess, Nina. He and Mrs. Lewis had just finished one of their weekly sessions and he was preparing to depart. "Well—good day, Ma'am." But Mrs. Lewis could not contain herself and stopped him as he was leaving: "Mr. Horn, tell me—what—how did they look?" Trader Horn came closer and, without having had the time to work out this detail of his tale, spontaneously replied—for all the world as if he were not lying—"I should say her eyes were kind but piercing. Aye. Kind but piercing."

Of all the places to which one journeys in the course of reading *Trader Horn,* it was the remote waterfall in the deep interior of primeval forest that most haunted my imagination and epitomized for me the glamour of African exploration. Samba Falls. Time and again Trader Horn had returned to Samba Falls, a day's canoe ride from the Woermann factory managed by Herr Shiff, at the mouth of the Remba Koi. Of the falls themselves very little description is given: "Next came Samba Falls which are not very high but are picturesque as they are wide." Nonetheless, I had a vivid image: the scene would be tinged by the green shade of the forest and for miles around there would be no noise save the thunder of its falling water.

Every person I approached in Lambaréné nodded in recognition when I mentioned the falls; but, disconcertingly, every person had a different opinion on where the falls were to be found and even what they were called, and the names Fougamou, Bongo, and Impératrice were invoked as often as Samba. The consensus was that I should go to Fougamou, a small town some sixty miles south, on the Lambaréné-Mouila road, from where I could either go directly to the falls or make an excursion to Sindara, an even smaller town a short distance from Fougamou; but I was assured that the falls could be reached from one place or the other. Importantly, there was a Catholic Mission at Fougamou, where I could stay.

Bus services are nonexistent in Gabon, and travelers must either hitchhike or rely on the *taxis de brousse.* Mother Jacques Marie, having driven me into town, inquired up and down the line of taxis about the cost of a ride to Fougamou, and then confronted the driver she had selected for verification of her research, which he stammeringly agreed to be correct. Mercifully, I obtained a place in the cabin, not the open back of the van, and we set off an hour later with the windows tightly closed against the dust.

Fougamou was only two hours away, but two hours on roads one does not trust is an extremely long time. We were run off the road only once; the greatest danger is usually presented by the lumber trucks, whose top-heavy loads of okoumé logs render them incapable of controlling either their speed or subtleties of direction, but in this case the culprit was an army truck crowded with drunken soldiers. When their dust had settled down, we backed carefully out of the roadside bush where we had sought refuge and continued on our way.

Fougamou was not in fact a town, but a village of concrete

buildings flanking a two-mile stretch of unpaved road. There was a sense that the building of the village had been begun with high spirits, dedication, and optimism, but that somewhere after the first mile and a half this enthusiasm had flagged. The official buildings—the infirmary, the school, the market, the police station—stood securely in dusty yards that had been energetically stripped of greenery, whereas the houses at the end of the road were sunk in high grass and foliage. River rushes formed a dark green hedge just behind the houses; the water I could see beyond them was the Ngounié.

The Catholic Mission at Fougamou was more modest in size and less cloistered than that at Lambaréné, but nonetheless was set back from the road and sheltered to some extent by its wide-spreading trees and garden. Like the rest of the town it harbored an abnormal stillness, as if we had caught it during its siesta. When the taxi pulled noisily into the mission driveway, the Sisters sitting in the cool calm of their living room turned their white-coiffed heads in startled unison. Rising together from their raffia chairs, they came out to meet me on the verandah with an air of bewilderment and caution. Yes, they verified, there was a room for visitors, but they would have to find the keys. While one of the Sisters went off to search for them, I handed over the mail I had brought from the Sisters at Lambaréné to the Mother Superior, who read it quickly and gave a report: "Mère Jacques Marie says that Carmen is doing well. There is still some pain, *bien sûr,* but this is to be expected. . . ."

I was led at length to another building, to the left of the kitchen, in front of the kitchen garden. The Sister unlocked its padlocked door with a cumbersome and antique key and swung it slowly open. Inside was a deserted schoolroom, half-filled with desks and benches that had been stacked and covered with dust sheets.

"Now it is closed," said the Sister, moving cautiously to another door at the far end of the room. Her whole manner was that of a person exploring new territory. I asked if it was closed because the school term had finished.

"Oh no; it is because it is too expensive." She had unlocked the back door, and we peered into a long dark corridor in which stood neat rows of empty beds, as in a hospital ward. The air smelled of dust and mildew.

The Sister walked in as if stepping over the threshold of a secret doorway that had been closed for twenty years. What can be here? her wondering expression seemed to ask. Every door-knob, cabinet, and chair was a discovery; she should have been holding a guttering candle aloft, but instead she was searching for the light switch.

"I seem to remember—I'm certain there is one. . . ." As in the fairy tales, there were many mysterious bolted doors, and I half expected to be given the classic admonition: "Remember, you can come and go in all the rooms you please, only the little door in the right-hand corner you must never enter. . . ." One of the doors was discovered to guard the bedroom where I was to sleep. The bathroom was at the farthest end of the unlighted dormitory, off a short and even darker corridor.

The Sister left me, and I heard her wrestling to pull the front door closed on her way out. The bedroom was in fact comfortable, if plain, furnished with only a bed, table, and chair, and bedside table. Heavy louvered shutters barricaded the windows, which were in any case almost overgrown by bushes. It was by now late in the afternoon, and I wanted to see the rest of Fougamou before it became dark.

Outside, I was greeted by a young man who appeared to have been waiting for me on the verandah. The Sisters, as it turned out, had recruited him to show me around. We strolled off in the direction of the more ragged part of the village, and he told me that he was a student at a technical school. I asked him if he found the work difficult.

"Yes," he said, holding up a mutilated hand. "I have already lost two fingers." Accidents of this kind were common, he told me nonchalantly, most students expected to lose *something*.

In the low late-afternoon light, the flat, uninspiring houses were beginning to sink back into their shadows while the foliage, as it darkened, was slowly becoming the more dominant feature of the landscape. Fougamou ceased to give the impression of being a planned community; it now appeared as a mass of dense greenery, ringed at its farthest end by the outline of remote mountains in which a few houses happened to be set. I had the names of two people I hoped to look up; one was a Peace Corps volunteer, the other a Protestant minister.

"There are two Peace Corps men here," said my escort. We had so far encountered not a single other person. All the houses, shuttered against the dust, had the air of being boarded up with storm windows and deserted for a season. "One of them has just arrived. He is very nervous."

I asked what he was nervous about. My companion shrugged. "He is new here," he said mildly. The other evidently was well established and had many friends; people visited him in his house, and he always bought drinks in the bar.

"This is Willis's house," he said as we passed a boarded building indistinguishable from all the others, and a hundred yards later he pointed again: "This is the house of Harvey." Willis was nervous; Harvey was not. Willis was a scientist and spoke very little French. Harvey taught English and had a bicycle. They taught at the same school.

"They are not here," he said, when I indicated that I would like to meet them. Harvey would be back in a couple of days; Willis . . . might be longer.

A group of young men ambling languidly in the dust now approached us. They were of roughly the same age as my companion, who, try as he did, could not conceal his pleasure at having been caught with an exotic foreigner. We shook hands all round.

"Your friends from the Peace Corps are not here," one of them volunteered, watching my face closely. I said I knew this. They nodded and eventually moved on.

"They fought in the street," said my companion. I turned to look after the departing men, but he corrected me: "I mean the Americans," he said.

It seemed that Willis, the high-strung scientist, nervous, newly arrived, and faced with the prospect of two years in

Fougamou, had accused Harvey of "not doing things the right way." Gregarious Harvey had responded with anger; there had been shouting, and the two came out into the one long street that was Fougamou and exchanged blows. Willis now keeps to himself more than ever, and the two men no longer speak to each other, although they live only a hundred yards apart and commute daily to the same school, Harvey leaving, one supposes, half an hour after Willis and sailing past him every day on his bicycle. Near the end of the town we came to the pastor's house. The pastor's wife was sweeping the compound in the growing darkness; the pastor himself was, needless to say, out of town.

While walking back I broached the question of Samba Falls. My companion knew of the falls and even of du Chaillu, but he had never seen the falls. They were called "Eugénie," he thought, and one got to them from Sindara. This was by now the answer I had expected; if the falls had been at Fougamou, I did not see where they could be hidden.

I parted with my friend some distance from the mission, faced with the problem of getting dinner. There were no shops to be seen anywhere, the market was closed, and I had not come across anything that looked like a restaurant. Walking past the mission and on toward the entrance to town, I at last saw a large pink building clearly marked "Restaurant," but when I went closer to investigate, it looked suspiciously unfrequented.

"It is closed," said a voice from across the way. A tall man dressed in a skullcap and caftan was sitting outside the house next door in a low chair, slumped over his Koran, which lay open on the table in front of him. He was the owner of the restaurant, which, he informed me, was now the only one in town; there had once been others when people traveling between Mouila and Lambaréné used to stop for a meal, even for the night. But now, *la crise . . .* However, he was willing to open it, and if I came back in an hour, his wife would have prepared a meal.

When I returned, a young boy solemnly escorted me through the back door into a large room painted turquoise from the floor to halfway up the walls, and hot pink from the rest of the way up to the ceiling. Some fifteen tables, covered with hot-pink oilcloth, were all—save one which had been set for me—stacked with upside-down chairs. A single long fluorescent bulb had been vainly affixed to the far wall to illuminate the entire room. A very good meal was brought in by the little boy, and I ate it in half darkness and utter silence. Coffee was brought the moment I laid down my knife and fork, as if, again, I had entered a fairy-tale world, where heroines in empty castles are served by unseen ministers who anticipate their wishes. I declined dessert, paid the bill, and left.

Fougamou was its most desolate at night. The few feeble streetlights did no more than give proof that nothing was capable of alleviating the darkness. A range of human activities was displayed through the open doorways of the line of roadside houses, but the people themselves seemed unapproachable and slightly unreal, as if they were merely participants in a series of scenes performed on tiny self-contained stages. The noise of frogs that arose from the river rushes above the soft and incessant whirring of the generator brought associations of a solitude of unpeopled lakes and marshes.

Although it had been dark for over an hour by the time I returned to the mission, it was not late, and there remained much time to pass until the morning. The door of the deserted schoolroom opened on the unnerving stillness of the empty dormitory, and my footsteps on the concrete floor had a foreboding ring as I groped my way toward the inner bedroom. Before I left Lambaréné, I had spent a day in bed with a low fever, which had not been serious, although it was uncomfortable; now, suddenly, the fever returned. I put chloroquine within reach on the bedside table and then lay in the darkness, uneasily trying to assess my temperature. The discomfort this time was accompanied by an acute sense of vulnerability; the two hours I had traveled from the security of the Lambaréné Mission and the Schweitzer Hospital now suddenly made a world of difference.

Harvey and Willis; Willis and Harvey. Harvey unmistakably was an exemplar of the energetic, personable, adaptable, well-rounded individual that the Peace Corps seeks to recruit; and poor nervous Willis was the kind of person one dreads discovering oneself to be, when in a dark night of the soul one awakes to the stark reality of a place like Fougamou. Whatever heady plans he may have made before he came, and whatever expectations he might have come with had failed him here. As for me, I found my imagination suddenly bankrupt, incapable of summoning even the vision of Samba Falls. The barren and despondent reality of Fougamou was inescapably overwhelming.

I awoke to the new day, feeling healthier, but still weak and somewhat dispirited, and decided that the best thing I could do was to get moving. I had been told that taxi vans to Sindara left from the hospital, and so I made my way back toward the entrance to town. Now there were signs of life; the market was busy, there were taxis waiting in the road, two small trucks were pulled over to the roadside, and the police barrier, which had been vacated when I drove in, was teeming with officious-looking gendarmes.

"Halt!" One of the gendarmes came skipping from his sentry house. I stopped and waited, and a small crowd drifted over from the parked trucks and taxis. The gendarme himself looked flustered; he had obviously acted on impulse and now had no idea how to proceed.

"Papers!" The word was hissed like a stage cue from the sentry house.

"Identity papers!" the gendarme shouted.

I explained that, *malheureusement,* my papers were at the Catholic Mission—where I was staying as a guest of the Sisters. Realizing, however, that means must be provided for the gendarme to exercise authority of some sort and save face, I produced a document from the Ministry of Tourism, typed on heavily embellished official paper and signed with many seals, which I had expended considerable energy to obtain in Libreville for precisely such occasions. While the gendarme turned the paper many times over, I allowed no uncomfortable silence to fall, but proceeded to recite the purpose of my mission: I was here to see the historic falls, the falls known throughout the world and discovered by Monsieur du Chaillu—the Sisters at the mission had told me that the taxis waited here. . . . When the gendarme looked up again, I asked him bluntly for his advice on how to get to Sindara.

The gendarme, and by vicarious association all his other comrades, now being publicly in control, became most helpful. More orders were shouted to the crowd—to Fougamou—in general, to the effect that immediate transport must be provided. One of the gendarmes suddenly pointed up the road and said excitedly, "Bakary!"

A man was sauntering toward the crowd with an air of sleepy good humor, as if he had just awoken from a pleasant sleep. He made his way to us slowly, for he stopped to shake the hands of all he met.

"Bakary, where are you going?" called one of the gendarmes. Bakary waited until he was within easy speaking distance before he answered.

"Sindara," he said, taking the gendarme's hand, but looking off somewhere into the distance. He was in his late thirties and was from Mali. His eyes were ever-so-slightly crossed, as if their gaze had been trained to look downward and away from the glare of desert sand. I shook Bakary's hand while the gendarmes explained that I wished to go to the falls at Sindara.

"Ah," said Bakary, again looking somewhere in the distance beyond us. "Samba."

One of the gendarmes stepped forward and announced that he would take Bakary's van to get petrol; this, as everyone knew, was an excuse to use the van for some personal errand before we departed.

"The keys are in the truck," said Bakary, who had not lost his lazy smile. He concentrated on taking a cigarette from the packet rolled in his shirt sleeve. The gendarme beckoned for me to follow him.

"No," said Bakary, smiling into the middle distance, "you go, and I will tell her about the trip to Sindara." He nodded his thanks as a matchbook was handed to him. "The brakes don't work," he said to me as he lit his cigarette.

This the gendarme had just discovered; after a briefly impressive roaring of the engine, he had attempted to turn the van in a tight circle, but at the speed he was going had almost succeeded in turning it over. He gave a shout of alarm before heading off toward an incline leading away from the opposite side of the road, where he gradually lost momentum. The risk of losing the van, it seemed, had been worth the pleasure of giving its driver a fright.

Bakary ran a taxi service to villages in the vicinity. Uniquely among all those I met who engaged in the transport business, he was unconcerned about recruiting customers, and I knew that our departure would depend not on whether the back of his van was full, but on when he himself felt ready to go. He was shadowed by two young companions of about seventeen, who had obviously chosen him to be their mentor. One of them, Muhammad, had elegant, almost Hamitic features, a head of long, glossy curls, and outrageously long eyelashes. The other, Ghan, also appeared to be non-Gabonese. His face was a slanting plane, a flat surface tilted back at an angle, and he surveyed the world by looking down his nose through the narrow slits of his eyes, which gave him a somewhat sinister air.

The returning van appeared cautiously on the horizon, where the gendarme was drifting in careful zigzags down the incline. Bakary, however, did not turn his head until the gendarme had dismounted and made his way back to the gathering by the sentry booth.

"Are we ready to go?" he asked and led us all to the van.

Once we were under way, Bakary showed me how he controlled the brakes, by driving with the brake pedal half depressed. He had picked up a few passengers in Fougamou, and now a young woman on the roadside flagged him down. Scowling into the van, she said something in Fang.

Bakary turned to Muhammad, who shared the driver's cabin with us. *"Respectez la femme."*

Muhammad's response was not in French but was unmistakably indignant.

"All the same," said Bakary, with his imperturbable smile, *"respectez la femme."* His downward-looking eyes gave him an expression of introspective inner peace. Ignoring the woman as he stepped out of the cabin, Muhammad sulkily surrendered his place and joined his friend in the back.

Sindara was notable for being imbued with yellow dust, not red. The well-swept compounds in front of the low wooden huts ran indistinguishably into the main road, which was clearly not to be used as a thoroughfare so much as a convenient avenue on which to promenade. A luxuriant shade tree growing at the crossroads marked the center of the village. Tall and distinguished-looking men in caftans were sitting in languid elegance outside the huts, and the women who stepped from inside were built on a strikingly large and healthy scale, lacking completely the ragged downtroddenness of so many village women. The unusual coloring, the uncluttered, clean space, and the sociable groups of people lent Sindara an air of sunny good nature.

Bakary was welcomed in the village as an old friend. I thanked him for the ride and prepared to seek out a guide. He was amused. "I am getting the guide," he said, tapping his chest. "*I* am taking you to Samba."

By the communal decision of the village, the guide selected was a little boy of ten or so, who went off self-importantly to borrow a machete. As Muhammad and Ghan insisted on joining in the excitement, there were five of us who eventually set out on the expedition.

Shortly past Sindara, our guide directed us down a road that was completely overgrown. The surface itself was not bad, but the grass in places would have stood above my head, and it gave no evidence of having been used by man or beast for some time. We rocked slowly along, seeing very little of the forest through the grass until we came without warning onto a wide clearing to our left.

"The mission," said Bakary. I caught a glimpse of a red-brick building through the trees and the unexpected sight of a bed of red canna lilies. "We will stop when we come back," said Bakary as we reentered the forest. "I know it is what you will want to see."

Not much farther on, with no intervening change in vegetation, we suddenly found ourselves in a bamboo forest. The individual shafts of cane grew in distinct clumps, forming fat pillars as in the megaron of an ancient palace. The canes had grown too high to bear their own weight, and their feathery heads curved unsupported toward the ground, like drooping plumes of ostrich feathers, forming the forest's low ceiling. There was no undergrowth, and the ground was clear except for the bamboo's fallen parchment-colored leaves, which covered the earth like a tiled floor. We stopped and got out to walk around: Bakary was unreservedly admiring, Muhammad was concerned that there might be snakes. Our young guide watched us with a tolerant, proprietorial air while leaning against the van.

The bamboo forest was left behind as abruptly as it had been entered. The little boy, who was riding in the back, banged on the roof to indicate that we should stop. We parked the van and followed him on foot down a trail that took us to the river. For some distance, trees overhung the narrow strip of beach, which then widened into a spit of yellow sand. On the opposite shore, no break was to be seen in the forest wall, which grew to the edge of the swiftly flowing waters. Samba was not a falls but a patch of surging rapids.

Bakary had begun to hunt, first for fish in the pools formed among the river boulders, and then, somewhat unexpectedly, for gold; some years ago, he assured me, Europeans had come and told the local villagers that they would pay for a certain kind of rock that was found in the river. The villagers had sold them pieces of this rock for very little money.

"They didn't know what it was," said Bakary, turning the sand in the river shallows over with his bare foot. Our young guide asked him what gold was.

"Gold?" said Bakary. He pulled a heavy chain that he wore around his neck out of his shirt. "This is gold." Ghan was almost asleep on a boulder in the sun; Muhammad was smiling with pleasure and suggested that we could all spend the day fishing.

Bakary looked lazily at the sky. "We must go back so she can see the falls," he said and began to walk toward the trail. "The big falls are at Fougamou," he added, smiling at my mystified expression.

He did not explain until we were back in the van. He, Bakary, had once before come to the rapids we had just seen and been told that they were called Samba and were the husband of the Nagossi rapids, some miles away. *But,* there was also a large falls, real *chutes* and not merely rapids, near Fougamou, which he had never seen: indeed he knew of few people who had seen them, apart from the local fishermen, which was why no one seemed to know exactly how to reach them. Some years ago, a team of Yugoslavian engineers had been sent to investigate the possibility of erecting a hydroelectric station near the falls. Their motorboat had stalled downstream, and they had been swept over the cascade. Four men had perished: "One white man and three *de notre type,*" Bakary said over my head to Muhammad, who was back in the cabin and following the conversation with close attention. It was said that the spirit of the falls had destroyed the men in his anger at their attempt to violate his waters with a hydroelectric station. One Gabonese man had been rescued by helicopter after clinging to a rock for a day and a night. "He was rescued, but he went mad."

Bakary wondered if there were not two traditions that had been conflated: a Samba-Nagossi tradition, in which the "real" falls was Samba, the husband, and the Nagossi rapids, Samba's wife; and a separate legend regarding the spirit Fougamou, which came to be associated with the same falls. Bakary's hypothesis was convincing, in spite of du Chaillu's different sequence: in du Chaillu's account, the so-called Nagossi rapids are not only located miles away from Samba but also are separated by the so-called Fougamou falls, which is strange if the two are supposed to be "married"—on which everyone seemed to agree. Furthermore, du Chaillu himself had first come to hear of the falls as Samba-Nagossi, which would presumably refer to a distinctive landmark, rather than to the unremarkable rapids. Mary Kingsley of course knew of the falls as Samba, as, needless to say, did Trader Horn.

When we returned to the first clearing, Bakary kept his word and made a detour to the mission. A large square had been cut in the jungle to accommodate a small whitewashed church, a row of schoolrooms, and a magnificent mission building, made of the ubiquitous locally made brick, with its distinctive orange-rose hue. A double row of mango trees led grandly to the mission entrance, reminiscent of the oak-flanked avenues of plantations in the American South. The arched colonnades that ringed both the upper and lower floors lent the otherwise plain building an exotic, somewhat Spanish flavor. Considerable craftsmanship was evidenced in the well-joined wooden ceiling beams and a dainty staircase of a similar dark wood, which led to the floor above. The rows of dark green, tightly closed doors still bore the name plaques of their former residents: St Pierre, Cardinal Bijawa.

From ground level, the mission looked well tended; the grass was being kept under control, hibiscus bloomed around the perimeter of the mission building, and there were the surprising beds of canna lilies. But, leaning out between the columns of the upper colonnade, I also saw that the little blue and white church, once surely the most important feature of the mission, sat forlorn and dilapidated on the unkempt outer fringes of the clearing, with the forest breathing down its neck. The mission had ceased to function as a mission many years ago—I found no one who could tell me exactly when—but the main building continues to be maintained by the French Army, who stay here when on maneuvers.

Back at Sindara, no one seemed to have stirred since we had left. Bakary stationed himself under the centrally placed tree to conduct an inquiry about a guide for the next stage of our trip while I bought drinks for all members of the expedition. The choice was limited to Fanta and Coke, as no alcohol was locally available, Sindara being chiefly a Muslim settlement. Pointing to one hut after another, Muhammad recited the nationality of each occupant: Malian, Malian, Malian, Cameroon, Nigerian, Cameroon . . . Due to its low population and previously booming economy, Gabon has relied heavily on imported labor and attracted a substantial immigrant population. In most of the towns I visited, the majority of small businesses were owned by foreigners.

Bakary rose from beneath the tree and marshaled us all toward his van. His inquiries had yielded the information that one André, who lived in a roadside village between Sindara and Fougamou, was the man we needed to consult. André was a great fisherman and reputed to be an expert on the paths and riverways in the region.

We made a few preliminary excursions for petrol and machetes, Ghan and Muhammad becoming visibly more animated and excited; the first trip seemed to have whetted their appetite for adventure. "We are going to Samba!" they called from the van as we drew up to each of the different supply points. "We are going to see the big fall!"

Our guide-to-be, the Ngounié's greatest *connaisseur,* did not at first sight inspire a strong degree of confidence. André made his appearance by stumbling backward out of his house, loudly sputtering angry words to someone still inside. When he turned to face us, he exposed—and I use the word advisedly—a pair of impossibly tattered shorts whose open front was held together by a piece of string. He listened to Bakary's request with great attention, screwing up his face and squinting as if he had been dragged forth into unbearably bright light. But he nodded wisely; well he knew the trail to Samba. He would take us there at once.

Bakary and I rejoined our cohorts in the van to wait while the man into whose hands we had placed our venture, if not our lives, returned to his house to make some preparations.

"He is not so drunk; he is a little mad by nature," said Bakary, as if I would find it comforting to know the precise cause of his derangement. André himself reappeared briefly in his doorway.

"I'll just get my gun," he called back matter-of-factly.

Even Bakary appeared somewhat perturbed by this announcement. He turned to me. "If he brings a gun, we don't go. For the hunt, yes. *Mais pour faire une promenade?* No."

Fortunately, this promise was unfulfilled, and our guide appeared with only a new pair of shorts and a machete. André's father made a fleeting but memorable appearance, long enough to establish that his son was but the inheritor of a family tradition: we left him standing in the middle of the road, somewhat unclad, grasping a bottle of beer so tightly in each hand that one had the impression they served as balances of a sort and were the sole means by which the old man managed to remain upright.

André directed us back onto the main road while repeatedly shaking his head, as if to clear it. The direct route to the falls was closed, he said, and it would not be possible to go there in the van; a large tree had fallen across it some time ago, and as the way was so little used, no one had bothered to move it aside. At his direction, we turned off the main road onto an overgrown trail and proceeded as far as we could through heavy overgrowth, until the trail broke off before a sharp decline, which we took as our clue to halt. We left the van in tall grass that was lanced with slim, branchless saplings, each surmounted by a single leaf banner, which en masse gave the impression that an entire legion had flung its standards defiantly into the ground. André had become markedly alert and voluble, but as he did not always speak in French, I could not always follow what he was saying. I had no idea how he intended for us to proceed, but contented myself with following Bakary, who I suspected was also somewhat in the dark. Ghan's face was unreadable, but I took his coming with us to mean that he was enjoying himself to some degree. Muhammad was scowling nervously around him, on the lookout for snakes. André made only one point that I caught: the way on foot was long, long, but by pirogue was shorter, better.

"Pirogue? Never!" said Muhammad, scowling under his ringlets more darkly then ever. "We go by land," he said, striking the solid earth with his foot for emphasis. The following discussion was indecipherable, but Muhammad looked less anxious, and I assumed that he had won.

We clambered down the steep incline and followed André as he cut his way abruptly into the forest, where a web of vines and

roots and foliage ensnared us. There was here no tawdry secondary growth to clutter the forest's original, grand scale; this was the
painted garden jungle of Le Douanier Rousseau's naive vision—
lush, squelching with juices that coursed through tuberous vines,
heavy with the ponderous burden of fleshy, sap-filled leaves. We
picked an uncertain way until the forest narrowed into a downward sloping tunnel and deposited us onto a dark, silty beach.
André's fishing camp stood just inside the tunnel mouth, a rough
palm-thatched bamboo shelter with a wooden stool and the
charred remains of a fire. The beach was fringed by the low,
vine-covered branches of a twisted tree and faced a higher bank
on the opposite side of a narrow channel of opaque green water.
Impossibly, and as if the scene that was about to be played out
had been prescheduled and the props prepared beforehand, two
pirogues waited handily on the far corner of the beach.

"Oh no, not in a pirogue," said Muhammad, backing away.
Ghan looked on, as always, without comment or discernible
emotion. Bakary had already ambled off to cut himself a pirogue
pole.

"Me, I know how to *faire le pirogue,*" he said easily, which did
not surprise me—I should imagine he could do anything. From
André's lips flowed forth a stream of incomprehensible direc-
tives as he busied himself in setting the pirogues in the water.
Once they were afloat, he underwent a remarkable transformation: careful, businesslike, fully in control, he divided us into
two groups. There was to be no question that he was the captain
of this fleet.

It is necessary to point out that there are pirogues and there
are pirogues. Those that are to be found in the busy waterways,
such as Lambaréné, and that are used on journeys of any significant distance, are modern, that is to say, roughly the size and
draft of a canoe and fitted with an outboard motor. The traditional pirogues are pole- or paddle-punted, and—most distinc-
tively—so shallow that their gunwales rise only inches above the
water level. It was pirogues of the latter type that André was
commandeering, seating Bakary and Ghan in the smaller of the
two, while he himself took Muhammad and me in the larger. I

eased myself in, sitting bolt upright on the floor, with my legs straight out in front of me, and André, Charon-like, took his standing position in the stern.

"Get in, get in!" he harangued Muhammad, who was scowling at us from the beach. Bakary was sitting comfortably in the stern of his pirogue, practicing with the pole.

"All the world knows how to swim except me," said Muhammad, but crept closer until, goaded beyond endurance by André's taunts, he lowered himself shakily into the space in front of me.

And so it happened: who could have guessed that this experience of forest and river would be wrung from dispirited, dusty Fougamou? Without contrivance and against all expectation, I had entered the world I had dreamed of, and fleetingly made contact with the past. André showed that however addled his wits might be, boating was a skill over which he had absolute mastery. He stood on the rear tip of the fragile shell, sure-footed and unshakable, negotiating his unstable bark over stones, sandbars, fallen logs, down into the rills and dells and minor rapids of the channel. Bakary had fallen some way behind us, but nonetheless made steady, if less elegant, progress: Ghan's face was split in an unexpected grin.

Only Muhammad was suffering: "But why is the boat trembling?" he cried, clutching the bow with both hands. His face had actually gone gray.

"It trembles because you tremble, you who are afraid, who fear water . . ." André's tirade was unceasing, a flow of unending and imaginative abuse, interrupted only with passages of self-praise: "I who, in this boat, have gone all the way to the *embouchure,* with my wife, with my three children, with *le bagage . . ."*

Seen from the perspective of near water level, the forest took on a different cast. One looked up into the umbrella trees' cupolas, which hung in clusters from each branch like tiny parachutes or brushed against the loops of creepers that drooped into the water. The sky was overcast and, if it had been the season of rains, would have threatened a storm. A few fat gray birds dabbled nervously at the edge of the river grass, and above our heads scythe-tailed swallows clipped in and out of the trees. The foreboding air seemed to have suppressed all noise except that of the boat going through the water, and André's voice. Our pilot now became a tour guide and pointed out interesting features of the landscape, such as the rows of crocodile holes on the higher nearby bank. Predictably, this caused Muhammad some alarm, and André relented enough to allow that the crocodiles would be asleep, "each in his hole," during the day.

But the damage had been done, and Muhammad began to look wildly around, to jerk himself in the opposite direction of every anticipated bump. It had to happen: in a patch of fairly active countercurrents, the pirogue overturned, and we were all spilled into the water. Momentarily, André's abuse ceased, presumably while his face was underwater, then rose and continued at a higher volume than before, inflected now with greater scorn. He nonetheless had his wits enough about him to drag the pirogue over to shallow water, where he could stand and see to getting it in order. Muhammad had apparently landed on a large boulder and was trying to summon courage to get from there to the shore; in fact, the water on the beach side was shallow enough for him to wade in. I had swum after and retrieved André's pole and extra paddle, and Muhammad's shoes, keeping an anxious eye on the crocodile holes all the while. Bakary had caught up to us but was laughing so hard that he had to pole the boat to shore, where he could draw breath, and Ghan too revealed unsuspected depths of humor. We helped Muhammad ashore and then all began to laugh, André and Muhammad uniting in a momentary truce. In fact, this was to be a turning point for Muhammad; the worst had happened and he had survived. Indeed, I had the uneasy suspicion that he now believed he could swim, and I hoped for his sake that he would not decide to test this theory.

Bakary took charge and ordered a reshuffling of our positions: "Madame goes with me," he said decisively. André was to take Muhammad and Ghan in the bigger boat. "Because," he explained with statesmanlike diplomacy, "you are by far the better boatman."

We reembarked in our newly appointed stations, Bakary poling at a peaceful, unhurried pace. André now fell far behind us, as the situation in his boat had become considerably more difficult to cope with. Muhammad, emboldened by the happy outcome of events and egged on by Ghan's deep sardonic laughter, no longer refrained from responding to André's invective, and their verbal dueling wafted to us across the widening distance between the boats.

The channel waters, up until now relatively placid, became swifter and more agitated, causing Bakary to content himself with letting the current carry us along while he turned his full attention to steering us through the fallen branches and sudden boulders. The little boat began to toss about. Stability was best preserved by sitting absolutely immobile, neither anticipating the steersman by trying to fend away from the obstacles encountered, nor clutching at the gunwales for support—a fatal move, as Muhammad had demonstrated. Minutes after entering the swifter water we were carried, for the first time, within earshot of Samba Falls.

André called to us, above the increasingly loud muffled booming of the water, to head for a nearby cove, where he quickly caught up with us; the novel threat of a more rapid current, dramatically underscored by the sound of the falls in the distance, had reduced Muhammad once again to silence. We moored the boats and followed André into the forest, which pressed so closely to the tenuous shore. A winding trail of black moldering soil, knotted with roots and creepers, took us into heavily canopied, gloomy woodland, permeated by the roar of water. The trail came to a dead end on a stony beach, where we confronted the Ngounié proper, wide, rapid, and the color of celadon, racing in from our right toward a long break in the forest on the opposite shore. Here the waters disappeared in a mist of spray that rose from the watery horizon: Samba Falls—but from the wrong side; the curtain of falling water was on the other shore.

We stood, still wringing wet, and watched it in silence.

"We shall get to the other side," said Bakary, who must have seen my expression of longing, and he promised that we would return the next day with a big pirogue, manned by at least two paddlers. "I too must see Samba," he said, surveying the tantalizing mist.

A small pirogue lay on the beach, which André identified as belonging to Henri, because it was surrounded by the footprints of Henri's dog. He straightened up from his examination of the beach and then without warning stepped into the boat and began to paddle energetically toward the ledge of the falls. After a brief pause of horrified silence, we ran to the edge of the river and began to call and beg him to return, but he only yelled back over his shoulder that he would show us that the river could be crossed: I could not decide if we had in some way impugned his honor as a piroguer, or if his mind was simply more unfathomable than we had known.

Bakary turned to me: "Tell him that you want to take his picture." I obeyed, and the effect was magic and immediate; instantly André maneuvered the boat around and paddled his way back to us. By the time he reached the beach, he was in an extremely good humor and had apparently forgotten his original intent.

Our return trip passed without incident and was chiefly notable for being harder going for the boatmen, who had to pull against the current, and for the tenor of André's monologue, which now ignored Muhammad and focused exclusively on self-praise. At the van, André chose to remain behind, saying that his wife, poor woman, would be joining him at his camp; by the time we pulled away, he had already turned back into the forest, with the preoccupied air of a man with much business to attend to.

Our return to the dust and noise of the main road signified a reentry into the hard modern world. On the outskirts of Fougamou, Bakary pointed out a small whitewashed building with blue shutters that he said was the mosque. It was just before sundown, and a row of caftaned men stood with their backs to us, their arms slack and their palms upturned, in the attitude of empty-handed humility that is the essence of religious worship.

Bakary sped into the mission driveway and came to a stop with a noisy and malicious halt, which produced the desired effect of bringing the Sisters scurrying onto the verandah.

"Oh, it is Bakary," they said, and looked much as Sister Carmen had when she saw that I was to be accompanied by a reliable member of the Peace Corps. I shook hands with my comrades, and Bakary promised to pick me up in the morning.

"Yes, Bakary is a good man," said one of the Sisters as we watched his van turn down the road. This second night, I was better organized and had obtained my own provisions; I was also exhausted and had no trouble falling asleep.

A rustling in the bushes outside my window on the following morning after breakfast, followed by an insistent rapping on the window, announced Bakary's arrival. Muhammad and Ghan were not in sight: Muhammad had been forbidden to come, and Ghan, as I imagined, had simply had enough.

We picked up our second boatman at another of the villages that lay between Fougamou and Sindara. This gentleman had none of André's color but appeared to be a solid, conscientious citizen. André himself, and his slow-moving wife, we met again just as they were about to turn onto the forest path that led to their camp. They were hung with woven fish traps and black cooking pots, and were carrying poles. André was considerably more all-about than when we had left him, and he greeted us with great warmth. His three small children emerged one behind the other from the forest, where they had run on ahead, and Bakary went over to tease them while our new boatman courteously shook hands. Everyone was already known to everyone else: I was always impressed by how well acquainted people were with the inhabitants of all the different villages in their area.

We followed André and his family down to their camp by the river, where André deposited his burden of traps and pots before going to see to the pirogues. His wife immediately applied herself to her domestic duties, and we left her building a fire. We set off in the two boats, Bakary riding with André, who was remarkably subdued, I with our new and careful boatman.

André's children escorted us for some distance, splashing along behind the boats in the river shallows until they were outdistanced. We left them, thin and naked, resignedly watching us until we vanished behind a bend in the winding channel.

The cove was reached without mishap, and against the background of Samba's muffled drumming we turned again into the forest. Stationed at the top of the moldering trail's final downward slope to the river was a tree that bore tiers of enormous sconce-shaped fungi up its trunk, as if to hold candles that would illuminate the way. The day was overcast; when we arrived on the rocky beach, the Ngounié looked dark and dull, and the swirl of foam on the horizon at the break in the forest opposite was not at all inviting.

A *grande* pirogue, larger, heavier, and deeper than those we had so far used, awaited us on the beach, arranged through the ubiquitous and inescapable communications network that informs all villages: André had contacted Henri, who had contacted another fisherman in the area who either owned the requisite vessel himself or knew someone who did. André took the bow, our grave companion the stern, and Bakary and I seated ourselves amidships.

Our crew did not appear to feel the strain of paddling until we were a little past midway, where they began to pull much harder. There was, for me, a moment of mild panic: at one point the three men stopped paddling and let the boat drift disconcertingly toward the ledge of the falls before pulling hard into a current that drew us rapidly toward the shore. That brief slackening of control, the quick slip into the Ngounié's hell-bent course, although it lasted only seconds, caused me to question the wisdom of the undertaking. But all ended well, and we beached safely on the other side, the noise of the falling water now loud in our ears.

Our new boatman took the lead, and we followed him into the forest, where the leaves were wet with spray blown from the falls. Like the rigging of a storm-torn ship, vines wrapped the forest in spectacular disarray, and from high in the trees finer creepers dangled like slackened halyards. We climbed upward over a rubble of great roots and boulders, where the earth seemed to have been shattered by a terrible infernal force. Whole trees lay sprawled across this scene of chaos, their disintegrating hulks already furnishing soil for the next generation of forest growth, and a bottle-green and beige motley dappled the trunks of the living trees, so that even these cut uncertain and disordered figures. The ground was littered with leaves that had decayed to fibrous skeletons and fragile tissue, like lace kept in an attic. We passed a deep hollow to our left, which our guide, shouting in Fang over the roar of water to Bakary, said was haunted by a spirit: not even airplanes could fly safely over its territory. We turned toward the river and exited the forest, where an impressive deposit of enormous boulders had been spilled onto the river's edge.

The cascades of Samba were wide rather than high, the whole river coming down over a low cliff, surrounded by an amphitheater of mountains. A rock island in the middle covered with trees broke the force of the water into two unequal parts. The cataract, as I had expected from du Chaillu's description, did not present one imposing sheet of water.

All of us found places on the great boulders that embanked the river and sat surveying the scene, within distance of the gusts of spray that were carried from the falls. Much later, we went farther downstream, walking from boulder to boulder, and ended up on a rock island in the middle of rapids, with a less oblique view than before, facing the outrunning caps of foam almost head-on. André, who had all this while carried a pole and basket, lost no time in expertly baiting a line with a crayfish that he had caught in one of the rock pools. Generously, he distributed lines to the others, and soon his basket was filled with thrashing fish. We walked farther downriver still and came upon Henri himself, his patient dog, and his wife, who was setting a black pot tightly sealed with a banana leaf on the fire. A pile of steamed manioc lay in neat fat tubes on a banana-leaf platter, next to two fish, one clearly dead, the other still moving its almost human lips.

Several hours later we started back and paused for my sake

once more by the falls. "Have you got it in your mind?" asked Bakary, laying a finger to his head.

Back through the devastated forest; back across the broad Ngounié, with a backward glance at the flying spray; back up the channel to André's camp, where the earth had been swept clean around his shelter, the pots hung in a row over a pole, the fire lit and the water boiling. With great feeling, I shook hands with the redoubtable André, and then Bakary and I and our unassuming guide returned to Fougamou.

It was after four o'clock when we got back, and as no one in their senses is willfully on the roads after dusk, this meant I would either have to find a ride to Lambaréné immediately or spend another night in Fougamou. The gods were kind and presented me with the situation every traveler in Gabon would dream of: a Muslim, i.e., nondrinking, driver of a big truck. One of the youths I had met on my walk that first afternoon came over to tell me that Harvey would be returning the same evening; but I had such a clear mental picture of the man, I could not risk spoiling it by meeting him in the flesh. I ran to the mission for my bags and then turned to say good-bye to Bakary: "I now shook hands with my best mate on earth," as Trader Horn had said of his parting with the friend who had shared his adventures.

We arrived at Lambaréné just after dark, and I was dropped off at the crossroads by the bridge. The mission was only a short walk away, and I soon saw the whitewashed chapel gleaming in the darkness over the mission gates. Like André in his little shelter, I felt I had come home.

•/•/•

TRADER HORN wasted hours of my life; although my investigations yielded many instances where his narrative was substantiated, there were also many dead ends. Thus, in attempting to identify the White Goddess, "Nina T," I spent an entire day poring over the genealogies of British noble families whose surname began with T—before discovering that in the British edition of *Trader Horn,* her name was Lola D. I spent another day reading about the history of Peru, searching for a reference to the father of Trader Horn's best friend, whom we are told in Chapter One was the president of Peru. That was before I recalled that later on in the narrative, his friend is said to be the son of an Englishman who had wandered to Peru and made his fortune in the silver mines. But this was a story I wanted desperately to be true.

Trader Horn (whose real surname was, unglamorously, Smith) died in his native England on June 26, 1931, at the age of seventy-nine. By the time of his death his book and a movie based upon it had made him a wealthy man. His obituary reported that he had been buried in the Catholic section of the Whitstable cemetery in Kent, and that he had left the sum of $8,520 to his daughter, Mrs. William Scales. His death was the most concrete and reliable fact of his life, and I decided I would go to see his grave.

On my return to England, I made a trip to the Whitstable cemetery on a sunny Sunday afternoon. The task of searching out the grave in the sprawling cemetery without directions of some sort was daunting, but I did not see anyone around to ask for directions until a lone car pulled into view. The driver was a young man, who introduced himself as Eddie. When I asked if he knew the whereabouts of the Catholic section, he replied that he did indeed, as he had just come from "visiting" his grandmother.

"There's some rumor that the world is going to come to an end either today or tomorrow at tea time, unless so many thousand Britons get together and hum. I thought it wouldn't be a bad idea to pay Grandma a visit, just in case." He checked his watch. "Well, we're safe for today." He asked me whom I was looking for and was interested when I said Trader Horn. "My mother's sister married a relative of his. And she knew the old man as a child—I've heard her talk about it." He gave me his mother's phone number and assured me that she would like to chat. "She's very open, is my mum."

He suggested that I ask the minister about the exact location of the grave and directed me to his house. "Oh, yes. Trader

Horn," said the minister, when he came to the door. "It's been—goodness—I should say at least nine years since I took anyone to his grave," he mused as he escorted me back into the cemetery. He led me to the grave site and then tactfully withdrew, leaving me to my own thoughts.

The wide slab of stone had been intended to commemorate more than one person, but no other member of his family had wanted to be buried here. The stone plaque was encircled by a low, rusty rail, and I had to sweep away leaves and twigs to read the inscription:

PRAY FOR THE SOUL OF

ALOYSIUS SMITH

(TRADER HORN)

DIED 26TH JUNE 1931

HOME IS THE SAILOR HOME FROM THE SEA

AND THE HUNTER HOME FROM THE HILL

R.I.P.

Eddie was right; his mother was extremely open and talkative. I telephoned her from London, and she asked me to come to tea. Catherine McMurray had been one of the legendary Bluebell Girls, who graced the stages of the Lido and Folies-Bergère. Slim and attractive, and at sixty-something still able to high-kick over her head, she was overflowing with her own memories. "All the family is in theater," she said. "It is our life."

She had first met Trader Horn as a child, when she used to commute for her dance lessons to London from her little town just outside Whitstable. "We'd both be coming back late from Victoria Station," she said. "He was usually with Dan Sherrin, a painter. They went boozing together." The train was not scheduled to stop at her station, but Trader Horn would pull the emergency cord and pay the five-pound penalty. She remembered him at a local church fête, sitting behind her mother's fruit stall, where a beer barrel had been hidden. He had not gotten on with his daughter, who had at one time done some traveling with him, before getting married and moving up north. Mrs.

McMurray's sister had married Trader Horn's grandson: "Sandy. He was always away traveling—Persia and so on. He worked on steel scaffolding." Her face hardened. "My sister was thirty-eight when she died. The family doesn't forgive him." She would not say any more.

Catherine was, justly, more interested in talking about her own adventures. Later in the afternoon, Mr. McMurray came home, a small, bent man with suspiciously black hair, who kindly offered to run me to the station.

"I hope you got what you wanted," he inquired, when we were in the car. "She . . . she talked about what you wanted to hear *too?*" He gallantly waited with me on the platform for the train. "Yes, we're all theater people," he sighed. A vaudeville personality who had just died came to his mind: the press had not picked up on this—it would be a real scoop. . . . The train was pulling into the station and people were making their way to the front of the platform, so I did not hear who this important personality had been. Doors banged open, and people stepped down from the carriages. Latecomers were running from the ticket office to the platform when Mr. McMurray suddenly stopped talking and touched my arm: "You went to Africa all alone? I'll bet you could tell some stories." (Sir, I could tell you—I've seen—)

·/·/·

TRADER HORN had read Mary Kingsley's *Travels.* "A clever woman and inquisitive to the way of things as they appear on the surface, but very little edge on what she had to say. A book must have Edge. . . . 'Tis an illusion based on Truth. To catch the Truth, George Bussey says, you're sometimes obliged to present it as an illusion."

The full import of this observation was to be impressed upon me time and again in the course of my travels. Every travel account has its own peculiar Edge, as every writer has his own idea of Truth and how best to present it. Temperament, the specific objectives of one's journey, prior expectations, selective memory, personal associations, the audience one is addressing—

all are determining factors that shape the interpretation and ultimate presentation of one's story. In making comparisons between my travels and those described by Mary Kingsley, it was at times difficult for me to accept the fact that, although I could retrace the route of her journey, I could not repeat—or, strictly speaking, even verify—her experiences.

For this reason, I am sympathetic with Trader Horn's fictive version of his adventures. Not only was it the best means of ensuring that his audience shared the excitement of the most memorable period of his life, it was above all an honest flagging of the interpretative process. His exaggerations can be forgiven: the story of his vanished, glamorous youth was, after all, told at the end of a long and difficult life, and from a doss house.

How, I wonder, in years to come, might I tell the story of my little expedition? Already Fougamou's row of desolate houses has subsided into the mental landscape of other nameless villages, and my initial depression has been virtually forgotten. The route to Samba Falls, as I choose to recall it, leads one deep into primeval forest, through the palatial grandeur of a bamboo grove, past a deserted mission and haunted valley, and by pirogue down a silent river channel. Samba is first glimpsed across a broad expanse of fast-flowing, dangerous water, perilously approached at risk of life, and beheld at last through spray and mist and jungle creepers: the scene is tinged with the green shade of the forest, and there is no noise for miles around save the thunder of its falling waters.

TALAGOUGA,
OR THE SIGHT OF WOE

E VEN AT THE TIME of Mary Kingsley's journey, the missionaries and traders of Gaboon's interior stations led isolated lives, the dangers and discomfort of long-distance river travel ensuring that their visits to the more "civilized" coast were infrequent. To travel from Lambaréné to the mouth of the Ogooué in local craft, for example, required on average five days, which might include a night in the open, if a friendly village had not been reached by dusk. In the season of rains, the spectacular tornadoes and electric storms that shook the forest rendered river journeys of even short distances unsafe. And in the best of times, there was always a danger of encountering bad-tempered or playful hippopotami, or of being caught in the crossfire of warring tribes.

The arrival of a steamer from the coast was a solace in this isolation. The boats brought mail and supplies and news, and offered too the possibility of comfortable and safe conveyance back to the coast, or farther upriver. When Mary Kingsley had been with her hosts the Jacots at the Kangwe Mission for two weeks, the arrival of one of these steamers, the *Éclaireur,* gave her the opportunity of joining it for the remainder of its journey up the Ogooué to Ndjolé, the river's farthest navigable point, and to the Talagouga Mission nearby.

Mary Kingsley did not seem to have had any definite object in mind when she embarked upon this trip, apart from a desire to see more of the interior. Her fellow passengers were a Mr. Cockshut, an agent of Hatton and Cookson's who was going to check on his subfactories, and the lively French official referred to earlier who was on his way to Franceville. It was on this journey, at the Ogooué-Ngounié confluence some little way out of Lambaréné, that Mary Kingsley had looked down the broad channel that led to Samba Falls.

"We go on up stream," she writes, "now and again stopping at little villages to land passengers or at little sub-factories to discharge cargo, until evening closes in, when we anchor and tie up at O'Saomokita, where there is a sub-factory of Messrs. Woermann's." Here, the crew and passengers disembarked and were greeted by the factory's young agent, "the only white man between Lembarene and Njole. He comes on board and looks only a boy, but is really aged twenty." Tragically, we are to hear of this boy-agent again: When Mary Kingsley returned to Lambaréné some weeks later, she was informed that he had committed suicide, an event that seems to have shaken her as much as any single incident of her trip, and that prompted her to dwell at length on the strain of living in isolation, "surrounded by savage, tiresome tribes." "No one knows, who has not been to visit Africa," she broods, "how terrible is the life of a white man in one of these out-of-the-way factories, with no white society, and with nothing to look at, day out and day in, but the one set of objects—the forest, the river, and the beach, which in a place like Osoamokita you cannot leave for months at a time, and of which you soon know every plank and stone. I felt utterly wretched. . . ." This impassioned reaction is noteworthy, for although ostensibly addressing the trials endured by the isolated traders, the passage is also a rare confession of sorts that Kingsley herself was not unacquainted with this degree of loneliness.

The company, including the boy-agent, dined on board the *Éclaireur* that first night. Mary Kingsley retired early to her cabin after dinner but continued to listen to the festivities carried on in the saloon next door. "That the French official is the leading spirit in proceedings I am quite sure, for I know his voice wherein he is now singing tunes," she writes. This is of course the same French official who was introduced as "a tremendously lively person" and "excellent company." Alone in her cabin, she continues in her usual tongue-in-cheek style: "I hear the French official, I am perfectly sure, trying to convince the others that I am an English officer in disguise on the spy." Then, safe in this ironic vein, she blurts out: "Wish to goodness I knew French, or how to flirt with that French official so as to dispel the illusion." (Wish to goodness one knew more about this lively French official!)

O'Saomokita, or Samkita as it is known today, is forty-odd miles upriver from Lambaréné, a little under halfway to Ndjolé. A French Protestant mission station had been established here in 1901, after Mary Kingsley's visit; but halfway as it was between the important sites at Kangwe and Talagouga, it never achieved particular importance. I decided to pay a visit to the site, although I was warned that there would not be much to see. An Agro-Gabon oil-palm plantation had been established a few miles downstream from the present village of Samkita, and this, I was told, was now the only reason one would want to take a journey anywhere near this region.

I was unsure how to get there; by road, one could go by *taxi brousse* as far as the crossroads that led to the plantations, but the village itself lay some miles farther east, on the banks of the Ogooué. It was obviously most accessible from the river, but it was difficult to find boatmen willing to embark on a journey of this distance in their small pirogues. On inspiration, while being ferried from the Schweitzer Hospital back to the island one day, I asked the piroguer, a taciturn and bespectacled man, if he had any advice.

He looked almost perplexed. "But Madame, that is near my village. We can go at any time."

I met him at the river's edge early the next morning, waiting amid the wet rushes on a cove of damp yellow sand. There was no sign of the sun in the washed-out sky, and yet I already knew that the day would be unpleasantly hot. An hour and ten minutes out of Lambaréné, we passed the entrance of the Ngounié, whose waters join the Ogooué so quietly as to pass almost unnoticed, and I looked around in order to take bearings from Mary Kingsley: "The banks of the Ogowé just above Lembarene Island are low," she writes, and "the blue mountains of Achango land show away to the E.S.E. in a range. Behind us, gradually sinking in the distance, is the high land on Lembarene Island." All of which proved to be correct.

The river became much swifter above the confluence, and we made slower progress against the current. On both banks, great blankets of vines and foliage covered the forest like dustcovers over bulky furniture, the vine ends dangling brown and bare and giving the impression of a frayed, unraveled skirt of fabric. We passed no other boats or people but saw a great number of water birds—white egrets, gray-blue herons, red-backed skimmers, and, incongruously, a pelican, in creaking, weighty flight, leading the vanguard of a flock of gulls.

Jean, the boatman, steered his boat with a frown of concentration. The river was low, and he had always to negotiate against the danger of running afoul of sandbanks. Jean, as will be seen, was later to play a central role in a longer and more complicated excursion. Each time we met anew, he disconcerted me: he seemed so grave, so stiff and somber, that I hesitated to intrude on his thoughts with anything but the most necessary matters, and yet each time I actually broke the silence, he would raise his head to respond with warmth and interest before huddling down again over his outboard motor.

The river narrowed somewhat past the jetty of the oil-palm plantation. We passed a few small islands, and Jean began to steer us toward the left bank, where we eventually ran ashore on a gravelly beach at the bottom of what Mary Kingsley would have described as a "dwarf clay cliff." At the top of a steep path that led from the river, we turned right and came to the old mission house, and the later church. The house was the most remarkable I was to see in Gabon and must be one of the few surviving originals of the old wing-eaved colonial type, such as Schweitzer's first house had been. The church behind was constructed of shining orange-gold wood, with a bell tower that had shown intriguingly above the tops of the trees as we approached in our boat. Jean was tromping loudly on the outskirts of the forest so as to frighten the snakes—watching me closely to see that I followed his example—in search of the old cemetery. It contained the graves of two missionaries, Rambaud and Rusillon, who had died in harness in 1919 and 1920.

The Pastor's wife met us as we passed by her house on our return and gave me a present of some grapefruit from the trees that she said the missionaries had planted. To my remarks about the survival of the old house, she smiled.

"It lasts longer if it is used," she told me wisely.

Samkita village lay at the other end of the path, two parallel rows of bamboo and thatch huts facing each other across a narrow dusty street. The huts did not have windows but only slits, made in the bamboo walls, like the lookout slots in a fortress. At this time of day, most of the villagers were away in their outlying banana and manioc plantations, but we were greeted with friendly curiosity by the few old women who had remained. In the center of the village, a strange bamboo platform elevated on high stilts was covered with drying fish traps. The village looked "old," that is to say exactly like the old photographs I had come across in books roughly contemporary with Mary Kingsley, and there was no corrugated iron or other "nontraditional" material to be seen.

Back in the boat, I looked up again at the bell tower through the trees, and then up and down the forest and river, which extended in either direction, trying to imagine what it would be like to live here, as Mary Kingsley had said, day out and day in, unable to leave for months at time. . . . Woermann's boy-agent was the first of many ghosts that would haunt me on this Talagouga trip.

On our return to Lambaréné, we passed a long series of egrets standing exactly equidistant from one another—nine seconds apart as we passed in the boat—and all leaning out at the same

forty-five-degree angle from under the fringe of shaggy foliage
that overhung the water. There was now more life to be seen,
and we passed the occasional shallow pirogue being punted quietly in and out of the almost hidden channels that filtered into
the river. In shallow water, an enormous and magnificent woman
was sitting stark naked astraddle an overturned pirogue doing
her washing while other ordinary-size mortals followed her example on river rocks behind her.

Back at the mission, I began to prepare for the next long trip.
My immediate destinations were Talagouga and Ndjolé, but I
planned to make my way eventually to Franceville, which is not
far from the Congo border, before coming back to Lambaréné.
Sister Carmen had been released from the Schweitzer Hospital
while I was at Fougamou and had met me on the evening of my
return to the mission, stepping shyly out of the night shadows
of the courtyard tree to greet me. She was now working valiantly
at her old duties, her injured arm strapped to her side in a sling.
Her relief at being back in her garden sanctuary was unmistakable, and she approached her comfortably familiar tasks with
renewed love and appreciation—the laundry room! So many
stacks of crisp clean linens to run her hands over! The bowls of
just-washed, new lettuce from the garden, glistening and green!
While the other Sisters took their siestas or were in town on
business, Sister Carmen happily roamed the premises, radiating
her contentment with all that met her eyes.

"If you have a little time, we could sit down," she said tentatively, patting one of the benches under the cool loggia by the
laundry room. My still wet, muddy clothes had not escaped her
notice on my return from Fougamou, and I had to tell her about
the overturned pirogue. She was, naturally, horrified, but oh! to
sit safely in the shade, looking out over the garden and talking
of these adventures with the stranger Alexander—this was all
delightful.

Sister Carmen had originally come from Buenos Aires, and her
family still lived in Argentina. She had been at this mission for
fifteen years. "I have not given a *thought* to leaving," she said in
her high, tremulous voice (how quickly the years had flown!).

Eventually, the mother mission in France would recall her, but she would hate to leave: "I love Africa."

On the day before my departure, she fluttered around as I packed, and locked a bag I was leaving behind in the laundry-room wardrobe. In the late afternoon, she appeared with a colored pencil and enormous calendar and requested that I indicate clearly the day of my return. I hesitated, and said I could not possibly tell. She looked alarmed: but I must have some idea! I made quick calculations and gave her a date some weeks away, with a safety margin of ten days, somewhere within which I assured her I would reappear.

From Lambaréné to Ndjolé is only two to three hours by road, but it is possible to make this trip by river if one wishes, as the boat that runs from Port-Gentil to Lambaréné continues onward to Ndjolé. It only goes once a week, however, and from my point of view the timing was inconvenient—which is not to say that I was overly dismayed to miss this opportunity of rejoining my old friend the *Ekwata* for another day-long voyage. Mother Jacques Marie once again volunteered to take me down to the *taxi brousse* line, and once again, she made a personal inspection of the selected driver and his vehicle. Before leaving the mission, I had left a present of some fresh fruit and biscuits on the kitchen table. Mother Jacques Marie now turned to give me her last words: "Me, *I* know how much the grapes cost," she hissed, wagging a finger in my face.

•/•/•

NDJOLÉ HAD BEEN established as the most interior French post only in 1883, by no less a person than the ubiquitous Count de Brazza. When Mary Kingsley visited, it had been a small settlement consisting of little more than the post, or government headquarters, and the factories of the usual European trading houses—Hatton and Cookson, Woermann's, and John Holt.

The *Éclaireur* stopped briefly to deliver mail at the Talagouga Mission, just downriver from Ndjolé, enabling Mary Kingsley to make arrangements with M. Forget, one of the resident missionaries, to stay at the mission on the *Éclaireur*'s return in two days' time. She then continued onward to Ndjolé, leaving M. Forget to break the news to his wife that they would be entertaining an unexpected guest. Ndjolé itself apparently offered the rare casual traveler little to do, apart from taking a stroll around the settlement and looking over the factory premises. As there was no accommodation available, she spent the following night again in her cabin on board the *Éclaireur,* before returning to Talagouga on June 25.

Her first sighting of Talagouga was dramatic: "The hills become higher and higher, and more and more abrupt, and the river runs between them in a gloomy ravine, winding to and fro." The Ogooué has narrowed, she reports, and its current has become so swift that it would "promptly whisk the steamer down out of Talagouga gorge were she to leave off fighting it." The mission station is "hitched on to the rocky hillside, which rises so abruptly from the river that there is hardly room for the narrow footpath which runs along the river frontage of it." There is a house set on poles some fifteen feet off the ground, a church that she claims is the prettiest she has seen in Africa, and—ambitiously—a sawmill, which is powered by a dammed-up stream.

"The whole station is surrounded by dense, dark-coloured, and forbidding-looking forest. . . . It must be a melancholy place to live in, the very air lies heavy and silent. I never saw the trees stirred by a breeze the whole time I was there."

Several streams cut the premises, one of which was spanned by a little wooden bridge, the handiwork of the energetic mission carpenter, M. Gacon. Another had carved a deep ravine in the hillside, on the opposite side of which stood the remains of the first mission house, built by the station's founder. And at the foot of the ruined house, illustrative of the "transitory nature of European life in West Africa," was the grave of the founder's wife, set "among the great white blocks of quartz rock, its plain stone looking the one firm, permanent, human-made-thing about the place." These great quartz blocks were to be important.

The founder of this mission station was Dr. Robert Hamill Nassau, whom Mary Kingsley had visited in Baraka and repeatedly refers to in her *Travels* as the leading authority on African fetishism. Nassau was a remarkable pioneer; he had also been the founder of the Kangwe station, and when he came to Talagouga, the region had been visited by only a handful of Europeans before him. Nassau himself tells us that Bruce Walker, the trader-explorer of Hatton and Cookson, had come this far in a steam tug, and that a white man called Smith had attempted to settle on Ndjolé Island, which at the time was known as Asange, some three miles farther upriver—this Smith, incidentally, was none other than Trader Horn. The creation of the Talagouga station, which Mary Kingsley found as a neat establishment of houses, church, school, and even sawmill, was one of the most formidable of the European feats of settlement in this region.

Nassau had come to West Africa as a missionary and medical doctor in 1861 and worked first at the Presbyterian Corisco Island and Benita Mission stations just north of the equator for ten years, before taking his first year's furlough in the United States. He returned to Africa in the spring of 1874, commissioned by his mission board to establish a new station on the Ogooué River. He labored here for another seven years, establishing first a station at Belambla, a short distance upriver from Lambaréné, which he was forced to abandon because of hostile treatment he received at the hands of the resident Bakélé, and then the successful Kangwe station at Andèndé. He took a second furlough in 1880, and when he next returned a year later, it was to establish yet another station, the most interior and remote of any European settlement to date, at Talagouga.

An account survives of the slow and terrible process of site prospecting, clearing, building, and equipping in what is to my mind the most fascinating sourcebook pertaining to the history of Gabon—Nassau's autobiography, which was published as a seven-hundred-page volume under the title *My Ogowe*. The book, written as a diary, is a fastidious record of his daily preoccupations and encounters with other people, yielding a portrait both of life on the edge of an isolated West African river, and of an assortment of African and European personalities.

Dr. Nassau himself was described by Mary Kingsley as possessing a "strangely gracious, refined, courteous manner." The autobiography substantiates this characterization but also reveals a man who must have—frequently—grated upon the nerves of his associates. His unswerving, scrupulous sense of propriety never condescends to make allowances for human imperfections, and time and again he makes a decision with full, presentient knowledge of the exact ways in which it will enrage a particular party. His unshakable belief in the correctness of a principle will at all times override practical considerations. While visiting Dr. and Mrs. Bacheler, the new supervisors of the Kangwe station, for example, he makes much of the fact that he has surrendered all authority over his old station to his successors and therefore resists taking any action that could be interpreted as presumptive of power: a sound, fair-minded policy, except that Nassau carries it to such extremes that he has to be solicited to contribute to the most ordinary tasks by an incredulous and irritated Dr. Bacheler. "I was a stranger, and only his guest," Nassau concludes after he has marshaled forth a series of arguments to back his position—arguments he had unquestionably prepared beforehand, precisely because he had known so clearly beforehand how his nonintervention would be interpreted. His dealings with the Africans are conducted in the same spirit of scrupulous bloody-mindedness: because he refuses to do business on Sundays, when some Fang traders arrive to deliver goods that he had purchased earlier in the week, he has them dumped into the river—and then on Monday renegotiates for the same items, compelling the bewildered Fang, one can only believe, to question the white man's sanity.

In the course of his many years in western Africa, and in Gaboon in particular, Nassau was associated, as founder or as missionary laborer, with several stations, but it was with Talagouga that he identified himself most closely. To appreciate why this was the case, it will be necessary to backtrack briefly to 1880, the period of his second furlough, his autobiographical account of which begins—startlingly perhaps for those who have not yet met Dr. Nassau, but in every way characteristic of his self-absorbed and unashamed pronouncements on all matters having to do with his own person—with the announcement that due to mental excitement and irregular eating, he is suffering from piles. Only pages later he announces, startlingly even to those who feel they now know him, that "even if there was no reason of impaired health for my furlough to the United States, I would have gone, for the sole reason, that, after ten years of widowerhood, I felt the duty of re-marriage. I even had gone over in my mind, the names of several ladies whom I had known, and, I had tried to guess where my best hope for success and happiness might lie. I reduced their number to three."

This number was soon further reduced to two, one of whom, it turns out, had unfortunately already married. The mother of the remaining lady deterred the good doctor by boldly stating her opinion that no man should take the woman he loves to Africa.

"I was at sea. Everywhere thinking of a wife. But, how could one know, on acquaintance of only a few days, the tastes and fitnesses necessary for a life companionship?"

How indeed? Particularly as much of this short furlough was taken up by his recuperation from an operation on an anal fissure, the details of which Dr. Nassau is pleased to relate to his reading public. But eventually, through the busy agency of interested female relatives and acquaintances, whose spheres of interest spanned much of the northeast United States, he zeroed in on a likely-looking candidate, one Miss Mary Foster, who was a teacher in Barnegat, New Jersey, and was active in the church. Some few months later he proposed by letter, and after several anxious days received a demure but positive response. They were married on Monday, October 10, 1881, and set sail for Africa on Wednesday, October 12.

I confess that when I later came across a photograph of Mary Foster, I was surprised. With her strong features and thickly coiled hair, she had a dreamy, self-contained, Pre-Raphaelite beauty, not at all how I had imagined a missionary's wife to look. Nassau was forty-six when he married her, and she was thirty-two. On December 5, they arrived in Libreville, and Mrs. Nassau, who professed herself interested in the strange people, animals, and flowers, seemed to have weathered the long journey well. They remained at the coast for a few weeks and then proceeded to Andèndé, where they were welcomed by the ringing of the church bell and a nocturnal torchlight procession to their house. Here, as we learn from Mrs. Nassau's own diary, her spirits began to flag: "Wed'y, Dec. 28. Very dull in morning; sun, in afternoon. Many women and men come; trying to nerves. In helping Mrs. Bachelor, and getting own things around, was very tired; cried. House in disorder; dirt around; strange language, seems as if I should never learn. Go to God in prayer for help . . ."

She and Nassau were together only briefly before Nassau embarked upriver upon his search for the new station site, which the mission board had stipulated should be "not less than fifty miles distant from Kangwe." Mrs. Nassau stayed alone in a dilapidated house on the Kangwe hillside; the Readings, the only other missionaries at the station, had moved from the hill to the Andèndé beach below.

Nassau set out with nine Galoa paddlers in a canoe laden with salt and other trade goods for the purchase of provisions on the way, and in the course of the next twelve days he traveled some one hundred and fifty miles upriver, passing through the series of rapids that terminate all steam travel just above Ndjolé, into the open prairie land inhabited by the Bakota. Three possible sites caught his interest: Asange, which was eventually to be the site of the Catholic Mission, the French government's Ndjolé post, and modern Ndjolé; Ndjolé Island, three miles downstream from Asange, which Brazza had used as a camp site en route to the interior; and two miles farther downstream still, a place named by the local Mpongwé for a nearby landmark, "a very large rock, in the river, near the right bank, which was called Talaguga (sight of woe)."

On his return to Andèndé, Nassau described the possible sites to his colleague Mr. Reading, who offered to accompany him to look them over, although it is clear that Nassau had by then already made his final choice. Asange he deemed too far away, and Ndjolé Island he understood to have been preempted by Brazza. That left Talagouga.

"Mr. Reading," writes Nassau, "was exceedingly displeased with me," and Nassau allows that they differed radically in their opinion as to the purpose of the station. Reading assumed that it was to be the site of a fully equipped mission, with a church and schools, for which the dramatically steep Talagouga hillsides were unsuitable building ground; Nassau understood its purpose to be no more than a convenient halting place at the head of a comfortable river navigation, halfway to an as-yet undetermined station farther upriver still.

Nassau's choice prevailed, and he began at once the daunting task of clearing and building. It was a slow process, and the only regular help he had to aid him were his crews, although he occasionally managed to recruit local Fang who stopped by to amuse themselves at the novel sight of a white man clearing land. All food supplies, for himself and his laborers, had to be bought from passing local traders or shuttled by canoe from Kangwe. Bamboo thatch for the house also had to be gathered and ferried to the site. Even as he was building, his work was undermined by white ants that ate the wooden foundations, or by rain that softened and rotted the wood. Nonetheless, by the end of June he had succeeded in building huts for himself and his workmen as well as a boat shed, and the foundation posts had been prepared for Mrs. Nassau's proposed hillside house. At this stage he decided that it would safe for his wife to join him in the tent in which he had so far been living.

In the first week of July, Nassau and his wife left Kangwe for their new home, accompanied by a small fleet of canoes laden with supplies. No white woman had ever been seen this far upriver, and many Fang visited the Talagouga camp to look her over. The Nassaus lived between the tent and the hut, cooking their meals over open fires, warding off the swarms of driver ants that would periodically invade their campsite, guarding and praying against an onset of fever. Finally, in February 1883, the "hillside cottage" was ready, and Mrs. Nassau was mistress of her first African home. They established a domestic routine, with Nassau continuing to supervise the further construction needed, and Mrs. Nassau busying herself with the laundry and food preparation. And in January 1884, Mrs. Nassau shyly told her husband that she was pregnant.

"Your mother was undemonstrative," Nassau wrote to his daughter years later. "I knew it before our marriage. But, I told her and I was willing to wait for her love to grow. It did. And she began to be demonstrative. But, her constitutional *reticence* she carried to the last day of her life."

By way of preparation, Nassau wrote to a doctor he knew in Liverpool, giving him "carte blanche to send to me everything of infant food, clothing, medicines, and appliances that he would deem necessary for a lady in confinement in Liverpool." He also extracted the promise from Mrs. Ogden, one of the missionary women at Baraka, that she would come to assist Mrs. Nassau at her confinement; in fact Mrs. Ogden did not come, for which Nassau never forgave her, or any of the other mission women. The appeal to Nassau's sister, Isabella, also a missionary of many years' standing in Batanga (in modern Cameroon) and the Gaboon, to fulfill this happy duty, did not bring about the desired response. "My sister, having deliberately chosen for herself the single life, caused it to be understood that, as she 'knew nothing about babies,' she could render no aid; adding an expression of opinion that children in a missionary's household were a hindrance to mission work."

The first sign that there was something terribly wrong with the pregnancy occurred in July while the Nassaus were in Kangwe, attending the quarterly communion. Mrs. Nassau began to hemorrhage, and although she was successfully treated by Nassau and Mr. Reading, she was subsequently confined to her bed for a week. Only a few days after she had recovered enough to leave her bedroom, she departed with her husband in a steamboat back to Talagouga, accompanied by Handi, a Christian Benga woman, who was to serve as housekeeper and nurse.

The days that followed their return to Talagouga were eventful. A leopard prowled into the camp and made off with a goat, whose half-eaten carcass was later found in the forest. There was trouble with some Fang men, who had wandered onto the Nassau "property" and begun to fell trees. The night of July 30 was especially trying: "That night, while compelled to sit up late, retreating from room to room before the vicious advances of an army of driver ants, we heard an outcry among the employees, about [another] leopard." The following day, July 31, Mrs. Nassau is, perhaps predictably, "not feeling comfortably. The loss of sleep, on account of the 'drivers,' and the much loud talking among the employees at the water-side, had tried her nerves."

Early the next day, in the dark of the morning of August 1, Mrs. Nassau was seized with her final, fatal hemorrhage.

"The life-blood was dripping away, from the first rush at 1 A.M. of the 1st to the last drop at 4 A.M. of the 8th. . . . During all that week, either Handi or I, day and night, were alternately watching by the bedside. There was no lack of medicines, waterbags, expedients, and rearrangements of bedstead, pillows, and bedding. . . . No lack of a variety of kinds and modes of preparation of food and drink. But, an inability to retain any of them, more than half an hour, until the patient became faint and weak with hunger." At length, the child was born at midnight on August 7, and Mrs. Nassau died five hours later.

"It would have been maddening," Nassau allowed, "if, in the reflections of those hours, there had been needed anything, for which there would be the regret, 'O! if I had only had so-and-so!' That Liverpool box from Dr. Adam had supplied every possible need for both mother and child."

Expedients! Water bags and rearrangements! *Watching* by the bedside as his wife bled to death over seven days in the remote forests of equatorial Africa! Had Nassau been totally blind to the unnecessary awfulness of his wife's lingering death? Had it not occurred to him, as a medical doctor, that a woman who had already suffered one inexplicable and serious hemorrhage might in fact have done well to go to the coast? Or that it would not have been amiss to have ensured the presence of another doctor?

Nassau knew all too well, but to face the facts squarely required more strength than he possessed. Once, fourteen years before, he had done so. Mary Foster was his second wife. His first had died in 1870, when in spite of Nassau's repeated pleas to his mission board for assistance, he and his wife had been left alone in charge of the Benita station. His wife had become seriously ill, and Nassau had made a desperate last-ditch attempt to save her by embarking on the open seas in an open boat, to take her to Gaboon, where he had hoped to find a doctor or a passage back to Liverpool. Toward the end of this nerve-shredding race against time, which lasted several days, Nassau had fallen asleep; and when he awoke, he had found his wife dead beside him in the moonlight and had turned the boat back toward Benita.

"I could feel more resigned if I looked on this as the Lord's doings," he had at that time written to the secretary of the board. "Humanly speaking she need not have died. She and I knew that both herself and I were failing, and you know how I have *plead* to the Church through you for relief. I do not blame you: I blame the church."

Perhaps it is easier to face such brutal truths at the age of thirty-five than it is at forty-nine; or perhaps they cannot be faced squarely twice in the same lifetime. Almost every one of the mission board's annual reports commences with a brief tribute to the missionaries who had died in the preceding year. With what illusions had the survivors shrouded themselves in order to continue with their service?

Nassau lived on at Talagouga until the end of 1890, with Mary, the little daughter who was born to him on that fearful night. He had made a solemn pledge to his dying wife that he would not be separated from the child until she was past her infancy, and consequently she was not sent home to be reared by relatives in the United States but grew up at Talagouga, learning Mpongwé as well as English, until she was seven years old. The station's inextricable associations with his wife and his daughter, around whom he came almost obsessively to center his life, coupled with the fact that he had been its sole founder, made this the station with which he felt the strongest emotional bonds, and he referred to that most remote of sites on the gloomiest stretch of the Ogooué river as "my Talagouga." Mrs. Nassau's grave was dug among the quartz boulders of the hillside on which her house was built. Nassau later erected a tombstone and marked the area off with a little fence. This was the grave that Mary Kingsley had seen at the foot of the decaying mission house.

The published portion of Nassau's autobiography covers the years from his entry of the Ogooué river in 1874 until his departure from Talagouga. The remaining years of his missionary life, which commenced in 1861 and ended in 1906, are covered by his manuscript autobiography, his diaries, his mass of unpublished letters, and his various other books and articles, which together have ensured that he is one of the best-documented figures of this region.

And happily so, for Nassau was so strategically placed in time that virtually everybody who played a part in shaping the history of Gabon in the formative years passed through his hands and narrative, right up until the time that Albert Schweitzer corresponded with him from Nassau's old Andèndé station. Some small highlighting detail is given to most of the individuals whom Mary Kingsley met. We hear, for example, that Nassau spent Christmas with Mary's Kangwe hosts, the Jacots, just weeks after they had arrived in Africa for the first time, and he remarks on the fact that they were going to a Christmas Eve party at the German trading house, which "was something new in the relations between missionaries and traders in the Ogowe." We learn that M. Gacon, the architect of the ambitiously built Talagouga sawmill, had been a Swiss cabinetmaker before coming to Africa. We are given a photograph of the *Éclaireur,* and can see that the crew or passengers hung their laundry from the lower deck rails; and we learn that the boy-agent who committed suicide at Samkita was called "young Dovey."

One of the chief values of this mass of papers is that it brings to life the various personalities that one otherwise only encounters at a distance, and, in its unashamed, personal relation of events, gives one a sense of the day-to-day realities of expatriate life at this time—an aspect missing from the generally optimistic and sanitized accounts of the other missionaries. It is the very mundaneness of the information that is ultimately so evocative; like sifting through the ashes of Pompeii and picking out the burned eggshells, or the broken homely tableware, Nassau's diary allows one to finger the texture of daily existence.

Nassau was also our only eyewitness to Mary Kingsley in Gabon—indeed, his journal provides a more precise record of her activities in Libreville at the beginning and end of her journey than she herself gives:

> Tuesday. May 23. A rainy day at intervals . . . At 4:50, went, with Mrs. Gault and Harry, to call on Miss Mary H. Kingsley, an English scientist, at Hatton & Cookson.
>
> Wed. May 29. Various jobs prevented me writing letter to America . . . Mrs. Gault went shopping to Holt's; & while she was away, Miss Kingsley came to call on her.

On Thursday Mary Kingsley went off with Mrs. Gault to a prayer meeting (of which Kingsley gives a mocking account in the *Travels*), and that same evening, Dr. Nassau extended a dinner invitation to Miss Kingsley and Mr. Hudson, the agent-general of Hatton and Cookson, for the following night.

> Friday May 31. Was occupied most of the day in preparations for the Feast in the evening of Friday. Mrs. Gault assisted, in directing the cook, and Anyentyuwa came, about 5 PM to relieve her, when it was time for her to receive the guests, who came shortly before 6 PM. Had an ample table, and cut the second of the 2 fruit-cakes Capt. Holt sent me for present last Christmas . . . Gave my guests music on the mandolins, and on the flute, & intended the guitar,—but the strings were broken.

These brief references contain several interesting points. There is first of all a minor discrepancy (both here and later in his autobiography) between Nassau's account of their meeting and that of Mary Kingsley, who claimed that Nassau had come down to the wharf by chance, looking for another missionary. It is also interesting that Kingsley represented herself as a scientist, presumably because she was collecting fish. In the long run, however, Nassau's references to Kingsley are maddeningly non-committal—whether because he was so self-absorbed as to be indifferent to all activity external to his own immediate concerns, or because Mary Kingsley struck this veteran of forests and rivers as being an unremarkable person.

Nassau is more forthcoming—on all subjects—in his letters to his missionary sister, Isabella. Having received a copy of *Travels in West Africa,* which Mary Kingsley had sent him, he wrote:

Gaboon Friday April 20, 1897

Dear Sister Isabella,

Miss Kingsley's book is quite complimentary of me. Her 2 chapters on *Fetish* are largely taken (by my permission) from my Essay on that subject. Her *descriptions* of *personal* incidents I discount to her vivacity. But her *statements* on Forest, People, Animals, Customs & co are very correct, & more graphically so than any book I have read on West Africa.

That Mary Kingsley owed her much-cited and praised chapters on fetish to his work is extremely interesting, for while she frequently acknowledged Nassau in the *Travels,* one is nonetheless left with the impression that she gleaned her information from their late-night conversations on his verandah, not from an already written, if unpublished, work. His judgment of her "statements" is a high accolade indeed, for few Europeans could claim to have known the country as well as he did, and Nassau was not a man who bestowed praise lightly.

Sister Isabella seems to have been less concerned with Miss Kingsley's views on Gaboon flora and fauna than on certain moral matters, and from Nassau's elaborate, careful answers in his next letter, it is not difficult to ascertain the questions that had been put to him by this upright lady:

Gaboon
Wed. Feb. 2 1898

Dear Sister Bella,

I have your letters of dates Dec. 24—Jan'y 15; Jan'y 17; Jan'y 21, all rec'd on Jan'y 26. Also the "Lyrics of the Lady" (will return it by Capt. Davis):—my copy of Miss Kingsley [which he had loaned his sister] (1) I have only condemnation for her misuse of the Divine Name. (2) In her Apology for the Rum-Trade, there is this to say, that, if Christians may *drink* Liquor, they may trade in it. British Christians, as a rule drink Liquor. *We* don't think it right: *she* does. If she is wrong, thousands of X'tians are wrong with her. (3) In her recommendation of Polygamy for uncivilised nations like Africans there is this to say (a) Some white missionaries to Africa have thought & still think Polygamy allowable in church members in certain cases. (b) Certain members of a Pb.y [Presbytery] in India think so (c) a Sec'y of one of our Boards w*d* allow it in certain cases. . . . (4) For her tolerant charity toward African women in their Marital Relations to white men, I have a profound respect; in that matter, I think she is nearer to the heart of God than any of my fellow missionaries, if I am to form an opinion from their treatment of some of the African women.

Nassau and Kingsley continued to correspond up until the year of her death, and only narrowly missed seeing each other again in 1899, when Nassau stopped briefly in Liverpool on his way to the United States, on furlough; and when he passed through England again, on his return to Africa in August 1900, Mary Kingsley was dead. His reference to her death in his diary is startlingly oblique:

Liverpool.
On Friday the 17 Spent the morning in writing. Wrote to

Mary [his daughter]: and to Mr. Kingsley, from whom had come a letter of notice of his sister's death. After noon lunch, was driven to the ferry, and went to Mr. Holt's office, and about 3.30 P.M., with him, went to the R.R. office.

Our single most hopeful source of information regarding Mary Kingsley in the course of her famous travels, then, yields disappointingly little. It is true, however, that when Nassau came to write his (unpublished) autobiography, he was more expansive; but here a cynic might point out that he was by this time writing with an eye to the fact that Mary Kingsley had become a famous personality:

Mary Kingsley, a niece of Canon Kingsley, of England, had been sent by a Natural History Socy. to examine fresh-water fishes of W. Africa. She also had a special interest of her own, for investigation of Comparative Religions. Stopping on the Coast at many points, she had inquired of all sorts of people, Government officials, traders, and missionaries, and had been given various points of view in regard to African Fetishism. . . . Some one said to her, "When you get down to Gaboon, there is a man, Nassau, there who has been investigating that subject." So, one day, word came to me from the house of H&C, at Libreville, that a Miss Kingsley was being entertained there, and that she wished to see me. I promptly called. This was the beginning of a friendship, which I have valued as one of the most interesting during my life in Africa. I called on Miss Kingsley frequently, and she visited at Baraka. I told her all that I had learned of the Philosophy of the Bantu Religion. . . . She was a wonderfully brave young woman. Armed with only a pistol [sic], and guided by a young native man who could interpret for her, she wandered in the forests, waded in the rivers, and slept in the cannibal Fanwe huts, attended only by her five hired porters. She was fearless, and was safe every where she had investigations for Science.

Nassau's papers serve a more profound purpose, however, than providing some insight into Mary Kingsley and the other minor characters in her story. "As a psychological study," Mary Kingsley writes at one point, "the carefully kept journal of a white man, from the first day he went away from his fellow whites and lived in the Great Forest Belt of Africa, among natives, who had not been in touch with white culture, would be an exceedingly interesting thing, provided that it covered a considerable space of time." And so it is, exceedingly. Nassau's autobiography and journal bring one as close as one is likely to come to understanding the pressures of the solitary existence that he endured and that destroyed young Dovey.

When Nassau first entered the Ogooué in 1874, as one of only six white men in the interior, to build the first inland mission station, the uniqueness of his task exhilarated him, and in this heightened state he was alive to the beauty of the strange world he was entering. "How wonderful that mangrove forest!" he exclaims. "For miles and miles, no other tree or plant!" His curiosity about the Bakélé people he has come to labor for is great, and he notes with keen interest their customs, their dress, their food, their social organization. Inevitably, he suffers from spells of loneliness, but he tackles these constructively by trying to play on his guitar, by writing letters or reports. But the years of this solitary living, of coping with the tedious and stressful business of clearing sites, gathering timber and thatch, collecting food for his workmen's wages, commuting back and forth from one site to another on lengthy and dangerous boat trips, let alone trying to proselytize, begin to take their toll; predictably, the novelty of the places and people wears off, and less and less mention is made of the world outside his immediate and increasingly narrow sphere of interest. His loneliness has worked insidious effects upon him; it is no longer something he combats in distinct and transient bouts, but rather it has become a chronic state of mind. Nassau himself is only occasionally aware that his personality has yielded to this pressure and been subtly altered.

"An incident that evening revealed to me how the climate and tasks were weakening me, and brought before me the *duty* of taking a furlough before I became any weaker," he wrote sixteen years after his arrival in the interior, during which period he had been on home leave only once. "Fanwe came to sell us plantains. I needed them; but, I refused to buy, because they mispronounced my name, calling me 'Nasi' instead of 'Nasa.' When I awoke to the consciousness of how foolish I had been, I began to be alarmed at the nervous condition that could cause such childishness in my manhood."

The autobiography chronicles the effects of protracted isolation on people other than Nassau: what, for example, is to be made of his sister's chronic neuralgia, which brings on such acute attacks of hysteria and which prostrates her in her bed for days on end, in such a state of hypersensitivity that she shrieks aloud when it thunders? "As a result of my sister's long nervous strain, her views had become abnormal," writes Nassau, matter-of-factly.

And there is the case of Brother Schorsch, who even before he came to Africa "had been known as eccentric." "Africa," says Nassau, "intensifies any prominent part of a foreigner's character." Mr. Schorsch's eccentricity developed into monomania: "On all other points he was sane. His mania was that he was in supreme authority." His violent tantrums and physical threats finally led the mission board to recall Mr. Schorsch to the United States—where he managed to persuade some sympathetic persons that he had been mistreated and should be allowed to return as an independent missionary.

As interesting as the individual case studies are the dramas that ensued when these various nervously strained personalities clashed. In 1895, there were twenty-seven American missionaries distributed among the six allied Presbyterian missions of Corisco and Gaboon. Mrs. Ogden, Mr. Ford, Reverend and Mrs. Gault, Capt. Peter Menkel, Mr. Kerr, Isabella Nassau—the same names appear and reappear through the annual mission reports and through the welter of official correspondence, now assigned to one site, now to another, and through the same sources one can watch them combine, dissolve, and recombine into their different factions.

In this ongoing heightened state of nerves, the pettiest events exploded into hostile encounters. Thus witness Mr. Menkel, the proud mission carpenter, break down and weep when Nassau shows him that the plumb line on one of his buildings is six inches off. Mr. Gacon, Mary Kingsley's amiable host at Talagouga, flies into such a rage at an African man who had been accused of stealing that he commences to beat the man, and Nassau has to intervene. In each case, although not directly the source of the original grievance, Nassau, as the witness, incurred the anger and resentment of the humiliated party.

In most cases, these animosities were of a petty nature. But the incident that almost broke Nassau, as a man and as a missionary, was motivated by darker impulses. The incident erupted in 1893, when Nassau was on leave in the United States, but it had been brewing for years before, and he was to reel from its effects for many years afterward. When Mary Kingsley visited him, it was very much on his mind, and, I believe, shaped to a great extent the report she eventually rendered of the time she spent in Libreville and Baraka, as well as of Nassau himself.

In 1882 a new personality had entered the missionary cast of characters. The Reverend Adolphus Clemens Good was a young man of only twenty-six when he arrived to serve at the Baraka station. He was by all accounts a natural leader, an athletic young man possessed of great physical endurance, and in his eventual twelve years of missionary service in Africa, he would also prove himself to be a first-rate linguist. From the beginning of his overseas service, he fretted over the classroom duties that were initially assigned to him as "a work I am utterly unfit to do." In 1885, he was transferred from Baraka to Kangwe, but here too he was restless, and spent most of his time away from the station on far-flung evangelical tours. "He was a missionary of the Livingstone type," an associate of his recalls, and it does not take long to surmise that Reverend Good yearns to blaze new trails: perhaps too he shares with his eventual successor, Dr. Schweitzer, the yearning for an "absolutely personal and independent activity." Consequently, he was not happy at Kangwe: "I am becoming demoralized men-tally, and especially spiritually. . . . I feel like running away," he wrote again to his wife.

From the Nassau autobiography's bland and even tedious narration, clear warning bells ominously sound. Why, for example, does the athletic young Reverend Good tell Nassau, who is by this time a man in his fifties, when they are alone one day at the end of a long walk, that he knows of "another path" back to Baraka and then lead him on a long detour in the equatorial heat? Why, when Reverend Good and Nassau are away together on business in the lakes around Lambaréné does Reverend Good suddenly embark upon an utterly fruitless and unnecessary excursion that delays their return to Kangwe by two days—and so ensures that Nassau just misses the departure of Anyentyuwa, his daughter's nurse, to Libreville? Why did this brother missionary, not long after his arrival in Kangwe, snap at Nassau, "You have the Benga and the Mpongwe; leave the Fanwe for me!"

The Reverend Good was a tireless advocate of the need to extend the mission's sphere of influence into the remote hinterland. He wrote lengthy letters to his mission board and particularly to the secretary of the board, whom he had made a personal friend, explaining in detail why and how this must be done; and from the beginning, he seemed to have assumed that he would be the man who would do it. He writes with not only confidence but urgency, telling the board that in the face of the French government's decree that all school instruction be given in French, the transfer of the mission's Ogooué stations to the French Protestant missionary society is inevitable and imminent, and therefore that no time should be lost in seeking fresh fields of labor. But the surrender of the hard-won Ogooué stations was still a much-debated issue, and it was not at all self-evident to either the board or the missionaries in the field that this transfer was the only solution to the increasing French authority. Nonetheless, at the end of 1891 Reverend Good at last received a mandate from the board to make a preliminary survey of potential mission sites higher up the coast, outside the French sphere of authority, in the hinterland of the existing Batanga station.

And in the intervening months between his departure into the interior and his reemergence, the mission correspondence is filled with references to the anticipated report of his findings.

The report arrived early in 1893, and its competence, thoroughness, and enthusiasm made a great impression on all who read it; it is impossible to assess to what extent it influenced the board's subsequent and swift decision to surrender the Ogooué stations and to build anew outside Batanga. As could only be expected, not everyone was happy with the decision—least of all Dr. Nassau, who had, after all, built the Ogooué stations in question single-handedly and from scratch.

The year 1893 was an eventful one. Dr. Nassau, who was on leave in the United States, was detained six months longer than he had anticipated when he was unexpectedly requested by the secretary of the board to stay and proofread a grammar of the Mpongwé language; he therefore was not present at the annual Presbytery meeting held in Baraka when an unusual motion was made by Reverend Good to the effect that single male missionaries be debarred from having native female domestic help.

Now, after his wife's death in 1884, Nassau had found it necessary to hire a succession of African nurses to look after his daughter. One of these nurses, as he says early in his autobiography, was to play an important role in his Ogooué life.

> This woman, known as . . . Anyentyuwa (by herself) . . . Jane Harrington (by most white people), and her younger sister, my dear friend Njivo, were the noblest native Christian ladies I met with in my entire African life . . . Of the two sisters, Njivo was the more beautiful, and witty; but Anyentyuwa was a stronger character, as a leader, and more intellectually brilliant, her education having been carried far by Mrs. Bushnell. . . . She had been sought by a score of white men, as a mistress. But, her virtue scorned their offers of wealth.

But this lady, when she came to Nassau, "had a past." Her story is a long and complex tale of misfortune and misunderstanding, which had begun when she was raped by an African church member and became pregnant. Mrs. Bushnell, her adoptive missionary mother, believed her story, but the Reverend William Walker, in charge of the Baraka mission at the time, did not: "She was driven from her Baraka home," Nassau writes. "After her child was born in August 1883, he summoned her before the church session, pointing to the child as proof of her guilt. He would not believe her protest. Apparently, the old man was not aware of the physiological fact that fertility does not depend solely on the consent of the female. She was suspended." In the brief period that Reverend Good was in Baraka, this suspension was transformed into an official excommunication. Ostracized by the community she had come to look upon as her own and after years of "civilization" unable to earn her living at rough manual labor, she took up with a white man who promised to make her his wife. Her situation goes from bad to worse; the first white man reneged on his promise and returned to Europe, and Anyentyuwa was approached again, and again accepted the second offer, which again ended in the same way. Her reputation was now in tatters, and few of the church community retained a belief in her virtue. Nassau did, however, and chose Anyentyuwa to be the nurse of his little girl.

The implications of Reverend Good's motion were therefore inescapably clear; indeed, the zealous Reverend Good found it necessary to write to Nassau in the United States and ask him bluntly if he intended to marry his daughter's nurse.

"I gave him the most explicit denial of any such desire or intention," wrote Nassau to his sister. "Nevertheless, with the letter in his pocket, he, at the Annual meeting of Jan'y 1893 directed his followers to strike me. . . ." Toward the end of this same letter, his voice rises with sudden and uncharacteristic passion:

> I will NOT, so *help me God*, dismiss this good woman,—undeniably the best and noblest of my church members. That there is any scandal in my church on her account is false. My white enemies make all the scandal that exists. I can

accept disgrace of recall, & retain my self-respect. To do the
cruel cowardly act of dismissal at the bidding of mere spite,
w*d* make me hide my head. This woman represents to me
my precious child; they are *inseperably* bound by memories.
. . . I can not, will not, see it any other way, for any one
whomsoever.

Reverend Good's motion was not passed, but nonetheless
enough trouble had been stirred up to cast doubt on whether or
not Nassau would return to Africa. Nassau did return, and with
the blessing of his board, but the affair was not to reach its final,
bitter conclusion for many years. Thus, on August 19, 1895,
while Mary Kingsley was resting in Libreville toward the end of
her journey, Nassau wrote to his brother from Baraka that the
missionary Mr. Ford had been appointed to spy upon his conduct and to report on his continued relationship with Anyentyuwa, and he added that he was being kept in these uncongé-
nial surroundings "because Mr. Good wanted me kept out of his
field."

It is virtually impossible that Mary Kingsley remained igno-
rant of this scandal throughout the weeks that she spent in
Libreville and Baraka, particularly as we know from Nassau's
journal that Anyentyuwa was, in defiance of the mission board,
very much a presence in his house at the time; it was she who
had served the guests at Nassau's feast in Mary Kingsley's
honor. Kingsley was a keen observer and a shrewd judge of
character, and it is most unlikely that she did not draw her own
conclusions; in this light, Nassau's letter to his sister, quoted
earlier, regarding Mary Kingsley's views on certain sensitive
issues bears looking at again: "For her tolerant charity toward
African women in their Marital Relations to white men, I have
a profound respect," he wrote, and toward the end of the same
letter he copied "Miss K.'s words on this subject taken from that
confidential letter of self-defence & explanatory of her life."

In the copied insert, Mary Kingsley's voice comes through
with its characteristic depth of feeling: "I can not understand the
view against the African women, held, as you say, so commonly.

They in their womanhood seem to me to quite hold their own morally with white women. Yet when one says this, as I often do, you see the white lady gaze at you aghast. . . . I dare say it may be some defect in my character, but I always think just the same of Anyentyuwa as I do of Lady Pembroke or Mrs. Green, or any other white woman." Surely this latter remark, let alone the whole tenor of the passage, is not fortuitous.

In 1899, while stopping in Liverpool en route to the United States, Nassau had received a message from Mary Kingsley, conveyed to him by his host, John Holt, "inviting myself, Mary & Anyentyuwa to her home." The sentence that immediately follows may be pointed: "And Mr. Holt said that if I w*d.* stay another week, he w*d.* take Mary & self as his guests for a week's sight of London." Mr. Holt evidently made no mention of Anyentyuwa. She is also included by Mary Kingsley in the preface to the *Travels* under her missionary name, Jane Harrington, as being among those people to whom she professes a debt of gratitude.

It is my suspicion that Nassau's predicament in that tiny, faction-ridden European community made a deep impression on Mary Kingsley. In particular, her often and strongly stated antipathy to missionaries in general should be borne in mind, together with the fact that Nassau is one of the few missionaries whom she singles out for praise, primarily for his unorthodox respect for African religious beliefs, which she shared. Nassau's diaries indicate that Mary Kingsley had visited him in Baraka far more often than one would realize from her book; Nassau was, in fact, in terms of both the amount of time Kingsley spent with him and the information she gained from him, a central figure in her journey though he receives only infrequent personal mention. One cannot but wonder if she did not deliberately downplay his presence and confine herself to careful expressions of gratitude and praise in part as a response to the scandal and difficulties with which he was then beset. The feast he gave in her honor, for example, is not even referred to, and yet it is perfect Kingsley material; the mandolin and flute and broken guitar—what a humorous tale she could have made of this! It may be that she resisted (as she did not, by contrast, in the case of Mrs. Gault and the Sunday service) because she did not wish to risk perpetrating an act of unkindness on this old-fashioned man of courteous airs. Indirectly, at least, she did him a great favor: in the longest passage of praise of him she wrote, she regrets aloud that Nassau has not published his unique wealth of knowledge pertaining to African geography and society. If he did, she says, "Dr. Nassau's fame would be among the greatest of the few great African explorers." Nassau himself had long harbored ambitions of this kind. "Years afterward," he wrote in *My Ogowe,* "other men traveled [to the interior], and wrote books, and told of things new to them and to the world, things of which I had known, but had been allowed no opportunity to verify"—one wonders if he had intimated this desire to Kingsley in the course of their long discussions. Several years later, the passage in Kingsley's book was brought to the attention of a member of the mission board, who consequently commissioned Nassau, at last, to prepare a work on African fetishism.

Reverend Good died shortly after he had made his trouble. In December 1894, he staggered back into Batanga after one of his by now near-legendary foot safaris, suffering from stomach upset, exposure, malnutrition, and fever. As his temperature rose to over 108 degrees in the following three days, he became delirious and died. The mission correspondence of this time shouts with the news, and much extravagant praise is mouthed: "He was a man of iron constitution and such amazing vitality of body and mind that it seemed impossible to associate death with him. The unnaturalness of his death impressed me as might some great convulsion in nature," wrote one of his associates, in bewildered grief. "There was something about Dr. Good that always reminded one of Livingstone." Reverend Good's last conscious words were, "See that I have not labored in vain."

And what of those heroic forays into the bush? In December 1892, Reverend Gault, a companion of Reverend Good's at Batanga, undertook to write to the secretary of the board a detailed account of how that first, benchmark expedition had been conducted. Up until a few days before Reverend Good's departure, it had been Gault's understanding that he would accompany Good, given that the board had authorized Good "and another missionary" to make the survey. Gault was suffering from a minor stomach ailment but was soon strong and ready to go. But to no avail, for it gradually dawned on him that Good had summarily deemed him "unfit" and had no intention of taking him along.

"The plain, simple truth of the matter is that Mr. Good commenced to make his plans, and his arrangements independent of me. . . . He did not make any excuse; he did not offer any apology. He coolly, deliberately, and unceremoniously dropped me. . . . I fully believe that Mr. Good *wanted* to go alone. As Bro. Godduhn says, 'He wanted all the glory of it to himself.' "

Reverend Good seems to have been possessed of one of those dangerous personalities that does not interact in ordinary human terms with other personalities but which combines with them, as in some mysterious chemical process, to produce results that could only with great difficulty have been extrapolated from the original elements. Many who should have known better seemed to have lost their wits in adulation of this man: the same missionary who compared the death of the Reverend Good to a convulsion of nature had personally been witness to a disturbing event that took place in Efulen, that most remote of stations that Reverend Good had so ardently desired: an African man accused of theft had been caught by the two missionaries and paraded through the village at a rope's end. Reverend Good then explained to his companion missionary, "with great reluctance," that the thief ought to be flogged in the presence of the people as an example. His companion almost quailed and confessed, "For myself, my mind was not quite clear that flogging was a moral necessity." But the thief managed to slip away, and amid the uproarious laughter of the village, was chased on the rain-slick clay byways by the Reverend Good. When the thief was eventually recaptured, the Reverend Good did a very strange thing: he wore himself out with "what would have been a severe flogging but that the strokes persistently fell about twelve inches behind [the thief's] shoulders." As the two missionaries returned to their station, Reverend Good referred to his cathartic panto- mime and impressed upon his worshipful companion "the moral propriety of not mentioning the incident to Mr. Kerr or any of the missionaries at the coast."

In January 1894, a Dr. Laffin went to survey the site of yet another station proposed by Reverend Good, still more remote than Efulen. He walked on many miles of trails and through many swamps: indeed the last four hours of his journey to this convenient station were through water. "Every where along the road," however, "the people were most friendly. As soon as I would enter a village the cry would be raised 'Ngudi Ngudi' (Mr. Good) and men, women and children would crowd around me. I found fresh evidence every day of what I saw while in Bule before, that, as an *evangelist,* he equals if not surpasses any man I have seen in Africa." Curiously, Reverend Good himself, in his final wild delirium, was heard to utter the statement, "It is strange that I have had to labor twelve years in Africa without a convert!"

The interaction of Reverend Good's personality with that of Dr. Nassau produced a very different chemistry. Clearly, part of the complex problem lay in his jealousy of Nassau's pioneering explorations, which explains in part Good's determination to cut Nassau's work off at the knees and to strike out alone. But why his persecution of Anyentyuwa? To Dr. Nassau at any rate the answer was clear:

The late Mr. Good (so extravagantly praised by Sec. Gilles- pie) gave to the Negro only a limited status; beyond that he was not to be raised. His open declaration in Pb.y [Presby- tery] in the faces of the native brothers was, "These natives must be taught to keep their places. Dr. and Miss Nassau are spoiling them." True, I "spoiled" them for him: taught them not to be sycophants. . . . Mr. Good hated the woman Anyentyuwa, for she, in her self-respect, did not bow the knee to him.

Anyentyuwa herself remains a background figure. Her name is everywhere, but she is directly described only once, in a pamphlet that Nassau wrote to bear witness to the harsh treatment she had received at the hands of his brother missionaries: "She was at that time [1900] 35 years old, but looked younger. She was petite, graceful, and quick in movement; not black, but of dark brown skin; neat, and scrupulously clean; industrious; skilled with her needle; vivacious; making herself a pleasant companion; intelligent and well-informed."

Did he intend to marry her? Perhaps he had briefly entertained the possibility, but I think he eventually came to see that the difficulties that would have been created, both for himself and for her, made this impracticable. But he undoubtedly loved her, as is shown in his letters to his sister:

> Can you beg, or steal, or buy from yourself or Miss Cox, or Miss Gault or Miss Babe, any ribbons for Anyentyuwa to trim a hat for herself? . . . I will repay you or the other ladies, whatever the ribbons may cost. I have no idea whether also, flowers, or even a plume wd. be appropriate . . . Anyentyuwa herself has taste and skill. . . .
>
> . . . In the afternoon, I went to Anyentyuwa's and planted 50 cacao trees for her.

And on several other occasions, he reported going to her house to plant flowers in her garden.

Tragically, Anyentyuwa contracted leprosy. Nassau built a little house for her in Gaboon, and visited her as long as he was there. Word of her death, of an ovarian tumor, reached him when he was on leave in the United States in 1903, and Nassau sent a tombstone for her grave.

He never got clear of the shadow of this scandal. The matter was dropped and resurrected repeatedly over the years in a tiresome and cruel pattern. Ultimately, it was used to force his retirement—due in any case—from his beloved Africa. Because his autobiographical writings bear the mark of his defensiveness and bitterness over this issue, they were generally suppressed or played down by the mission board. His outspoken contempt for the racist beliefs held by some of his fellow missionaries also ensured that his works were unpopular in the same circles, and this may account to some extent for the obscurity of his life and work.

What a web of humanity, what a tangle of emotions, is contained in those dry archival mission papers! Love and hate, spite and loyalty, generosity and courage, madness and megalomania—nothing is lacking here. How many dramas could be made out of the lives of only a handful of those lonely men and women! I was snared, caught utterly by this web of life: the Nassau papers plunged me into the living color of that vanished world, brought me face to face with a host of otherwise shadowy characters. And the temptation was very great to track down and hound through the reams of reports, correspondence, pamphlets, tributes, and cross-references the ghosts of as many of these characters as I could lay my hands on. The behind-the-scene glimpse of Mary Kingsley in the Nassau story further warmed me to her: her friendship with Nassau, I believe, reveals a wise and gentle insight, a softer edge to her usual public voice.

I HAD BEEN WARNED that modern Ndjolé would remind me of a truckstop and that I would find little more to do here than had Mary Kingsley. Ndjolé exists because all trade from the interior, whether bound for Port-Gentil or for Owendo, Libreville's port, must pass through its stretch of river. The Trans-Gabon railway, which will run from Owendo to Franceville when completed, may eventually divert some of this traffic, but at the present time Ndjolé is still, as it was when Kingsley visited, the crossroads one must pass, by boat or road, entering or leaving the interior.

A steep winding descent brought us into Ndjolé, where the *taxi brousse* delivered its passengers at the market compound, which lay between the main petrol station, the bakery, and some small shops. Awkward wooden shop stalls and a riverine petrol stand paralleled the Ogooué's bank, and an unpaved road behind them led up into the hills, where most of the town's cement-block houses stood. It was hard to gauge the size of the town; once in the hilly residential section, with its school and churches, Catholic and Presbyterian, it seemed sizable and populous. But along the Ogooué waterfront, strictly speaking the center of the town, it did indeed appear to be little more than an isolated depot.

The Ogooué and the surrounding forest had nowhere else appeared so dramatic. The river was narrow here, and the waters markedly swift and dark. At Lambaréné, the river's width, the complexity of its waterways, and the fact that mainland and island were alike cleared of immediate forest had given an illusion of airiness and open space, in which one could forget that one was essentially in a clearing of immense forest. At Ndjolé, the proximity of the high-banked forest of the opposite shore dispelled any such illusion. One confronted two profoundly incongruous worlds, coexisting but apparently unintegrated with each other: the busy depot town and the unscarred forest and river.

The Hotel St. Jean was a real hotel. From the outside it appeared to be a simple square of concrete blocks that could have been designed by a child, but inside it was resplendent with a wood-paneled, air-conditioned dining room and bar, and air-conditioned bedrooms with hot showers and televisions. Jollet, the proprietor, a short, bustling, moustached man, received me with the disinterested kindness characteristic of the expatriate French. He had a cook and chambermaid working for him, but the full weight of all the diverse duties of his establishment clearly fell on his own shoulders. He was working full-time in the bar but snatched what spare seconds he could between serving drinks to slice the bread for dinner, wipe down the dining room tables, run into the kitchen to give orders. And it was he who personally conducted me to my room, whisking my bag out of my hand and racing outside and up the steps that led to the top-floor bedrooms.

"Dinner begins at eight," he said. Although beaded with perspiration, his pale face held a steely, almost expressionless calm.

I walked up and down the dusty river road until it grew dark, looking out over the water. Almost opposite the hotel was a long, low-lying island with a triangle of tawny beach at one end. This, as a passerby told me, was Ndjolé Island (formerly Asange), and so it was here, then, that Trader Horn had tried to establish an independent factory when there had been nothing at all on the river banks save the forest.

When I came down to dinner, the bar was crowded with European men, who, I learned later, worked as foresters for foreign lumber companies. An amiably rough-looking crowd, they were freshly showered and dressed for their evening festivities. One man in particular stood out, a giant of nearly seven feet, whose white singlet, brawny build, and handlebar moustache gave him the air of a lion tamer or strong man in an old-fashioned circus. Jollet, who was again occupied as bartender, found time to rush me to a table, where I was to eat my dinner in queenly isolation. The air-conditioning worked so efficiently that the room was cold, and a nonending tape loop was playing the same songs I was to hear every night I stayed here, a concoction of Beatles hits sung in English by Frenchmen. Dinner was a four-course French meal, concluding with an impressive cheese board and excellent coffee. The men at the bar gave me a curious glance as I nodded good night to Jollet; I had the impression that I had left them just as their merriment was really getting under way. Outside, I caught myself looking hard into the night in the direction of Ndjolé Island, and I realized that I had been looking for the embers of a campfire.

I had mentioned to Jollet when I arrived that there were two people I particularly wanted to meet: the abbé of the Catholic church and the pastor of the Presbyterian. To my surprise, the following morning after breakfast, Jollet himself, who had served the breakfast, looked hard at his watch, did some quick calculations, looked around the bar, and then announced that he could take me now to see the abbé. Like Mary Kingsley, I constantly found that someone always assumed responsibility for the unexpected visitor.

The abbé lived in one of the cinder-block houses on the residential hill, and we found him alone, sitting bolt upright in the armchair of his bare-walled, sparsely furnished living room, staring into space with wide-open eyes, as if in rapt and amazed meditation. Jollet hastily took his leave, and the abbé and I conversed about the role of the church in settling this area. The Catholic Mission, always on the heels of the American Presbyterians, had established itself in 1897 on the opposite shore, on one of the two sites that Nassau had rejected, in the shadow of the French government's Ndjolé post. The site had been deserted in the 1950s because the local people had found it too out of the way, and the modern church was located, more sensibly, in Ndjolé.

The abbé himself escorted me to the pastor, walking stiffly in his careful old age, his face registering an expression of perpetual mild astonishment. We came to a prosperous-looking house, with a large garden and several cars, and were escorted into a long rectangular room that was completely edged with sofas. The entire family—the aged pastor in his stiff white shirt, his wife in her head kerchief, the pastor's charismatic son, and his gentle wife and their children—all congregated in the room to discuss my Talagouga trip, and all seemed to be fired with a genuine interest in the project. Daniel, the pastor's son, took charge: the Talagouga site was well known, he said, for information about it had survived in local traditions, but it was rarely visited. He knew someone who occasionally went to gather mushrooms in the area and would contact him; he would arrange everything.

Daniel had the rare facility of being completely at home in disparate worlds. He had been educated in France, and traveled often to Europe and sometimes to the United States, and so was conversant in things European. But he had also retained his Fang language and a keen sense of his heritage and had extensive knowledge of Fang traditions and lore. His personal household seemed to maintain a comfortable balance between these two outlooks.

Daniel was a source of much varied information. Did I know, he asked me, that the Fang considered themselves to be related to the Jews, on account of certain shared customs, such as circumcision, food taboos, the concept of a centralized cult? "In the old days, the Fang carried a box of relics with them on their wanderings, and they associated the ark of the Old Testament with their ark." I had heard of this lost-tribe theory in other parts of Africa but had never known that it was self-ascribed in this part of the continent.

Daniel was adamant. "Oh, decidedly. The Old Testament was a very effective means of evangelism, although the missionaries themselves may not have known it. This was true at least among the Fang—of the other tribes, I cannot speak."

Daniel's aunt had worked for Albert Schweitzer: *"Oh, yes—* the stories she tells. When patients came and greeted him as *'Docteur,'* he corrected them—*'Le* Grand *Docteur.'* He did not move from his first hospital at Andèndé because there was an epidemic; he moved because he wanted to set up his own village— he wanted to be both medicine man and priest. He allowed the patients to come with their families and set up camp in the middle of the hospital, so that they would create a real village community, and he could be its chief."

Daniel insisted that I leave the arrangements of hiring a boat and guide to him and not attempt to do this on my own. "You are a stranger," he said tactfully, "and I live here."

He arrived at the hotel early the next morning to take me to the boat, which was pulled up on the sloping beach opposite the market. The boatman was a slim, loose-limbed man with—unusually—a thick beard. He was wearing a knitted red hat and clothes that seemed to be held securely to his thin frame only by his tightly drawn belt. Evidently, it was he who occasionally went to pick mushrooms on the Talagouga premises. Daniel had also loaned us his gardener, a sly-looking man, who was to help with clearing a path in the forest. Daniel himself stood on the beach studying us, as if making a last-minute check of everything we needed.

"Well, *bon voyage,*" he said at last and nodded to the boatman to proceed.

Is it always overcast at Ndjolé? Is it the nature of Talagouga to be wrapped in gloom? Neither Nassau nor Kingsley had given me any reason to expect it to be otherwise; I thought of Kingsley's description of it as a place that harbored a perpetual and foreboding stillness, and of Mr. Reading's start of displeasure when Nassau had first conducted him to this site; "Mr. Reading was exceedingly displeased with me. . . ." And no wonder Reading had been appalled; there could be few more inhospitable sites on this whole long river. The dark, powerful current, the narrowness of the river between the oppressive forest-covered banks, the impossible inaccessibility of the quartz-bouldered hillside, under the perennially brooding skies—this was a strange place to select out of all possible others in the course of the one hundred and fifty miles Nassau had traveled from Andèndé.

Even if the site had not remained well known, one could in any case have located it by the landmarks Nassau noted when he first came prospecting: a large rock in the river opposite the mouth of a little creek, two miles below Ndjolé and a short distance below the even bigger Talagouga rock. We landed with difficulty, as there was only a scrap of silty beach among the roots of the trees, which grew right down to the river. Once we had scrambled ashore into the forest, there was no trail at all to follow, and the two men began to cut a path with their machetes.

From the boat, it had been possible to trace the rough squares of secondary forest growth along the immediate river shore that represented the later mission buildings. Once in the forest, I used Mary Kingsley's directions to find the site of Nassau's original mission house. Here were the enormous quartz boulders, here was the ravine from which a thin stream bravely seeped in spite of the decaying wood and foliage that clogged it, and here on the other side of the ravine and high up on the hill were the great white blocks of quartz rock, and a discernible square of an overgrown clearing.

The air was close and dim under the low roof of intertwining branches where we picked a difficult path through the creepers and roots and fallen trees, and at the end of our crawling ascent of the steep, moldering hillside we were clammy with sweat. I stood in the hard-won square above the boulders while the men, with impassive, unreadable faces, watched me turn slowly around. What had I expected? Even when Mary Kingsley had visited, the house had been in ruins. Yet I felt an unexpected panic rising within me, and I made a sudden determination to find Mrs. Nassau's grave, described by Mary Kingsley as the "one firm, permanent, human-made-thing about the place," which I knew to have been laid among the white quartz blocks below us.

Thus began several hours' search, in which the boatman joined me with some fervor, and from which the gardener sought to dissuade me by a variety of ingenuous and persistent tactics: (sadly) "Ah, it will be gone by now, Madame, it cannot have survived"; or (with inspiration, pointing to a boulder) "Here! I have found it here!"; or (a petulant last resort) "It would only be another old rock anyway." But for the boatman and me, the discovery of the grave quickly became an obsession, and we ceased even to hear our comrade's grumbling. We traced again and again the square outline of secondary growth, looking at each other and saying firmly, "This is the house." We went back and forth over every one of the large quartz boulders, groping among them and clearing them of overgrowth and decay, and eventually we allowed ourselves to be led astray as we roamed higher and higher up the hill, lured by the next boulder and the next, until the clearing was out of sight. The boatman was perplexed and seemed to have taken the search as a challenging puzzle that must be solved; and I was goaded by an irrational sense of failed responsibility, by a belief that I alone could rescue this site, and its vanished people, from complete oblivion. At last, when we were wringing-wet with sweat, and not a glimmer of hope remained that I would ever find the tombstone, I submitted and agreed that we should depart. We re-embarked in our awkwardly moored boat and drew away out into the swift water, where the boatman spun us in a last farewell circle, so that I could study the unrelenting forest line one final time.

When Kingsley had come here, the Mission Évangélique, the French mission that had taken over from the Americans, was in the process of transferring the entire station to the nearby

Talagouga Island (called Njoli Island by Nassau), "owing to the inconveniences of being hitched precariously on a hillside," as they then were. Kingsley visited the island in the company of M. Forget to look over the new site, and I now took the opportunity to do the same. The island lies roughly halfway between Talagouga and Ndjolé and would still be an ideal spot on which to build: it is low-lying, and although covered with forest, is accessible by a long tongue of attractive white beach: this was the site that, in Nassau's opinion, Brazza had preempted.

It was here, and not on the mainland, that the boatman picked his mushrooms, and so he knew his way around and was able to lead us expertly down vague paths that required only occasional clearing with his machete. Termites had wrought fantastic structures—long, bullet-shaped mounds that lay on the forest floor like unexploded bombs—and the foliage was here and there covered with their sandy-yellow dirt, giving the impression that the entire forest was corroding. Perfect, archetypical mushrooms, such as one would find in a Walt Disney haunted forest, ascended in tiers the trunks of many trees. The boatman, from force of habit, was gathering what forest fruits he could and stood contentedly nibbling what appeared to be a red toadstool while I looked around and the gardener grumbled.

Farther still, and we came suddenly upon an archway, a domeless vault of stone rising surreally into the forest heights. This, a brick chimney, and some iron posts were what remained of the second mission that had been so ambitiously built in stone and steel. The boatman was swinging his machete nonchalantly while he searched the ground for more mushrooms, and the gardener began to fidget and eye me sidelong, trying to guess how much of his time I would waste at this site. I said that I had seen enough, and we turned back.

It was by now late in the afternoon, although the sky, so overcast in any case, appeared no darker than when we had begun. Our final excursion was to Asange, on the mainland opposite Ndjolé, the site that had been chosen by the Catholic Brothers when they came out to contend with their Presbyterian brethren for the souls of the Africans.

Disembarking, we followed a path that had so far escaped the advancing forest and was overgrown only with weeds and grass. The surface beneath our feet changed suddenly, and I saw that we were walking on a lichen-covered pavement at the foot of an overgrown flight of steps; at the top of which we were confronted by the formidable sight of a two-story dormitory and a grandiose red-brick cathedral, both overwhelmed and ensnared by the forest.

The steps sagged, the floor creaked beneath me as I climbed the dormitory's outer stairs. The doors and shutters and palm-matting screens that flanked the long cool walkways had sagged and slipped into the jarring angles of decay. The forest's long exploring branches had reached across the verandah and were delicately tap-tapping at the Brothers' bedroom doors.

Downstairs again, I approached the cathedral, whose heavy double doors surmounted with great bosses stood closed with an air of finality, as if they had been sealed shut irrevocably and forever; yet they swung easily open when I pushed them. I stepped into the cavernous cathedral nave, which, stripped bare as it was of all pews and of every scrap of decoration, resembled a medieval dining hall more than it did a church. Dangling eerily on its broken chain above the choir loft was what appeared to be, but surely could not have been, a censer, spotlit by the weak light that entered through the large porthole window immediately behind it. All along the high side walls, the jungle had come peering in each window, groping with its sinuous tendrils into this private darkness, and leaf by leaf consigning it to a forgotten secrecy, like that enshrouding Sleeping Beauty's palace. Impossible to describe the feeling of desolation harbored in this grandiose and gutted structure, standing at the end of the long line of successive abandonments that I had wandered through that day! From site to site there had been no sense of continuity; each had seemed an isolated failure that had added nothing to the next attempt. Modern Ndjolé existed across the river as an entirely unrelated entity, so that the cumulative years of effort seemed to have led to absolutely nothing; one imagined that many years ago, some solemn deliberative council had been held one night, in which the governing body had finally stood up and, shaking hands, agreed, "No. This will never work," and the next morning packed up all the miscellany they had gathered and simply left.

What kind of outlook is shaped by an environment in which natural forces claim a man's artifacts within his lifetime? In climates that have allowed the achievements of successive generations to survive and clutter the horizon with battlements and towers and spires, it is easy to conceive of such optimistic ideas as the endurance of human toil and ingenuity. But life in the Great Forest Belt of Africa fosters no such illusions, and as a consequence, very different ideas evolve about the worth of human effort. The missionary reports, Mary Kingsley said, were written "not to tell you how the country they resided in was, but how it was getting on towards being what it ought to be." The forest societies among whom the missionaries were laboring did not possess this view of world improvement; their generations-old traditions were all geared to handing the world over to their children in the same condition in which they had found it. The missionaries had been repulsed by the dark superstitions that ensnared their African brothers; but superstitions arise in part through fear of death, and in the starker world of the forest, the power of death is a very difficult thing to hide.

When we had arrived, the great double doors of the cathedral had looked as if they had been deliberately closed behind someone, and the key carefully taken away. Now, as we were departing, I turned and saw that the gardener, careless of the atmosphere with which I felt this spot was fraught, had left the doors standing open. A strange tightening in my throat had strained my nerves, and I snapped at him, "Close the door."

When we returned to the mainland, I walked through Ndjolé almost without seeing it and made my way directly to the Hotel St. Jean, where I went straight to my room and locked the door. After I had showered, I turned off the lights and went to bed. The tightness in my throat had brought me to the verge of tears. I lay waiting—for what? I was not sure, and when at last I knew, the answer startled me. I was waiting for word to come that Mrs.

Nassau, her lifeblood dripping away over seven days, had finally died.

Later, I learned that her grave had been moved to the new mission station, on Talagouga Island, and had been placed with other missionary graves in a little cemetery by the house; I must have stood beside it without knowing. But this realization did not reduce for me the impact of my desperate scramble among the quartz boulders on the Talagouga hillside.

So, to update Mary Kingsley's impressions: the original mission house is not in ruins, it is gone. And the grave of Mrs. Nassau, once among the great white blocks of quartz rock, looking the one firm, permanent, human-made thing about the place, no longer exists.

HUNTING RAPIDS

By 1895, the Ogooué river from the coast to Ndjolé, accessible as it was to steam vessels, was well traveled and well known, but beyond this point one embarked upon a different order of venture. Behind its low-lying coastal plain, the Gabon hinterland rises to a rocky escarpment, extending to the north, east, and most of the south, that has been etched into distinct ranges by the descending interior rivers. The intersection of the Monts de Cristal and the Ogooúe river, beginning just beyond Ndjolé, forms the Okota rapids, which prohibit further navigation to all but the smallest, slow-going craft. Mary Kingsley's lively French official, for example, faced a journey of at least thirty-six days in his fleet of Adouma canoes from Ndjolé to Franceville. Kingsley notes that at the time of her writing little was known even of the important Okano river, which enters the Ogooué from the northeast only twenty miles upriver from Ndjolé.

The first Europeans to ascend these rapids had been two traders: Bruce Walker of Hatton and Cookson, in 1866, and Emil Schültz of Woermann, in 1871. Several tribes inhabited this stretch of river: the Bakota, the Apindji, the Okandé, and in the region of the tributary Ivindo, the Ossyéba and the Adouma, but the Okandé were the premier masters of the rapids. At the time of Kingsley's visit, the Fang had recently become an established presence. This tribal distribution, although diminished, is much the same today.

Mary Kingsley's ascent of the rapids is one of the most memorable of her feats related in the *Travels,* and her description of this journey one of her most successful pieces of writing. Her decision to make this journey, she says, was prompted by her desire to collect fish: "All the balance of the time I was at Talagouga I spent in trying to find means to get up into the rapids above Njole," she writes toward the end of her Talagouga chapter, "for my heart got more and more set on them now that I saw the strange forms of the Talagouga fishes, and the differences between them and the fishes at Lembarene." Doubtless, she was interested in her fish, but it may be too that her appetite for this adventure had been whetted by that intriguing French official who had given her a "lively and dramatic" account of these rapids, "rolling his hands round and round each other and dashing them forward with a descriptive ejaculation of 'Whish, flash, bum, bum, bump.' " She mentions the lively official again at the conclusion of this adventure: "I personally deeply regret it was not my good fortune to meet again the French official I had had the pleasure of meeting on the *Éclaireur,* " she writes but notes that she had come upon the ashes of his campfires—had she, one wonders, been on the lookout for such signs?

The trip had been difficult to arrange, as a spare boat and crew were not easy to come by, and the French authorities who manned the Ndjolé post had not been happy about granting her permission to advance beyond their station. Eventually, however, between Hatton and Cookson and the Talagouga Mission, an *équipage* had been assembled, consisting of a canoe and a crew of eight Galoa boatmen equipped with long-handled paddles with leaf-shaped blades. "I establish myself on my portmanteau comfortably in the canoe," she writes. "My back is against the trade box, and behind that is the usual mound of pillows, sleep-

ing mats, and mosquito-bars of the Igalwa crew; the whole surmounted by the French flag flying from an indifferent stick."

Her account of the ascent itself takes some twenty-five pages
and gives the impression of an endlessly diverting and exciting—
if dangerous—journey: "Great masses of black rock show among
the trees on the hillsides, and under the fringe of fallen trees that
hang from the steep banks. Two hours after leaving Njole we are
facing our first rapid. Great gray-black masses of smoothed rock
rise up out of the whirling water in all directions." As the river
narrows, and becomes more congested with boulders, it becomes
more dangerous and foreboding and is "forested with high
rocks, looking, as they stand with their grim forms above the
foam, like a regiment of strange strong creatures breasting
it. . . . huge monoliths rise from the water, making what looks
like a gateway which had once been barred and through which
the Ogowé had burst." When the river boulders became too
difficult to negotiate, she and her crew had to disembark and pull
their canoe along from the rocky shore, which they did so often
that they seemed to have spent almost as much time out of the
water as on it.

The drama apart, the trip would have been memorable for its
beauty. "These rocks have a peculiar appearance. . . . When the
sun shines on them they have a soft light blue haze round them,
like a halo. The effect produced by this, with the forested hillsides and the little beaches of glistening white sand was one of
the most perfect things I have ever seen." Thousands of beautiful vanilla-scented white lilies were to be seen growing in pools
between the black-gray rock. The two nights she spent beside
the river produced two unforgettable sunsets: "The *Erd-geist*
knew we wanted something, and seeing how we personally
lacked it, thought it was beauty; and being in a kindly mood,
gave it us, sending the lovely lingering flushes of his afterglow
across the sky, which, dying, left it that divine deep purple
velvet which no one has dared to paint. Out in it came the great
stars blazing high above us, and the dark round us was be-
gemmed with fire-flies." As a crowning touch, she had been

accompanied throughout by the singing of her boatmen, whose "M'pongwe and Igalwa boat songs are all very pretty, and have very elaborate tunes in a minor key."

The conclusion of this chapter is triumphant: "I hope to see the Ogowé next time in the wet season—there must be several more of these great sheets of water then over what are rocky rapids now. . . . I do not fancy however it would ever be possible to get up the river when it is at its height, with so small a crew as we were when we went and played our knock-about farce, before King Death, in his amphitheatre in the Sierra del Cristal."

That this had been a special trip for Kingsley is shown at several points. Her use of the word *Erdgeist* is particularly telling: in the tribute to her father that she wrote after his death, she repeatedly characterized him as "one who was under the thrall of the *Erdgeist.*" And in this chapter, too, she momentarily drops her habitual flippancy and speaks to the reader directly and at some length about the stirrings of her soul. Of her contemplation of the rapids in the darkness of the first night she writes:

The majesty and beauty of the scene fascinated me, and I stood leaning with my back against a rock pinnacle watching it. Do not imagine it gave rise, in what I am pleased to call my mind, to those complicated, poetical reflections natural beauty seems to bring out in other people's minds. It never works that way with me; I just lose all sense of human individuality, all memory of human life, with its grief and worry and doubt, and become part of the atmosphere. If I have a heaven, that will be mine, and I verily believe that if I were left alone long enough with such a scene as this or on the deck of an African liner in the Bights, watching her funnel and masts swinging to and fro in the great long leisurely roll against the sky, I should be found soulless and dead.

Of all Mary Kingsley's adventures, this was the one I had most looked forward to repeating. I had known before I came to Gabon that it was unlikely I would be able to duplicate her trip using the same method of conveyance—for one thing, European tradesmen are no longer in the position to loan out their personal Galoa boatmen to be used at the whim of unknown travelers. Nonetheless, I had an image of myself making my way through white water, accompanied by perhaps two boatmen in a little outboard boat, and occasionally being called upon to fend off from dangerous rocks with an extra paddle. My mother had suggested to me that I might want to take a life jacket, but I had disdained her advice: my trip was to be as adventurous as Kingsley's.

"In fact," Daniel said cautiously prior to my departure from Ndjolé, "they are not really 'rapids'; but the water does get a little rough," an observation that did not at the time make much impression on me. From my point of view, the expedition involved no organizational problems whatsoever—Daniel had simply arranged everything for me and turned up at the hotel, as he had on the morning of the Talagouga trip, to take me to the waiting boat. My crew was made up of the mushroom-picking boatman of the day before and a newcomer, an older man, gnarled and stocky with graying hair, who spoke little French. Our provisions included a bottle of water, several heavy metal containers full of petrol, and the mushroom picker's gun.

The landscape immediately beyond Ndjolé has been spoiled by the squat cement-block houses perched on the bare hills overlooking the Ogooué, by the roadway to Franceville, and by the Trans-Gabon railway line. Once we left this suburb behind, however, we entered again the familiar world of forest and river where, briefly, the Ogooué seemed wider and friendlier, as the forest on either bank did not tower over the water but stretched benignly away from its low-lying shores. When the river did again narrow between mountainous rock, the scenery still had none of the harshness and foreboding that characterized Talagouga. The banks even admitted an occasional substantial beach, and these long bands of pale yellow sand, acting as bright buffers between water and forest, lent the scene a cheerful air. The sun had come out, and both water and sky were a dazzling, unrelentingly bright blue.

Eventually the current became mildly agitated, and I began to brace myself for the rough ride that would inevitably follow. The shore became rockier, and a jumble of boulders and splintered islands so congested the river that it was impossible at first sight to select the correct route from the hundreds of illusory channels. I continued to look around expectantly for the first sign of white water, puzzled that it was taking so long to appear. I became confused by the landmarks and felt I had lost my bearings: half an hour may have passed before the slow-dawning, sickening realization came to me that this swift current, dappled with patches of uneven water, which experienced from a motorboat one hardly noticed, were in fact the rapids I had come to shoot.

The dictionary definition of *rapid* is "a steep descent in a river-bed with a swift current," an accurate enough description of what I encountered. As used by Kingsley, however, the word had conjured up a picture of a foaming river course shattering itself into white water against the rocks it met headlong. The most distinctive landmarks of her journey were easily identified: the imposing and seemingly perfect round hole of darkness in the cliff face on the southern shore that marked the entrance to the Boko-Boko cave; the blunt-topped cone of Kangwe mountain to the north; and near the journey's end, just beyond the mouth of the Okano river, the swirling Alemba rapids, which race downstream between the northern shore and the outlying island of Kondo Kondo—and had it not been for these unmistakable features, I could not have believed that I was following Kingsley's route.

It is obviously one thing to cover a stretch of rocky water in a boat paddled by Galoa boatmen and quite another to do so in a motorized canoe. Apart from the difference in the speed in which our boats made this journey, we necessarily saw the river from very different perspectives. A paddle-propelled canoe had to hug the shore, where the current was weakest and not beyond the strength of its crew. The chief dangers to a motorized pirogue, on the other hand, are of running into rocks or hitting shallow water, and the modern boatman steers for the deepest water, in the middle of the river. Thus, whereas Mary Kingsley's ride was continually disturbed by the necessity of fending off the exposed rocks in the river shallows, my boat was able to hold a steady, if duller, middle course. Kingsley and her crew had been forced to engage with their surroundings; I observed them passively at a distance. Finally, Kingsley may have found the river level somewhat higher, as she was told by the Adouma of Kembe island, where she passed her first night, that "the rapids were at their worst just now."

Even bearing these considerations in mind, I could not entirely reconcile the wild discrepancy between our impressions. Comparison with other accounts of this same trip were not altogether helpful. Brazza's official report of his first 1875–78 expedition gives little detailed description of this stretch of rapids, apart from noting that their inception delineates the limit of steam navigation, and farther on, that the Alemba rapid, some short distance beyond the mouth of the Okano river, is the most powerful that one encounters in the Bakota territory. On the other hand, Brazza's more expansive account, published in the popular journal of travel and exploration *Tour du Monde,* speaks of the "currents and countercurrents that render the passage difficult," as well as his company's fatigue at the end of the first day of their ascent: "Fatigue weighed us down; yet the difficulties overcome were, it appeared, only a preparation for the harder labor of the days ahead."

Nassau too passed this way, in January 1882, when he was prospecting for the Talagouga site, and rendered a characteristically laconic account amounting to little more than a paragraph: "There were a series of mountings of the cataracts, by the passengers landing, and walking around them." He notes too that "Miss Kingsley has described those falls, in a most graphic manner," words that recalled to me his review of Kingsley's *Travels* in the letter he wrote to his sister, in which he stated that "her *descriptions* of *personal* incidents I discount to her vivacity." At this point too I recalled, somewhat sourly, the testimony of a contemporary who had known her when she lived in Cambridge, that "Mary Kingsley was, with the exception of her father, the most brilliant conversationalist I ever met. She could meet with more adventures crossing 'Parker's Piece' than some folks would in crossing the Sahara, and could relate them with a vivacity and piquancy all her own."

Kingsley of course wrote with the intention of giving a personal account of this, the first adventure of the *Travels*, while the seasoned, perhaps more jaded explorers had made their trips in the line of business and had been preoccupied with surveying the surrounding countryside with an eye to its suitability for future settlement and development. In spite of her assertion about her desire to collect fish, the trip was for Kingsley not merely the way of proceeding to some farther interior point; she had embarked on the trip to do some sightseeing of the rapids themselves and was therefore obviously more inclined to dwell on every rock and boulder, promontory and sandbank—on all the details that make her account so graphic.

At no point were my impressions more at odds with hers than when I witnessed the Alemba, which—though it struck me as a potentially dangerous patch of swirling water—was hardly a phenomenon of nature I would call haunting. For Kingsley, the viewing of the Alemba seems to have been a transfixing experience: "Nobler pens than mine must sing its glory and its grandeur," she hymns. "Its face was like nothing I have seen before. Its voice was like nothing I have heard. Those other rapids are not to be compared to it; they are wild, headstrong, and malignant enough, but the Alemba is not as they. It does not struggle, and writhe, and brawl among the rocks, but comes in a majestic springing dance, a stretch of waltzing foam, triumphant."

According to the French explorers Marche and Compiègne, who explored the middle Ogooué in 1874, and also to Nassau, the first real rapids are entered some short distance beyond the Bakota village of Isangaladi (or Sangalati), over a full day's travel from Ndjolé—a fact that does not square with Kingsley's assertion that she encountered the first rapid "two hours after leaving Njole"; Kingsley herself reports coming to the "Sengelade Islands" on the morning of her second day on the river. In his report, Brazza stated that the rapids commence where "some large isles and shoals divide the river in two branches" (these are perhaps the "Sengelade Islands"), one of the isles being almost opposite the embouchure of the Okano—which Kingsley reaches toward the very end of her account. Moreover, in summarizing the geography of this part of the Ogooué, Brazza wrote as follows: "The points where the most violent rapids are to be found are in the territory of the Okota, a little above the Okono river; close to Mount Otombi, in the territory of the Apingi, at Boumbi in the territory of the Okanda and that of Booué in the territory of the Ossyéba." In other words, according to Brazza, the most significant of the Okota rapids *commence* at Alemba ("a little above the Okono river"). This fact perhaps explains a certain uncharacteristic coyness on Kingsley's part regarding the terminus of her ascent: "I will not weary you further with details of our ascent of the Ogowé rapids," she declares, "for I have done so already sufficiently to make you understand the sort of work going up them entails. . . ." Given her characteristic preciseness in matters of geography, her vagueness on this important point is suspect. I had to wonder, therefore, if Kingsley too had missed seeing the rapids she had heard so much about.

My boatman took us a little beyond Alemba to a convenient beach, where he secured the boat and then led us up the adjoining hill. I knew nothing about this boatman, not his name, or where he came from, or even how Daniel had known him. I now discovered that the wood-frame house at the top of the hill facing a broad meadow was the boatman's home. A tall man was standing in its doorway, dressed in trousers that had frayed off somewhere just below his knees, giving them the appearance of knickerbockers, which, with the short vest he wore open over a shirt with rolled-up sleeves, lent him the air of a country squire who had perhaps just stepped outside his house to see to his pack of hunting dogs. He met us in the patch of dusty ground outside the house and then stepped aside to let us enter.

Inside was a scene of unspeakable squalor. Streaks of dirt stood in relief against walls that had once been yellow, and the junctures between ceiling and wall were caked with ancient wasps' nests. A pile of excrement lay conspicuously near the center of the room, and the stone floor was littered with debris. The only furniture was a scarred wooden table and bench and some chairs with filthy blackened covers. A man and a woman were sitting sideways in the chairs, their legs dangling easily over the arms, swigging in turn from the spout of a tin kettle. They greeted us lazily and offered me the kettle, which I declined.

We sat down, and our guide chatted for a while with his relatives. The squire of the estate asked me if I would like to see a view of the Okano-Ogooué confluence. It was just over a mile away, he said; but I wisely prepared myself to walk at least twice that distance. The elder boatman pulled himself to his feet and, taking his leave of this agreeable company, led the mushroom picker and me outside.

The walk took us for some long time down the sunbaked tarmac of one of Gabon's few paved roads, bordered by unremarkable secondary forest. We ambled along, three abreast, as there seemed little likelihood of meeting traffic. Indeed, farther along we came upon a village where a young man was lying comfortably at full length in the road while he talked to a woman inside one of the houses.

Terrific screams and the sound of something crashing through foliage exploded from the roadside bush, noises which our guide identified as the sounds of chimpanzees fighting. This event greatly interested the mushroom picker, and he left us to study the scene more closely, his gun, which he had been carrying like a yoke across his shoulders, now held at the ready by his side.

The old boatman and I continued on until we came to a lookout point where the road level was high enough to see over the tops of the hillside trees to where the Ogooué mingled with the Okano below—there is always, for me, satisfaction in obtaining a god's-eye view of natural phenomena and verifying that they have been properly mapped by man. Some distance farther on, a second lookout over the Okano itself made one understand why Mary Kingsley had written that even at the time of her journey little was known about the nature of this river. It is congested with such a rubble of boulders that even an agile pirogue would have great difficulty in making headway up its waters, and it is still the case today, my boatman said, that the river is rarely visited.

We wound our way downhill, where there was a small shop at a junction of roads. We bought drinks and went outside to sit under the shade of a wooden shelter that resembled a bus stop. A sturdy-looking woman, wrapped in a dirty blue and white cloth and with hair that appeared to be caked with mud, came out and sat heavily on a stool opposite us, setting a battered black pot in the thick dust between her straddled feet. She took no notice of us, her attention being absorbed entirely by the contents of her pot. A wooden object in the dust beside her turned out to be a large spoon, which she used to ladle a lumpy stew out of the pot and directly into her mouth, a feat of some difficulty, as she had to bend low over the ground from her stool to do this. Her satisfaction with her repast was noisily evident, but at length she looked up and, transfixing me with a not overly friendly eye, demanded bluntly, *"Vous êtes pourquoi?,"* which I took to be an inquiry as to why I was there.

This was a question I myself was pondering. An explanation of Mary Kingsley's journey would be, I thought, in these circumstances, somewhat too elaborate, and so I merely pointed to the boatman, who was staring at the woman blankly, as if to say that I had come expressly to visit him. She grunted and turned back to her pot, and I suggested to the boatman that we might be getting on.

Kingsley's account of her return journey is brief, but she points out that to descend rapids is more dangerous than to ascend them. "Going down those rapids was like bumping down a flight of stairs," Nassau had written. For me it made little difference—going as coming, the journey was made swiftly, the river's difficulties ironed out by the speed of the boat; but the return trip was the more beautiful. A late wind had arisen, and the trees along the riverbank seemed to be shaking the heavy heat of the day from their branches. The water ahead of us was gunmetal black and its ripples silver.

Whatever the ambiguities of Kingsley's account, she had undeniably returned with a memorable adventure, I with but a tourist's day outing. And in every way befitting the touristy tone of my excursion was the palaver over wages that sadly arose at the end of the day. It was one of the very few occasions that I had any problem in this respect, and sadder still, it involved my comrade the mushroom picker. I had not consulted Daniel on this day's fees but assumed that what I had paid the day before would be appropriate; the same amount of time had been involved and far less effort, for whereas previously he had been boatman, guide, and path-clearer, today he had merely been a passenger. But he was highly and genuinely indignant and insisted that we take the matter to Daniel. We did so, and in presenting his case he revealed a logic that was enlightening: "Pah," he said, "I don't care about the time, and the work was nothing—but the distance was far, far." And Daniel gently explained to me that this trip had taken him far from his home.

The elder boatman too was far from home, and it was only now at the journey's end that I came to understand how he fitted into the picture. He, the inhabitant of the squalid hillside house, was none other than the brother-in-law of the starch-shirted elderly Pastor! More to the point, he had been summoned to Ndjolé by the Pastor's family expressly to take me on this trip, waiting in readiness for at least one day, perhaps two, with his wife, who had accompanied him. They took their leave shortly after five o'clock, ensured of a night ride and navigation of the river's many isles and rocks in the darkness.

I returned to the hotel a sadder and wiser traveler and stopped in the bar, where two young Frenchmen were talking to Jollet. Here I took stock of the day: it seemed to me altogether too shameful to leave matters as they stood. Perusing my one, and generally unreliable, guidebook, I discovered that at Lopé there was the possibility of joining the Okandé piroguers who guide the convoys of okoumé logs ferried downstream from the interior. This, the guidebook intoned, was the only opportunity one had nowadays of experiencing a river journey as it was conducted "as of old." Lopé is the only town of any importance in the swath of savannah that borders both sides of the river in the

Middle Ogooué region. It is also the site of one of Gabon's six national parks and game reserves. There were also rapids in the area, and I began a plan to put together my own adventure.

One of the men sitting next to me saw that I was studying a map and asked me where I was going. He had a mane of dark hair that fell to his shoulders in carefully tended ringlets and was dressed nattily in white shorts and a safari shirt.

"Lopé?" he repeated when I replied and, drawing languidly on his cigarette, volunteered that he was an experienced hunter and that there was little game in Lopé. I explained that I was not going to hunt, and that I had anyway understood Lopé to be a protected reserve.

He ignored my answer and, looking dreamily through lowered lids, outlined, between puffs of his cigarette, a plan of such torturous complexity that I began to wonder if I was really understanding his French: I would go with him and his friend to a certain town, where we would cross a river on a ferried raft, and then proceed by pirogue that he would arrange to have ready for us by radioing ahead to a friend of his who was hunting in the area. We would then go to the hunting lodge, where I would meet more men like himself (plucking the front of his safari shirt), and where someone, he was sure, would be able to take me to a road that was some five hours away, where I could be sure to get another ride to Lopé. "It will be fun," he concluded, stubbing out his cigarette.

"You are not going hunting?" Jollet asked when the men took their leave somewhat later, and when I replied that I had decided to stick to my original plan and proceed by a more direct route, he nodded his head and said he too thought that this was best.

·/·/·

JOLLET TOOK ME to the marketplace the following morning, squeezing me in between the nonending whirlwind of errands he had to run to the post office, to the bank, to the petrol station. He was evidently a well-liked figure about town; at the marketplace, he was delayed by several people who strolled over to shake his hand, courtesies to which he responded with detached good nature, as if his faultless good manners stemmed from a resigned sense of duty.

The best way to catch a ride to Lopé, I was told by the gendarmes who drifted around the market, was to wait by the market stalls until someone going in that direction came by: it was assumed that anyone passing through Ndjolé would stop, and that his destination would be common knowledge. Jollet came over briskly to say good-bye, having just delivered an armload of *baguettes* from the bakery to his little van. A truck began to pull away from the market compound, and Jollet, ever efficient and ever at hand, stepped out to direct it backward, halting it suddenly with a warning upturned hand while he darted forward to move a rock out of its path: all in a day's work.

I seated myself on the platform of an empty fruit stall and waited. Traffic, mostly trucks bound for Libreville or Lambaréné, came and went. The gendarmes lolled against the stalls and smoked and peered around at passersby. Few customers came to the market, which was stocked principally with bananas and manioc, and the vendors dozed and chatted with each other. Women ambled by on their morning errands to the shops or to the waterfront, where fish was being sold straight from a beached pirogue. European clothes could be seen put to novel use: a stout woman strode by dressed in a pink nightdress embroidered with lace and ribbons, carrying a shopping basket on her arm. A group of three women built like sumo wrestlers swaggered up from the waterfront, covered, but hardly clothed, in dark blue strips of cotton wrapped around their burly frames. The circumference of their biceps was so immense that their naked arms hung somewhat away from their sides, which gave them an aggressive air, as if they were spoiling for a good fight.

An oil truck pulled up to the petrol station just up the road, and I went over to talk to the driver, who by good fortune was on his way to Franceville and passing Lopé. He was from British Cameroon and spoke English as well as French.

"Good," he said matter-of-factly. "I can practice my English."

I was breaking new territory when we pulled out of Ndjolé. This was as far inland as Mary Kingsley had come before turning back to Lambaréné. The road to Lopé zigzags through the usual forest until a little beyond the Alemba crossroads, where suddenly, as if shaved away from the underlying hills, the forest has simply gone, and one finds oneself driving through yellow savannah grass, between bare horizons. The change in terrain is not so startling as the unexpected open vista, and the sudden dominance of the broad blue sky was almost unnerving; from the truck's elevated cabin, I felt we were precariously teetering near the roof of the world.

Lopé had been the site of one of the principal slave markets for the Upper Ogooué, held annually in February among the Okandé, Enenga, and Galoa tribes. The Okandé acquired the slaves from tribes yet higher up the river and sold them to the Enenga and Galoa, who in turn ferried their merchandise downstream for sale to the coastal Orungu, who sold directly to the European and American slavers. "The time of the market past," Brazza wrote, "everything is deserted and not even a village is to be found there." Lopé today is one of the stations on the new Trans-Gabon railway line, a modern "town" made up of the neat rows of houses that had been built for the railway construction workers and their families.

Jollet had told me that I should ask for Monsieur and Madame Fernandez, who were the supervisors of the reserve. The driver therefore dropped me off just outside the town, at the entrance of the park. I asked him what I owed him.

"Oh, enough to buy a drink," he said offhandedly.

The feeling of precariousness, of sudden naked exposure to an overwhelming sky, was accentuated after I had left the truck. I felt myself to be the tallest object anywhere around, that my head would strike the heavens if I stood too straight, too quickly.

A short distance from the road was a smart *boutique,* backed by a gravel courtyard that was enclosed by wooden railings. A young woman with a round, gentle face and her hair in rollers greeted me in the entrance and told me that either Monsieur or Madame Fernandez would be bringing workers from the reserve back to their village at half past five that evening and would stop at the road where I had been let off. It was by now just after half past two, and she invited me to wait, pointing to some well-scrubbed tables and benches standing under the *boutique's* overhanging shingled roof.

Untypically, it was the women here who had leisure time, and the men who were away at their work on the reserve, or on the railway. My hostess came outside to unroll her hair and arrange it with the aid of a broken mirror. She was joined by two female friends, who watched her attentively, and not much later by a thin little girl, who wore a precocious streetwise expression on her alert face and looked no more than twelve years old, although she was carrying a baby on her hip. More women strolled in and out of the courtyard from the houses across the way. A plump woman seated herself in the center of the group and began a low, plaintive monologue, which the others listened to, their heads lowered in sympathy. My hostess finished styling her hair and, smiling with satisfaction, disappeared into the house, to return with a plate of what looked like boiled potatoes, which she had kindly prepared for me. The baby began to cry, and the women turned around to look sharply at his young nurse, who slapped him gently on each cheek, accidentally loosening her hold on her charge as she did so and letting him slip between her knees to fall with a spine-chilling crack on the stone floor.

"Ahh!" All three women drew their breath and looked angrily at the girl; but no one made a move toward the baby until it had begun to howl again. "Shut up!" said one of the women firmly and, lifting it by one arm, gave it a resounding slap. After which all was quiet.

The afternoon wore on, and the houses on the plain in the distance began to blend hazily into the horizon. The rare traffic that passed hummed pleasantly from the road. In the late afternoon my hostess appeared to tell me that the Fernandez truck was coming from the fields, and I went down to the main road to meet it.

The driver was Madame Fernandez. She had a sunny, friendly freckled face and thick auburn hair pulled back into a ponytail. There was a surprise: she was English, and when I began to explain the purpose of my trip, her smile broadened and she said, "Hop in."

Her name, too, was Caroline. She and her husband had lived and worked on the Lopé reserve for seven years, conducting research on gorillas and chimpanzees for the Centre International de Recherches Médicales de Franceville (CIRMF), for whom they were an adjunct field station. The center is a state-of-the-art research institute that, although supporting various secondary projects, is, as its publicity booklet informs, primarily concerned with "the different elements related to fecundity," with the object of finding means of increasing Gabon's birthrate. (Gabon, it has been said, suffers from an underpopulation complex; outside estimates calculate the population to be well under a million, but Gabon government statistics claim nearly one and a quarter million.) Caroline Fernandez had first become interested in Africa, she said, when she had been given a child's version of Mary Kingsley's *Travels* when she was twelve years old.

"I always keep two copies of the book on hand: one to keep and one to loan." She knew the book better than I did and could recite whole passages by heart.

"Don't think *I* haven't thought of redoing her trip," she said. "My father has always told me I should."

Their field station lay well within the reserve; no sign of it was visible from anywhere near the entrance. Deep-green clumps of surviving forest showed as dark islands against the low-lit savannah grass, which was cut by narrow lanes that served as firebreaks as well as paths. An oddly shaped building appeared in the distance ahead of us, which Caroline said was their station.

Michel Fernandez was a handsome man with a deeply suntanned face, black hair, and the air of an outdoor man who is perpetually squinting in the sun. Stephanie, a young Scottish woman working with them, a classic British beauty of silken hair and creamy skin, was engaged in making a delicate sketch of a gorilla's bone.

The Fernandez station was the embodiment of that abiding

western fantasy of going Robinson Crusoe–like into the wilderness and creating a self-sufficient empire. The entire compact and efficient complex had, astonishingly, been built virtually single-handed by Michel. On three sides of the main building the walls stood only chest-high, as in an East African safari lodge, leaving a wide gap between them and the wide eaves of the deeply sloping triangular roof, and thus admitting an unobstructed view of the savannah, as well as maximum ventilation. The building was essentially one large room that doubled as living room and dining room, with a small study area at the top of a half flight of steps against the back and only floor-to-ceiling wall. A wooden deck ran around this central room, onto which the kitchen, storeroom, and laundry room opened. Three independent satellite units, lying some distance from the station's hub but connected to it by sheltered catwalks, housed the bedroom units. Even a layman's quick glance affirmed that the whole was an extraordinary feat of design and carpentry; the alignment of the buildings and the pitch of the roof had been calculated with a view to the heavy seasonal rains, as were the elevated, slatted walkways, which ensured that one's path was never mired in mud. Capacious cupboards and drawers were hidden in otherwise uselessly narrow spaces; automatic lights along the catwalks were set to allow enough time to get safely to one's bedroom before cutting themselves off—every detail had been accounted for.

The Fernandez research was principally concerned with census taking and the study of the coexistence within a contained habitat of two primate groups, the gorilla and the chimpanzee, for which Gabon is one of the world's few remaining habitats. "A nice project," said Caroline, "except that we can't always find the animals." Although Gabon's dearth of human population has ensured that there are extensive tracts of uninhabited forest in which the animals can survive, hunting is nonetheless prevalent, and the animals have learned to be elusive. The gorilla in particular has had historical importance for Gabon: du Chaillu's much-maligned "gorilla book" brought the ape to the attention of the western world and, published as it was in the wake of

Darwin's *On the Origin of Species,* was responsible in great part for inducing successive explorers to come to equatorial Africa, in the hope of hunting down this animal that many had come to see as the "missing link."

Over dinner, my plan of finding a way to the Lopé rapids was firmly squashed. In vain did I appeal to the wisdom of my guidebook. No boatman, I was told, would be willing to make the kind of trip that I desired. Caroline thought my best chances would lie yet farther up the river, at Booué.

We talked until it was late, and then made our way to our respective bedroom rondavels, the magic lamps along the cat-walks lighting our way in the night. Michel was concerned about a firebreak that was being blazed on the reserve to forestall the more dangerous, random fires that would be lit later in the season by local villagers: the wind had changed and the fire was not following the course originally predicted. We went to sleep with the noise of the flames crackling through the dry grass not so very far in the distance; and when I awoke late in the night, the sound had come much nearer. Through my window, the flames showed in a jagged line of red and yellow, but it was not possible to tell in which direction they were moving.

The morning was hazy with smoke. Stephanie and Caroline, dressed in what looked like combat fatigues and galoshes, went out to make their routine surveys along the rivers while I went for a walk out of range of the smoke from one forest clump to the next, in the vain hope of stumbling upon gorillas. In the course of my somewhat aimless walk, while reflecting on the Fernandez work, I was revisited with the uneasy sensation of being merely a tourist. For seven years the Fernandezes had lived and worked in this country, and their research had taken them through the length and breadth of the land. Pioneerlike, in the tradition of the first European settlers, they had cleared their land and built their station, and the work they were engaged in demanded a sustained and demanding commitment. I suddenly felt vague and insubstantial. Once again, I seemed to be skimming over the surface of someone else's deeper experience. Mary Kingsley had inspired Caroline Fernandez to come and stake her claim in Africa, and I began to feel that I might have slyly usurped a project that was hers by right. Her father had been correct; this was a journey she should have made.

I had decided to go to Booué, where there were reputedly both rapids and pirogues. It was Caroline who drove me to the station. "Well, *bon voyage*," she said, echoing Daniel. I was about to step into the carriage when she gave me an impulsive farewell kiss on the cheek; and I hoped this meant that she did not think I had entirely let her heroine down.

•*/*•*/*•

AT THE BOOUÉ STATION, a Senegalese taxi driver almost snatched me from the train as I disembarked and stowed me away in his truck with the other passengers he had garnered, then drove in circles around the parking lot, on the prowl for more.

"All right! That's it! Now I go," he screamed out of the window, threatening the crowd with his departure as he whirled off toward the road—where his bluff was called, and he came slowly back to circle the parking lot again.

There was only one hotel in Booué, and to this, the driver announced, I would have to go. I was his last passenger. The old woman he had delivered before me had stood in the road beside his car, straightened her headscarf, checked her bundles, and tentatively queried the fare.

"Oh, this is not the first time you have come to Booué," he had said sarcastically and, putting his foot to the floor, had left her in the dust.

The Hotel Cascades had the attractively seedy air of a once-elegant colonial watering spot, and its situation high in the hills gave it a heady view over the Ogooué river and the Booué cascades. Its centerpiece was a verandah with dainty wrought-iron work and vine-wrapped railings that looked directly down the hillslope to the river. The garden abounded in a profusion of untidy plants and red hibiscus.

I was met by the *patron*, a Frenchman of middle age and bearish build, who was dressed in baggy pink trousers that resembled harem pants and a shirt that he had buttoned the wrong way.

I found him on the verandah, giving the final touches to the tables that had optimistically been set with red cloths and candles in stubby glass holders. He beamed his welcome when he saw me.

"Is your bag heavy?" he asked. I replied that it was.

"Carry it!" he barked at a cross-eyed African woman who had poked her head around the corner of the adjacent bar. "She will show you to your room," he said, smiling. The woman, hastily scrambling for the bag, accidentally dropped it.

"On your head, on your head, you fool!" he bellowed, coming forward to manhandle the bag into position. "The rooms are down the hill," he said, turning to me and speaking normally.

I followed the woman as she careened down the hillside steps to the bedroom wing, which, with its stone patio and view, must have been very beautiful at one time. The bag had begun to slip to one side of the woman's head, and it was with great difficulty that she balanced this and opened the door. My room was filthy, with grimy green walls, ancient wasps' nests, tattered curtains, and a powerful smell of mildew. This, I soon discovered, was the very least of difficulties a guest faced at the Hotel Cascades, which was a kind of Gabonese Fawlty Towers, a masterpiece of awfulness, a monument of chaotic madness of such colossal and magnificent proportions that after prolonged experience anger subsided into a kind of awestruck admiration.

The successful attainment of this peculiar excellence has to be attributed in the main to Monsieur Jaoul, the *patron,* but he was aided in no small degree by his wife, a pretty Mauritian woman with a disarmingly sweet smile. She was incapable of being ruffled; when her husband chased the cross-eyed *femme de ménage* around the verandah tables or ran through the bar brandishing a knotted rope, or when her baby crawled onto the table where her guests were eating, or the pack of dogs hurtled between their legs, she sat calm and smiling, fresh and cool in her pink frilled blouse, her distant femininity rendering her beyond accountability for the many mishaps perpetrated within her establishment. Shortly after my arrival, the electricity went off; this was before I had come to appreciate that my experience of such a high degree of inspired lunacy was privileged and rare, and foolishly, my voice betrayed an edge of anger.

"It goes off every day," Madame had told me, with her sweet smile. There was nothing at all to be said to this, and abruptly turning away, I decided this might be a good time to take a stroll around the town.

Booué itself, like the Hotel Cascades, was imbued with an aura of faded colonial elegance. It had formerly been the capital of the Haute Ogooué, one of the nine administrative districts into which Gabon is now divided. Founded by Brazza in 1883, near the juncture of the Ogooué's sharp westerly bend from France-ville toward the coast and the Ivindo, its most significant north-ern tributary, Booué held pride of place in the region until the advent of roadways diminished the importance of its choice riverside location. In 1958, the district headquarters were moved northeast to Makokou, and Booué became little more than a rarely used resort. Even without knowledge of its history, one would surmise that it had been planned for a way of life that no longer existed. The Place de l'Indépendance, a parade ground near the center of town, was flanked by two processional roads of red clay lined with tired palms. The houses in this immediate area were built of whitewashed mud-brick, not wood, with slanting red tin roofs, often standing in close rows, like servants' lines. The town lies just inside the farthest edge of the savannah belt; Booué itself is airy and light, while the Ogooué riverbanks, hidden from view on the far side of the soft hills that enclose the town, are dark with forest.

An off-duty gendarme stopped me for a chat. He took evident pride in Booué's charms and history and ran inside his house to get a book he thought would interest me. It was a history of Gabon, illustrated with photographs, which he explained: "There is the town in 1960, and there is the white district pre-fect; there is the black who will replace him. There is the white district subofficer; there is the black district subofficer who will replace him. . . ." He told me that I ought to meet the Catholic Father and pointed the way to the church, which lay at the end of a long road that wound downhill and through the town, past the shops of the Hausa merchants and the Fatima Good Time Bar, past all the other houses, in a little dusty clearing of its own.

The doors of the white wooden church were firmly barred shut, but the Father himself could be seen through an open doorway writing at his desk in the small mission across the yard. He was an extremely genial Frenchman, who addressed me with his head somewhat lowered so as to look over his glasses, which he wore on the very end of his nose. He told me the route of his favorite walk, which led high, high, he said, into the hills, above the river.

"I usually go in the evening at about this time," he explained, trying to peer over his glasses at the late-afternoon sky, "but today . . ." He waved a hand over his papers. "You know, it will soon be Sunday. . . ."

Following the Father's directions, I took his walk into the green hills that divide town from river, making my way eventually to the beach at the foot of the long incline that led up to the Hotel Cascades. The Booué cascades were really small waterfalls and looked unapproachable by boat; but in the white water beyond them, I saw the silhouettes of two men paddling a pirogue to the near shore. My ride on rapids, then, was at least a possibility.

I returned, as instructed by the *patron,* at half past seven for dinner on the hotel verandah, which was looking festive with its lighted candles and scattered small vases of flowers. At eight o'clock, a thin man turned up to take my order, after which there was another lengthy interval during which Madame came out to enjoy the night air with her baby. At length a robust woman clad in a hot-pink dress and turban made her way to my table and, breathing heavily, commenced to take away my plate, glass, and silverware, with which she began laboriously to set the empty table behind me. I made a slow and careful survey of the restaurant to confirm my impression that I was indeed one of only two diners in the establishment and, having done so, leaned back in my chair and advised the woman that I shortly anticipated needing the articles she had just removed—a statement I had to repeat several times, with increasing unease, for the woman was staring at me with narrowed eyes and breathing heavily like an enraged bull.

Outside, a succession of slamming car doors announced the arrival of another party. A large man, fat, gleaming, and prosperous, made his entrance, followed by an entourage of younger men holding themselves self-consciously in expensive suits, and a woman wearing a tight, low-cut dress of blue silk, who looked almost breathless with fright. They took the long corner table, where the fat man directed the seating arrangements and the ordering of drinks. He had a little moustache, and his invariable smile revealed tiny gold-capped teeth. "Fried potatoes for everyone!" he cried, beckoning for the distribution of this surprising largesse.

The woman in hot pink approached with a basket of bread, but when I asked for butter she point-blank refused. By now, a dawning appreciation of the uniqueness of the Hotel Cascades made me eager to give its staff scope to reveal their powers to the fullest, and so I repeated my request each time that she put in an appearance. At last I elicited a response. "Quoi?" she said, returning slowly to the table, her chest heaving.

I was this time echoed, thunderously and unexpectedly, by Monsieur Jaoul, who appeared from the kitchen holding a spatula, his face wet with perspiration, his shirt buttoned with one button fewer than when I had last seen him, and his trousers slipped low around his hips. "Give her the butter!" he roared, and a moment later the woman banged the dish in front of me in fury. When she bore down on me again, she had my dinner in her heavy hands.

The food—astonishingly—was very good. The waitress returned to clear the table, approaching her task from the opposite side, leaning bulkily across the table and tipping my plate sharply so that the knife and fork fell into my lap. Dessert passed without incident, but coffee was served in the distinctive manner I had come to expect; the waitress appeared carrying a fragile, rattling tray with exaggerated care. Halfway across the floor she was struck by a sudden private fit of laughter that shook her so much that she upset the tray. M. Jaoul appeared from the kitchen in time to witness her recovering herself by bending over my table, her face buried in folded arms.

"More coffee?" he called to me, with admirable sangfroid.

I went down the hill to my bedroom shortly after the fat man at the long table had rolled away to his, clutching his escort firmly above her elbow. The sheets in my room looked clean enough, but I decided, nonetheless, that it would probably be wise to use my sleeping bag.

At breakfast the next morning, I was approached by a short, plump Frenchman with black hair and a neatly combed moustache.

"May I?" he asked politely, taking the chair opposite me. He introduced himself as Gregorie and said that he had been told there was a foreigner at the hotel who had come to see the rapids. He wished to take the liberty of asking me if I would like to join him on a little excursion: he had some friends visiting from Libreville who had never been *en brousse* before, and he was showing them around. I thanked him and said that this was very kind.

He shook his head. Not at all. Once before he had guided a visitor around, and he had enjoyed it very much. "He was an American who had come to do some research. He was interested in *les âmes sauvages.*"

On the way to his house, which lay a mile or so away in the hills on the outskirts of town, he explained that although he had lived in Booué for several years, his *home* was in Paris, and his wife and children were there now. He worked for a foreign engineering corporation—one of the foreign companies responsible for the Trans-Gabon's reputed over $4-million-per-mile ratio. Of Boué's population of two thousand, there were seven Europeans, he said: four French, one Italian, and two Belgians. Most, like him, were involved in the construction of the railway.

His friends were waiting at his house, which was one on a street of modern bungalows with Range Rovers and jeeps parked in their driveways. They were a family of five: a tall, beefy, red-faced man; a wan, weakly pleasant woman; and their three pasty, slit-eyed children. While the father gave his family directions on how to pack their car, Gregorie raced through the house making his own preparations.

"You can look at these while you are waiting," he said, tossing me an envelope. The photographs inside were of Gregorie and his European buddies posing, guns in hand and cigarettes in mouth, beside a variety of slaughtered game, all of which were endangered species. A beautiful leopard strung up between two poles exposed to the camera a creamy belly that had been slit open; Gregorie bared his teeth over the head of a gorilla—a gallery of haunting, not-to-be-exorcised images.

Wearing a blue peaked cap and strapping an ammunition belt around his hips, he came back into the room as I was laying his envelope on the table. His every action was now suddenly made with frenetic haste. He darted to a locked cabinet and snatched up another gun belt, which was loaded with heavier slugs, the size of flashlight batteries.

"For the big game," he said. His rifle was yanked from the cabinet, and the ritual testing of the bolt made with the same brutal impatience.

"*Alors*, we can go."

Gregorie and I led the way at breakneck speed in his light "bush" jeep, from which the doors had been removed—"so as to get out quickly when one sees the game." His rifle was wedged between our seats, its silver butt resting beside the gearshift, its barrel against my seat, not far from my ear.

"The safety is on, it cannot fire." (Click-click.) "You see?" (Click-click.) Behind us, the city man hung valiantly to our tail, determined not to be outdone on this, his first safari. Once we had plunged headlong down the hills, we whirled out into the forest that skirted Booué. A maze of narrow trails threaded through the trees and brush.

"Each European has his own trails," Gregorie shouted, plunging us with such violence in and out of potholes that on more than one occasion I bounced out of my seat and hit my head on the roof. "We respect each other's territory," he added gravely.

Our first halt, he said, would be at a village, where he knew the chief—the box of bread in the back of the jeep was for him.

Our bush road came to a sudden dead end, where we all trooped out and followed Gregorie down a narrow footpath. He was striding along the trail now, his rifle slung jauntily across his shoulder, and his arms full of french bread.

We emerged in a clearing in which stood a row of shelters, made of bamboo poles supporting roofs of bamboo thatch. Low platforms of bamboo and wood, lashed together with vines and padded with verminous-looking dry grass, formed a continuous line from shelter to shelter. Every one of these rough beds was occupied by one if not two people, some wearing dirty rags, some nothing at all. They were Fang and, according to Gregorie, a two-family group. Between most of the beds a black pot covered with banana leaves steamed over a smoky fire.

"Hello, hello!" Gregorie called, waving the bread around. An elderly man, bent and desiccated, came toward us on stiff, faltering legs. Gregorie seemed genuinely welcome.

"Take pictures," he called out, walking slowly past the shelters while the chief shuffled along behind. It was Gregorie who gave the village tour, pointing out the shelters, the trails, the fishing grounds, where an elaborate dam of split bamboo had been skillfully constructed to funnel fish into a waiting trap. The system yields two panniers of fish a day, Gregorie said, the chief beside him nodding his head in agreement, and the villagers supplemented their diet with small game, which they caught in traps, one of which we saw—a kind of miniature open cage, with a pile of rocks set on a platform to fall and crush the game when the trap is sprung.

Our whirlwind tour completed, Gregorie bade adieu to the chief. Most of the other villagers had remained, sleepily and indifferently, on their smoke-wreathed platforms. Keeping the frantic pace Gregorie had set, we raced back to the cars and headed for what seemed to be the main forest road. We traveled only a short distance before Gregorie ground to a dusty halt beside a patch of hillside that had been scraped bare of foliage and a shallow indentation gouged in the underlying red clay.

"Elephants!" Gregorie whispered. He had crouched down in front of the bared surface and was running his fingers over the grooves that ran like longitudinal chisel marks in the clay. The elephants ate the clay to soothe their stomachs, Gregorie explained, and the marks we saw had been made with their tusks. "The marks are fresh," he said solemnly, rising and looking around him. The paterfamilias suddenly pushed through the reverent semicircle we had formed around Gregorie and passed fumbling hands over the marks.

"I can feel them, I can feel how they are fresh," he said, looking from Gregorie to his wife. The city man was undergoing a transformation, provoked at least in part by his wife's marked deference to Gregorie, who with his jaunty hunter's cap and ammunition belt and, above all, the silver-butted gun that he carried with such careless ease, cut a masterful figure. Above all, the city man was hypnotized by this gun, and at one moment his thick fingers actually curled as his eyes strayed from Gregorie's face to that instrument of power. My fears of being involved in a hunting expedition had subsided some time before: it was clear that no one of our party was capable of bagging anything at all without the knowledgeable guidance of an African tracker. Nonetheless, the city man struck me as exactly the kind of person who causes accidents to happen, and I hoped that he would not get a chance to wrap his hands around the rifle. Gregorie seemed to have sensed that he had acquired some kind of aura, and he now played this to the hilt: ripping off the gunbelt he was wearing, he strapped on the belt of heavier ammunition.

"There are elephants around," he said. We got back into the cars, but we crept forward now with extreme caution, looking warily about us into the forest. The road ended some distance ahead in a semicircular clearing.

Gregorie got out with a finger to his lips, and obediently we followed him in silence. The song of cicadas was grating the air. There was a sound of scampering high in the trees ahead of us, and some branches dipped and rose.

"Monkeys!" It was a hiss. "Remain here!" Bent low, as if he were going into combat under a rain of fire, Gregorie scurried across the clearing and then disappeared from our sight into the arc of forest, where we heard him making his way through the trees. There was silence, followed by the roaring of a gun, which presumably had been loaded with the elephant shot. The pale woman grimaced and then smiled, the children covered their ears, and the city man bit his lower lip. There was another silence, and Gregorie reemerged, shaking his head.

He had been too late. But he had seen the monkeys disappear. "If we had come a minute earlier . . ." He gave an account of a monkey he had shot some time ago, and this led to a gorilla story, which he was not content merely to relate but felt compelled to reenact, taking the roles alternately of both himself and the threatened gorilla. It was an extraordinary performance. The gorilla he portrayed by standing on tiptoe with his arms extended from his sides and his face hideously contorted; himself, by crouching on one knee with his gun braced coolly against his shoulder, pointing directly at his audience and prompting me to move cautiously to one side.

The city man, by way of applause, exploded with a declaration of a secret yearning: he would love to kill a gorilla, it would be something he would always remember—to hunt and kill a big beast like that! Would it be possible to arrange . . . ?

"Well," said Gregorie as we drove back, "you have had quite a safari." We overtook two African men who were sauntering single file along the forest road with guns across their shoulders, each carrying a trophy of the chase, a small antelope and a monkey whose tail had been tied around its neck so that it could be carried like a shoulder bag.

"Good hunting!" Gregorie exclaimed, stopping the jeep. Eventually he came around to asking them how much they wanted for their game. A deal was struck, and cash and goods exchanged. Gregorie flung the monkey and the antelope behind our seats. The antelope's eyes were like glazed blue marbles, and it was oozing blood from a wound I could not see.

The family behind us had also stopped their car.

"I hate *les bêtes,*" the pale woman said to me, wrinkling her nose.

"I know someone I can give these to," Gregorie explained as

we got under way again; but I wondered if he had felt he must return from the forest bearing flesh and blood.

The family returned to the hillside bungalows, but Gregorie and I continued on down to the riverside villages, a broken string of wooden huts set off from the unpaved road and facing the water. Gregorie marched straight into one of the houses, with the antelope slung over one shoulder, his gun over the other. In the center of the room, an old man was reading a Bible at a table set uneasily on the beaten dirt floor and looked up with blank, unfocused eyes as we came in. Gregorie slapped him heartily on the shoulder and called out through the back doorway, which looked onto the banks of the Ogooué. A thin, worn woman with sagging skin, dressed in a ragged *pagne,* or length of cotton cloth, came in, followed by a tall, slender young man with an enormous smile.

"Here, take this for the pot," said Gregorie, slinging the antelope at the young man. The woman put her hands on her hips and began to scold. Gregorie laughed. "She is asking me why I didn't bring food for her—women cannot eat antelope." (A missionary writing in 1912 had observed that "women are prohibited from eating certain kinds of meat, or certain parts of an animal—usually by a strange coincidence the very parts that the men like best.")

"Oh, greedy woman!" Gregorie exclaimed, gripping her by the throat and pretending that he would shake her. "She is my mother-in-law," he said unexpectedly, and it turned out that the wife in Paris had come from this village.

The antelope was carried to the smoke-blackened kitchen behind the house, where it was appreciatively examined by the young man. Gregorie called the youth over to the riverbank, talking with him earnestly and pointing first at me, and then upstream. The young man smiled.

"Bon! You will see your rapids," Gregorie said to me. "François will take you after lunch."

It was Sunday, and on Sundays the Cascades had a buffet and barbecue lunch. The verandah tables were already full when we returned, mostly with Europeans who either lived in Booué or had come in from one of the several lumber companies in the area. Madame Jaoul was drifting serenely among the tables, serving drinks, but as she never carried more than one glass at a time, orders were processed slowly. Jaoul had worked himself up to such a pitch of excitement that I did not see how he survived this institution more than once a month. He could be glimpsed through the doorway that opened onto the bar, lumbering back and forth to and from the kitchen, his hair plastered to his head with sweat, his clothing baggier and less securely fastened at every sighting. There were the usual diversions: the assistant cook came plunging into the crowd of expectant diners after a cat, whose neck was gaping open with what appeared to be an old machete wound. The *femme de ménage* scurried out with a shopping basket, pursued by Jaoul.

"Onions and eggs!" he roared after her, "and today, not tomorrow!"

At the tables, the conversation was confined wholly to hunting and game. A string of encounters of escalating danger involving the speaker or a close friend with buffalo, leopard, hippo, and gorilla were related. We helped ourselves to salad from the buffet.

"I am a taxidermist," the man to my right said, once we were back at our tables. "I don't kill to eat, I kill to stuff." Some time later, following a loud clatter in the kitchen, Jaoul appeared like a clumsy cave man dragging the cooked carcass of an unidentifiable but very large animal, which he heaved onto the buffet table, aided by the assistant cook.

"Lunch is served," he announced with an almost manic grin.

Chasse, gibier, game, meat—the words hummed obsessively around the table. It seemed the subject was inexhaustible. Thinking of Caroline and Michel's work at Lopé, I girded my loins to enter the conversational fray: was it not true, I ventured, that many of the animals they were mentioning, such as leopards and gorillas, were protected species?

The diners turned on me in a body: "We give them to the Gabonese! We feed the Gabonese! It is meat for them!"

The taxidermist explained that the white man's duty was to

provide game for the Africans: he had the jeeps, the guns, the ammunition, which the African could not afford—a convenient rationale that allowed the European the fun of the chase without the necessity of having to prepare and actually eat the unpalatable meat. I pressed on: could not the money spent on the hunting equipment, which was undoubtedly expensive, be used to acquire food for villagers by a more direct means? Was it possible to eat species that were not endangered? But there was a gap between my logic and theirs that no amount of discussion was going to close.

After lunch, Gregorie took me back to his in-laws.

"I have a plane to catch to Libreville and I must leave you," he said. He scribbled his address on a piece of card. "One word, only one little line!" he cried, squeezing my hands in his before he dashed off to his car.

François led me to the river, where his shallow pirogue was waiting in the water, wielding, to my delight, a long paddle with a small, leaf-shaped blade. It had become a sparkling blue day, and the river below the Booué cascades seemed swift and playful. Once out in the water, François labored against the current and miniature foamy breakers. Patches of whirling water appeared between the many gleaming rocks, and we struck out for the farther shore, where the current was not so strong. Rapids!

The water creamed toward us between low boulders, gently but gratifyingly, rocking the shallow boat and trembling beneath us. Here and there we came upon men fishing from their drifting pirogues. Women waved to us from the occasional sandy breaks in the forest line, where they had come down to do their washing. It seemed as if a veil had been whisked away and the world unmuffled; the blue and white of the speeding water seemed suddenly clearer, and there was an explosion of new sounds—of calling birds and rustling trees, of running water and the distant rush of the Booué cascades. In calmer water beside the river rushes, we surprised kingfishers and egrets and one grave heron. At one glorious moment, I saw Mary Kingsley's white lilies growing among the rocks on long, floating stems. Only the blue-haloed rocks were lacking.

The patient and long-suffering François brought me back to his village just as the light was turning to dusk and the river was almost navy blue. I faced a long walk back to the hotel along the dusty riverside road, but was nonetheless triumphantly happy.

My contentment was shattered on my return to the hotel. The electricity was working, but the water was off. For some reason, the trains going in the direction of Franceville run only in the middle of the night, and as I was departing from Booué that evening, I now looked forward to taking this ride without having had a shower. Madame handed me a heavy plastic bag that was dripping with water.

"It is your laundry," she said. "It could not be washed when the water went off," she explained as I continued to stare at her, "but we had started to soak it." I asked her why it had not been begun several days ago, when I had first given her the clothes.

"We only started it today."

Perhaps to make up for this blunder, Jaoul himself came to me that evening at dinner with a present. "It was the largest I could find," he said, dropping onto my plate an enormous rhinoceros beetle, which began to kick and buzz as it tried to turn itself right side up.

I had planned to try to sleep for a few hours in my room before I left for the station, and so I paid my hotel bill after dinner.

Monsieur Jaoul proudly presented me with his card, in case I had friends to whom I might wish to recommend the Hotel Cascades.

"Apart from the water, were there any problems?" asked Madame with her sweet smile. As the unmatchable chaos achieved by her establishment could under no condition be relegated to the lowly status of a "problem," I was able, with complete honesty, to say that no, there had been none.

END OF THE LINE

AT TEN O'CLOCK on the evening of my departure from Booué, there was a knock on my bedroom door. I opened it to find a woman and two enormous men in the dark passageway outside. The woman smiled. "We were in the bar having drinks with a friend when Monsieur Jaoul told us that you were taking the night train." She spoke French with a heavy Spanish-sounding accent. "We are going to keep you company."

Her name was Victoria, and she and her husband lived *en brousse* with her husband's brother in a lumber camp twenty-five miles from Booué, she said, indicating one enormous man after another. She was Brazilian, and the men were Portuguese. They had worked in Angola as foresters before coming to Gabon. "Are you already packed? Good. We will bring the bags with you."

We climbed the hillslope steps toward the lights on the verandah, where their friend was waiting and still drinking in the bar. He was a Frenchman of alarming thinness, with long, lank hair tied back in a ponytail and a melancholy expression at odds with the disconcerting sharpness of his eyes. "Never mind my name.

Call me Le Couteau [The Knife]," he said, raising his glass with a flourish. He insisted that we should all go to his house, for a party.

One of the brothers carried my bags to their Range Rover, which was parked behind the hotel. In the disorienting darkness I vaguely gathered that Le Couteau's house lay in the opposite direction to the station. Le Couteau sat in the front seat, gazing out of the window into the night with a look both intense and dreamy. Victoria's husband was driving. Both brothers had glossy black hair and long black sideburns, and both were absurdly shy. Victoria told me a little about herself: "I was very alone when I first came. I did not speak French; I have learned since I was here. It was difficult. And the forest always the same on every side of me. I turned to my religion, which I had practiced in Brazil. It is a Japanese religion, with an English name," she said, brightening. "Perhaps you know it? It is called 'Perfect Liberty.' "

Her brother-in-law suddenly spoke up from beside her. "Oh, I am enjoying myself already!" he exclaimed.

Le Couteau's diminutive house stood on a scrap of cleared land in an alcove of the forest. The bare yellow bulb above the door seemed to cast more shadows than illumination. Inside, the house was partitioned into tiny cubicles, ill-lit by colored lights and decorated with infinite care. All the furniture—the sofa and several chairs, the bookcase and bar that covered nearly an entire wall—had been made of bamboo by Le Couteau himself. Flowers had been placed around the room in containers made of cross sections of a bamboo cane. A table constructed from the thick slice of an enormous tree trunk filled all the space between the sofa and the bar, where Le Couteau had gone to prepare the drinks.

Reaching to a shelf above his head, he selected one of three tape cassettes. "Country music! *You* will like that," said Victoria's brother-in-law, turning to grin at me.

The walls were covered with stencil outlines in black paint of palm fronds and ferns, and by a single charcoal drawing, which depicted a man who looked like Le Couteau embracing a woman whose face showed reluctant acceptance.

"It is a mother and her child," said Le Couteau from behind the bar, when he saw me looking at it. He was the artist. The few books on his shelves were all about the Second World War. One shelf had no books, but a line of bullets of different sizes standing on end, arranged according to height. A bamboo canopy descended like a funnel-shaped air-extractor over the bar, where Le Couteau was fastidiously wiping down the counter. There was not a superfluous scrap of paper, not a thread of excess to be seen.

"For this occasion," said Le Couteau, "we will have champagne." Victoria's husband stood shyly beside the bar, bulky and grotesque in the reddish light. Victoria herself sat sleepily on the chair beside her brother-in-law, who was telling me how happy he was that I had come. We turned obediently to watch Le Couteau pop the cork.

"It is too bad I didn't know you were coming," said Victoria. "I have photographs at the camp I could have shown you. I have pictures of a dead elephant being cut up—picture by picture, you can see the whole process."

They had lived in Gabon for thirteen years but spoke less of it than of their former homes in Brazil and Angola. I still was not clear what Le Couteau did.

"Mind your own business," he replied when I asked, in a voice curiously devoid of hostility. He had been slicing the cork of the champagne bottle with a hunting knife but now stopped. It was, I guessed, not yet midnight. My train left at five minutes to two. Victoria was half-asleep, and her husband said they should think about leaving; I appreciated that they had a twenty-five-mile ride down rough bush roads ahead of them, and that the brothers had to be at work by half past six.

"You are always trying to spoil my fun," said the brother-in-law, beginning to pout. "How many times do I have a chance to talk? How many times do I meet someone? And now here is a young lady, and you want to take me home."

Le Couteau disappeared into one of the rooms at the back of

the house and returned with a camera, saying he wanted to take pictures of his party. The brothers began to argue, Victoria's husband continuing to assert with shy firmness that they had to leave.

"I won't! What do I care what time I get to work?"

"I think," said Le Couteau looking at me, "that we would like to know a little more about our traveler."

Victoria eventually unwound herself from the sofa and left to get a bag she had stored in another room. From a shelf below the bar, Le Couteau brought forth a folded piece of material, which he handed over to me. It was a flag.

"Yes, Le Couteau was in the Legion," the brother-in-law said, seizing gleefully at this topic. He had turned almost sideways on the sofa so as to gaze directly into my eyes. "Le Couteau walked from Chad—"

"That's enough," said Le Couteau. "No, keep it—it's for you," he insisted as I tried to return the flag. I protested; it was neatly ironed and folded, and had been looked after with evident care.

"Take it!" I thanked him, but said no.

"Then I will burn it," he said, and holding it at arm's length in one hand, he ignited his lighter in the other.

"You see," said the brother-in-law in delight, "he says he will burn it. You will have to take it now." The flag safely on my lap, Le Couteau began to ransack his meager possessions for more gifts. He turned up a long porcupine quill, a piece of ebony carved to look like the barrel of a gun, and an old coin. Victoria and her husband were standing awkwardly by the door until the brother-in-law at last sighed deeply and rose from the sofa, holding out his hands and looking me mournfully in the eyes.

"I am so glad we got to know each other," he said. He collared Le Couteau by the door and impressed upon him the necessity of making copies of the photographs that he had taken.

"Good-bye," said Victoria as her husband stood beside her, smiling in embarrassment. "Le Couteau will take you to the station," she said over her shoulder as they departed. Le Couteau closed the door.

There was a long silence, in which Le Couteau pulled up a

chair opposite me and sat leaning forward with his hands clasped between his legs. He seemed to be caught between two moods, and weighing up which of them he would indulge. I made no attempt to conceal the fact that I was watching him as closely as he was studying me; in this case, there was, I thought, nothing to be gained by pretending to be more at ease than I was. At last he drew in his breath, pulled his chair closer, and secure perhaps in the knowledge that he would never see me again, proceded to relate his life's story.

He had been with the French Foreign Legion for fourteen years, and had "left" two years ago, from Chad. He had done some "security" work here in Gabon, at the highest level. His father had been in the Legion before him; of his mother he did not speak. The Legion had done to him what the Vietnam War had done to the veterans in my country; he had read about their adjustments and their problems and would deeply like to meet and talk with them—it would help. For now, he said, waving an arm around the room, his carpentry helped to relieve the tension, the force inside him.

"Here I live, in my little house of wood. Sometimes I think I will go mad. Sometimes I think I will kill someone. In France, I know I would. I think I am safe here."

It was quarter past one. Hesitantly, I said that I should start for the station soon. He slapped his knee and rose to his feet, pacing the room. What was I going to do in Franceville? he demanded.

Stammeringly, I explained that I had numerous appointments to keep.

He pulled on his ponytail. "With whom?" With people who were expecting me, I replied. He continued pacing around the tiny room.

"I will meet you in Franceville," he cried, with inspiration, and outlined a dreamlike project. "I will take you to the plateau, the Bateké plateau. We will walk there along trails I know. We will walk to the edge of the canyon and look out over its peaks, we will walk to the edge of the Congo border. *Your lady* would have

gone on and on," he said, turning on me with a suddenly accusa-
tory tone.

I repeated that people were expecting me. He stopped still,
caught again between moods, and studying me as if his cue lay
in my expression. At length he looked at the floor and said,
"Come. I will take you to the station." While he led the way out
the door with my bags, I furtively left the flag and other presents
on the corner of the bar; I could not bear to walk away with his
scanty trophies.

We drove in complete silence through the night, Le Couteau
leaning forward over the wheel as if to pantomime the extreme
caution with which he was slowly driving. Perversely, all taxis
cease business after nightfall, and the crowd of passengers that
filled the station, having no means of transportation of their
own, had been waiting there since dusk, many killing the intervening seven or so hours by drinking. On the platform, people
swayed and shouted, embraced and pushed one another around.
Le Couteau surveyed the crowd.

"You will get a first-class ticket," he said and stood close
beside me at the ticket booth, to ensure that I followed his
instructions. We went into the restaurant, where people seemed
to have reached the maudlin stage of intoxication and were
quieter. The word went around that the train was delayed, and
I told Le Couteau that, please, he did not have to wait with me.

"Do you think that I would possibly leave you here alone? All
right, why even ask?"

When we heard the train approaching, we joined the crowd
on the platform, which had become noisier and more confused.
Le Couteau handed my bags up to me as I stood on the threshold
of the almost empty first-class carriage.

"If you return, there is always a room. No need to go to a
hotel." He walked along the platform, looking into the train
until he found the window where I was sitting, and stationed
himself outside, legs apart, hands stiffly behind his back, the
Legionnaire's at-ease. Another twenty minutes passed before
the train's engine started up, and through all this time he faith-

fully held his post, staring directly and unselfconsciously through the window until we finally pulled away.

•/•/•

IN FACT, I was going not to Franceville, as I had told Le Couteau, but to Lastoursville, where the pretext of a prior engagement would by no stretch of the imagination have been convincing. I had not realized until now how much I had been relying on Mary Kingsley's companionship and guidance. Although strictly speaking I had parted company with her at the Ndjolé rapids, that experience had carried me through to Booué. Now I felt myself to be very much on my own, and there seemed a kind of arbitrariness as to where I should go next. As I was within striking distance of Franceville, the last important town on the Ogooué, it seemed foolish not to "complete" this journey to the end of the river. But should I go straight to Franceville, or should I break the trip? Why not, after all, turn back from Booué? Suddenly this had become my own journey, and I had to ascertain and follow my own inclinations. Eventually, one particular feature of Lastoursville caught my attention: there were, according to my fallible guidebook, grottoes on the mountainside, where one could "admire stalactites and stalagmites." Conveniently, there was also a mission.

It was four-thirty in the morning when the train arrived. The station platform was floodlit by harsh yellow overhead lights, but beyond their pool of illumination the night was black. I found a cab and settled cozily into the cabin while the driver went off to see about other passengers. My tiredness, combined with the heightened sense of anonymity, almost of invisibility, that arrival in a strange town by night confers, gave me the not unpleasant sensation of withdrawal from the world, of being reduced entirely to a spectator. I was glad that once again I was the last of several passengers to be delivered, for I enjoyed the dreamlike ride down roads and past dim outlines too indistinct to demand my real attention. The Lastoursville station, like all the stations on the Trans-Gabon line, was inconveniently distant from the town. We crossed what seemed in the dark to be a bridge of extraordinary length spanning the black abyss of a great river. I had the impression from the sleek tarmac road and ranks of streetlights filing away into the gloom that we were on the perimeter of a modern city. It was too dark to see the houses and buildings we passed in any detail, but the roads we followed seemed lengthy and complex. We stopped outside a number of low houses, where lanterns were burning in readiness for the anticipated traveler. Whole families came pouring out of doorways as the taxi van rumbled up, but their voices, too, seemed indistinct and blurred in the darkness.

All the other passengers had been delivered when the driver came to take me to the mission. We turned onto a road that seemed to be winding uphill through the forest. We turned again, and the silhouettes of palms on either side indicated that we had come to an entrance avenue. A towered church loomed ahead of us, which we passed to the right, stopping moments later before a high wrought-iron fence with a padlocked gate. The bright van headlamps made the iron gates gleam but shed no light on what was beyond.

The driver thought that I should wait inside the mission grounds, even though everyone would be asleep. He lifted my bags over the gate, lowering them expertly down the other side.

"Softly, softly," he murmured. Instinctively, we both spoke in whispers. He gave me a leg up and over the gate.

"Good night, Madame," he bade me courteously. His every action had been so sure and noiseless that I could not help suspecting that these were activities in which he was practiced. I landed hard on the other side of the gate, falling backward to the ground as an enormous dog came bounding toward me out of the shadows and, before I could get to my feet, placed a heavy paw upon my shoulder. A door in a building I had not even seen in the darkness was suddenly flung open, and the figure of a bent woman holding a lantern appeared in silhouette at the top of its stairs, demanding in an alarmed voice to know who was there.

The dog, turning joyously at the woman's appearance, let me free to struggle to my feet. I made my way to the lantern light and explained that I was a traveler who sought accommodation.

"Alas," said the woman, "the Sisters are on holiday in France. I must go to the *Père* and get the keys." Now that she had looked me over, her manner was maternal. I hastily told her not to wake him, that I could wait until he got up; it would soon be dawn.

"Oh no. He should be up for his matins anyway," she replied almost grimly. I followed her to the arched colonnade that lay to one side of her house and saw in the lantern light that I had returned to comfortable rosy brick mission architecture. We stopped before a closed, slatted door which the woman began to pound vigorously.

It was opened by the Father, a tall, handsome, silver-haired man dressed in a knee-length velvet bathrobe, with a cigarette hanging down from the corner of his mouth. "Eh? Yes?" he said, listening as the woman narrated all that had come to pass, while I stood apologetically behind her.

"Mmmm? Well? Is that what happened?" the *Père* replied, his every word and even hum suffused with irony. "Well, I see that we shall have to get the keys." He withdrew his cigarette from his mouth with his thumb and index finger. "And do you always travel this way?" he asked, his ironic tone making it impossible to know if he meant did I always stay at missions, or did I always climb gates in the early hours of the morning. The old woman stepped forward to help me carry my bags.

"It is wet," she said in a startled voice, looking at me and then at the *Père,* and holding the plastic bag that Madame Jaoul had been so kind as to give me for my laundry before I left Booué.

Feeling suddenly shabby and unshowered, I told them that the bag contained my laundry.

"Your laundry? And you find it easier to carry it with you, ready to be washed?"

The arched walkway ran entirely around the long mission building. On the opposite side, the Father unlocked one of a line of closed doors that opened onto a tiny suite of rooms, comprising a living room with a desk, chairs, and bookcase, and a bedroom with a high box bed covered with mosquito netting. The shower was down the walkway, a grim room of bare, mottled cement and stone and medieval-looking iron pipes.

"The hot water—see? You turn it here," the Father demonstrated, in the tone of tolerant good nature with which one would address an idiot. His old-fashioned lathering brush and cutthroat razor lay on a shelf, which he tidied up to one side.

I had my long-deferred shower and returned to my room to sleep. When I awoke, the mission was deserted, save for one woman whom I found doing laundry in the shower. The mission's premises were much larger than I had ascertained in the night, built, as were all the missions I visited, in more optimistic days for an entire order to live and labor in. There were essentially two separate residential wings, one where the four Sisters who were in France lived, one for the lone Father. The steepled church lay in wide, grassy grounds that were barely being kept under control. Some distance behind the wing in which the father and I were sequestered were the servants' houses, which also appeared to be deserted.

I passed more huts as I made my way down the avenue of palms toward the road, where I learned from a passerby that Lastoursville lay two miles down the hill. I was unprepared for the reappearance of the forest, which I had last seen at Ndjolé. Now the world was reduced again to a palette of two colors: the forest's great green height and the red dust of the road, which was here so thick that it yielded beneath my feet like drifts of sand. Red and forest green: both seemed to absorb and hold the heat—the most oppressive colors in the spectrum.

If I had been asked to draw a map of Lastoursville based on my perceptions of the night before, I would have drawn a wide, sprawling complex of residential streets, with scattered modern shops and offices like those in Libreville in its center. The new tarmac station road, with its lines of modern lights and above all the bridge, which had seemed to me to be a kind of elevated freeway, had set me up for these delusions. Lastoursville, I discovered by daylight, amounted to no more than a handful of splintery shops and stalls run by West African merchants, and an open market straggled out along a riverside road, with residential streets randomly leading off it here and there. The forest wound around the town, dogging the road that coiled down from the hills into its midst. Several small islands in the river directly in front of the town center made the Ogooué appear even narrower than it was and brought the forest that much nearer to the mainland. The most striking feature of the river, however, was the color of its water—a deep, opaque green, the color of a lagoon or a stagnant pond. "The interior": until Lastoursville, this term had been for me roughly synonymous with "inland" or "upriver." Now I appreciated its resonances to the full; "inside," "innermost." Lastoursville seemed contained by the forest. The river here did not strike one as being a highway in and out of its environs; it drifted through, thickly green, idle and unused. The character of the river above all else gave Lastoursville an air of wildness: an interior town, hanging on, ostensibly fulfilling little function, in danger perhaps of disappearing, of being just let go.

The precariousness of Lastoursville's survival is also evident in its history. Brazza had come this far up the river in 1877, but it was not until 1883, in the course of his third and most important Congo expedition, that a post had been officially established on a site chosen by a young engineer in the expedition company, François Rigail de Lastours. At the time of its foundation, the post had been called "Maadiville," or "oil town," in deference to that important commodity, the oil palm; but when Lastours died of fever two years later, it was renamed by way of tribute to him. Lastours's grave can be seen today among the graves of other Europeans from different stages of the colonial past, a stone tablet with a raised iron cross in a small cemetery set in a bamboo grove, some distance off the main road.

Prior to the arrival of the Europeans, the site had been known chiefly for its important slave market. Subsequently, it had become the principal supply depot for all expeditions passing through to the Upper Ogooué. The Catholic Mission of Saint-Pierre-Claver had been established near the government post in the year of Lastours's death, but was abandoned fourteen years later, after being attacked by local people, and was not reinstated until 1940. In 1896, an uprising of the Awindji tribe resulted in the abandonment of the administrative post (the Awindji and the Adouma are the same people, their different names referring respectively to whether they live in the forest or along the river). The French colonial administration reinstated the post in 1909, but the hostile incidents continued, incited in the main by the colonialists' demands for tax and service duty from the local tribes, the most famous and serious being the uprising led by the hero-rebel Wongo, chief of the Awindji, as late as 1929. Lastoursville briefly enjoyed its reputation of being the headquarters of the Ogooué-Lolo region, but ultimately its fate, like that of Booué, was linked to the declining importance of the river. In 1960, the year of Gabon's independence, the official capital of the province was moved to Koulamoutou, leaving Lastoursville with little to distinguish it from any other out-of-the-way interior town. Supposedly, the Trans-Gabon railway and the exploitation of the important Mounana and Moanda mines closer to Franceville have instigated a resurgence of Lastoursville's prosperity. If this is so, and one is then to believe that Lastoursville today is in a state of rising fortune, it is but a testimony to the sad state of decline to which it must have previously sunk.

It is customary and advisable to "register," or check in, with the resident district officer of a new town, and so before returning to the mission, I made my way to the prefecture, which lay at the far end of the waterfront in a concrete building with peeling paint and bare stone floors. I was welcomed by a round jovial man, who listened to my formalities with unbounded delight, nodding and smiling as I spoke. When I concluded by saying that I had come as a visitor to pay my respects, he beamed.

"It is entirely normal," he replied.

Back at the mission, I spoke to the Father about my interest in seeing the grottoes.

"Ah yes, the grottoes," mused the Father. "Oh yes. *Le bon Père* who was in charge before me told every visitor he must see the famous grottoes. 'The water! The stalactites! The columns of stone!' But had *le bon Père* ever been there? Never in his life." Nonetheless, he said that he knew the person to contact regarding a guide and would see to it the next day.

I wandered around the mission grounds until dark. The purpose of the mission, I had discovered, was to run a dispensary and two elementary schools, the former being under the supervision of the absent Sisters. The long avenue of palms distanced the mission buildings from the dust and annoyance of the road and settled them in the secluded calm that seemed to be as requisite a feature of the missions as their rosy-orange brickwork. At six o'clock, when the light had fallen, the sound of a choral chant suddenly resonated from the church. I had been outside for several hours and was incredulous that an entire choir could have entered the building without my noticing, and went over to peek inside the church door. Only three persons were responsible for the full, rich, amplified song—two elderly women and one old man, bent low as they faced the altar.

Le Père had invited me to join him for dinner. We dined in a large room at one end of the mission building, with windows on two sides looking out onto the trees and grounds, and a back door opening onto a small pantry—the kitchen, as was common, being outside. A group of worn but comfortable-looking armchairs arranged around a bookcase were positioned on one side, the long, dark dining table being at the very back of the room, directly facing the doorway, which was usually kept open. Two places had been set side by side so that the Father and I could both watch the television that was wedged over the door and that was broadcasting the results of the national election of local officials. For the sake of the television, too, the room was in near darkness.

We sat down at our places, staring directly ahead at the flickering screen. A man came through the back door carrying the first course.

"Ah, Joseph," said the Father, staring closely at the well-done mutton on his plate. "Can you tell me? Charcoal—is it good or bad for the health?" A bat flew through the open window slats, circled around the room, and then skillfully left through the same window.

The Father indulged me with a running commentary on the

election results. "Only ninety-eight percent in favor! Down from last year. Officials last year were elected by at least one hundred and ten percent." The outcome of one-party political elections rarely keeps one in suspense.

A sports program followed, featuring the highlights of an international track meet. The Father stopped eating, his knife and fork in midair while he leaned forward with a look of real interest. "Incredible," he said after one close finish. "Ah, yes, that final surge."

I ventured at this point to find out when the Father had first come to Gabon.

"I first came out after the war. I had no idea where I would be situated—South America, Africa, the East—one never knew. Gabon was *mal, très mal* at that time—the fever," he said, waving his knife at his head. "Worst of all was Cayenne—two years, three—then finished. All dead."

I asked him if he liked Africa.

"Like it? I am habituated," he replied.

He was Dutch, he told me, and was returning to Holland for his leave at the end of the month, where he would stay until Christmas. He lived in Hilversum, he said, his voice momentarily dropping its habitual irony, nor far from Amsterdam, not far from Utrecht—not too far from anywhere.

The end of each course had been signaled by the Father ringing his knife back and forth against his beer bottle until Joseph heard and came running in from the kitchen. When the meal was finished, the Father returned to his study with another beer, and I went down the silent walkway to a storeroom where I had seen a large collection of books. In addition to the expected religious texts, there was also a wide selection of Agatha Christie mysteries and the novels of A. J. Cronin—many of which had not been translated into French or Dutch. My eyes narrowed in suspicion: I had never yet met a Dutchman who did not speak fluent English, and I began to wonder if the good Father was holding out on me.

The doctor of a nearby town, it seemed, was the person to be sought as a guide to the grottoes, and the next morning, the

Father, dressed as usual in casual slacks and a print shirt, went with me into town to find him. The doctor was not in his office, but we learned that he was in a bar down the road, "celebrating the election results." The festivities could be heard before they were seen, and the Father entered the bar with his hands conspicuously over his ears. The bar was a narrow, murky room decorated with Christmas lights. One couple was half dancing, half shuffling around the sandy floor, while everyone else leaned slackly against the bar or the bare, chipped walls. We found the doctor in that genial stage of intoxication that warms one to all mankind, and he flung his arms around the Father's shoulders. He listened with good-natured, bleary-eyed attention to my request, but sadly shook his head; he professed an ardent desire to go to the grottoes, but unfortunately foresaw that he would be occupied for several days. He recommended a Belgian woman, yet another Caroline, who worked in a natal-care clinic for the Association Française des Volontaires du Progrès, the French equivalent of the Peace Corps.

Caroline lived in a large wooden house on a narrow street behind the main road. The windows and doors had been barricaded with boards and cushions in a vain attempt to muffle the noise from the disco that ran twenty-four hours a day directly opposite. She was a striking woman, engaging, but with an air of private distraction. Her curvaceous figure was shown to great effect by her skin-tight, green leopard-patterned trousers and short, sleeveless shirt.

"Why Father Kurt, you never visit any more," she chided. "What can I get you to drink? Orangina? Toni-Cola?"

"I'll have a beer," said the Father, comfortably settling himself in an armchair. Her house was full of plants and local basketwork. Caroline was agreeably willing to undertake the grotto trip. "I have only been twice before, but I am sure I can find the way," she cautioned. I went to look at a map of Africa that covered one entire wall, and Caroline joined me, running a slow finger from Casablanca to Capetown. "I shall never see it all," she said, suddenly burying her face in her hands. It was agreed that she would come to the mission for breakfast the next day, and that we would leave together afterward.

"Well, success! We got what you wanted," said Father Kurt, when we were back outside in the twilit street.

At breakfast with Caroline, Father Kurt ostentatiously crossed himself before breaking bread, something he had never done when alone with me. Caroline had brought *les nécessaires:* a machete, an old-fashioned oil lantern, and a book of matches. For the expedition she was dressed in rubber thongs and blue leopard-patterned slacks.

A trail led from behind Caroline's house through parched plantations of manioc and bananas, taking us high enough into the hills so as to have a view over the Ogooué to the north. We continued through shoulder-high grass and overgrowth, which Caroline occasionally cut back with an impatient swing of her machete, until we reached the edge of the forest. The entrance to the grottoes lay down a descent so steep that one did not climb down it so much as slide.

"L'inconvénient," said Caroline, brushing the dirt off the backside of her pants, *"c'est les serpents."*

While I was pondering whether *inconvénient* was in this instance best translated by its English counterpart, Caroline lit the lantern. From the grotto entrance, one could see the roots of the forest overhead dangling precariously over the cliff face. Long fingers of water filtered over the grotto walls, which were plastered with broad leaves that clung leechlike to its rocky, claggy surface independent of any apparent plant. The shrilling of bats could be heard even outside, and as we entered the grotto they rose in a cloud of agitated flight, flying distractedly back and forth across the ceiling. The path inside took another downward swoop into a dark, silty hole. Caroline held the lantern up above her head, verifying that the passage ahead of us was the one we were to take. I took a last look behind us and saw that the bats were still whirring in the entrance hole like enormous moths, the membranes of their wings softly transparent against the entering outside light.

The passage ceiling shortly and abruptly dropped to only a few feet in height, and we had to continue by crawling on our elbows and stomachs over cold, pebbled ground beside a feeble stream of icy water. The tunnel opened into another cavern, where we could stand but not avoid the water, into which Caroline plunged knee-deep, rubber thongs and all, without breaking stride. In the swinging yellow uncertain light of the lantern, I could see that the rocks on either side were encrusted with crabs and guarded by unyielding cockroaches with foot-long feelers. We made our way along a farther tunnellike passage, once again on our stomachs in water several inches deep. I watched with some anxiety as Caroline inched the flickering lantern ahead of her, carefully setting it down at each advance where the water seemed the shallowest. At length, a chamber in rock the color of old, yellowed bone opened into a kind of circular amphitheater, so theatrical that one felt there must be a balcony in the upper shadows.

In the course of her ascent of the rapids, Mary Kingsley had paused at the entrance of two caves in the rock that came right down into the river. One looked "suspiciously like a short cut to the lower regions," the other was Boko Boko, whose great circular opening I had noted. "As we had no store of bush lights we went no further than the portals," she wrote, continuing, however, that "strictly between ourselves, if I had every bush light in the Congo Français I personally should not have relished going further. I am terrified of caves; it sends a creaming down my back to think of them."

Why *does* one seek out caves? In part, perhaps, for the challenge of doing something that can be terrifying; in part for the same reasons that one climbs a mountain—because "it is there." But perhaps, too, from some primal belief that an odyssey through life is incomplete without a journey to the Underworld—whence, tradition has it, one emerges to the upper world possessed of new knowledge, direction, and sense of one's destiny.

This belief is reflected in the traditional use of the grottoes that Caroline and I had entered, which were used for rites of initiation, and are even today regarded with a kind of circum-spection: some villagers we passed along the way, for example, had shaken their heads and told us that the caves were "bad." Reputedly, initiates were required to pass a prescribed amount of time without food, water, or light in these innermost chambers before returning to the outer world.

One of the most fascinating manifestations of this belief that by simulating death one thereby wins new life is to be found in the initiation rite of Gabon's most important secret society, the Fang "Bwiti." Initiates are required to eat the root or root bark of the eboga, a common plant in the equatorial forest, which taken in small quantities acts as a stimulant and a represser of fatigue but taken in the massive quantities required of the initiate induces visions (and sometimes accidental death). The initiation process starts in the morning, the initiate ingesting eboga all the while, so that by nighttime he is virtually comatose. According to the most thorough study of this rite, the visions of the different initiates show a remarkable similarity: the initiate sees himself traveling by some uncommon means down a long, often red road that crosses rivers or streams of various colors and that ends with an abrupt change of landscape, usually from forest to grassy uplands. In the course of the journey he encounters his deceased relatives and sometimes monsters or dangerous animals (and on a few occasions, his dream progress is checked by a white official who seeks his identity or demands his papers—an eloquent indication that the European has left his own images of horror on African consciousness). The initiate then wakes from his visionary odyssey to the realm of the dead to a new identity and new life, as a Bwiti member.

At the end of our expedition, Caroline returned me to the mission, where we said our good-byes. I found Father Kurt leaning over the low cloister wall, smoking a cigarette.

"And was it all there—the rocks, the bats, the water?" he inquired. When I told him that I planned to leave for Franceville the next day, he raised an eyebrow.

"So soon? You feel you've seen it all, eh?"

•/•/•

I DECIDED to break the short journey to Franceville by stopping
at Mounana and Moanda, the sites of the important uranium
and manganese mines. The ride to Mounana, the first and
smaller of the towns, some seventy miles from Lastoursville,
proved to be eventful. In theory, the Trans-Gabon railway is
completed and goes all the way to Franceville, but in practice the
final stage of this journey has so far only been made by dignitaries and diplomats on official excursions, and I was therefore
forced to seek out the inevitable *taxi brousse*. Once at the main
road, I discovered that most of the taxis going in the direction
of Franceville had left very early in the morning, and that only
one was still waiting to depart. Its cabin was occupied by the
driver and two of his friends, so I got into the open back, where
other women sat wrapped in cotton shawls and turbans with
their market goods. They were aghast to see me join them and
told me emphatically that I should sit in the cabin and that the
two men beside the driver should let me have their seats. I
replied that I was content to be where I was, but they continued
to murmur indignantly.

The morning air was cool, and once we were under way, it
became extremely cold in the open back of the fast-moving
truck. I had not been entirely well for some days, and I inadver-
tently began to cough.

"Ohh!" The women gazed at me with pained expressions, and
one of them rose shakily in the bumping truck to take matters
into her own hands and began to pound on the cabin window.

"A woman in the back! A sick woman in the back! While two
men are sitting in the cabin!" The driver stopped and with jus-
tifiable irritation explained that his friends had come beforehand; I interjected again that I was all right, that I was not sick
but had a "biscuit-crumb cough." But the woman were aroused,
and from this point on, at every village halt, they would stand
and shout to the village population about the wickedness of the
men in the cabin:

"A sick woman! Traveling alone!" they would call, clapping their hands together above their heads. Villagers came running to the truck and clicked their tongues in disapproval. Village men pounded on the cabin door.

"Why are you doing this? What is wrong with these *garçons* who sit like fools beside you?" In desperation, the driver rolled down his window to shout an explanation, but he was silenced by the jeering women. I became increasingly uncomfortable. Although it was impossible not to be touched by the protectiveness of the women, it was also impossible to overlook the real issue at stake: my place was felt to belong in the front of the cabin not because I was sick, certainly not because I was a woman, but because I was white.

At last, at a crossroad where the driver stopped for two old women, I decided to get out and wait for another taxi—there were too many halts to be endured between where we were and Mounana. I had already climbed down from the truck and was saying good-bye to the women when another taxi traveling in the opposite direction pulled up on the other side of the road. Immediately the women raised anew their chorus of complaint and derision. Out of the crowd of people packed into the back of the other truck, there arose a massive, immaculately clad gendarme, who called for silence and then began to question me by shouting across the road.

"Why are you getting out at the crossroad?"

Feeling trapped, I explained that I was going to wait for another taxi.

"And what is wrong with this taxi?"

I said nothing, but here the women answered for me. The gendarme silenced them again. "Is it because you must sit in the back?"

I replied that there was no room in the front. The gendarme interrupted me.

"Oh, but there is room in the front," he said, speaking decisively and very slowly. "When those two *garçons,* those men who are more women than men, those men who make one ashamed of Gabon get out, you will have plenty of room. Get out!" he thundered. A small crowd of curious people had drifted over to the crossroads. At the gendarme's almost operatic declamation, a man stepped forward from the crowd and jerked open the truck door. The two men got out, keeping their faces low and avoiding looking at the jeering crowd. The women were beside themselves with glee and began to sing and clap and laugh mockingly at the two men, who understandably declined to sit in the back but positioned themselves by the roadside. A young boy sprang from the crowd to hold the cabin door open for me.

"*Madame, ascendez-vous,*" he said gallantly, his expression indicating that he had never in all his days witnessed such a shameful and shocking event.

This was not a victory I was proud to have won. I got into the cabin, and the driver and I sat in a chilly, bitter silence for the remainder of the trip.

Mounana, the site of the uranium mine, was a small, depressing settlement of yellowed concrete houses exposed to the main road. But Moanda, the manganese mining town, was, as I had been told in Libreville, a *petit* Paris. Gabon is one of the foremost producers of manganese and possesses one quarter of the world's assessed resources, a fact that accounts for the striking prosperity of the town. Here one could again obtain pastries and croissants and small luxuries from fashionable *boutiques.* There was a multitude of West African restaurants, a modern supermarket, expensive cars, and a sudden predominance of European faces. A grand hotel stood in the town center, surrounded by wide lawns and patios and a pool deck. In the hilly area around the town, houses where the mining staff lived were arranged in tree-shaded gardens behind painted decorative wrought-iron fences.

From here too, the road had an excellent tarmac surface, allowing my *taxi brousse* to cover the remaining forty miles to Franceville with terrifying speed. This city had originally been the farthest station founded by Brazza in Gaboon territory, and was at one time part of the Congo colony. It remained an inaccessible, isolated outpost until 1970, when a connective roadway was at last built to integrate it with the rest of the country. A modern town of over thirty thousand inhabitants, it is now the capital of the Haut-Ogooué region, sprawled without apparent plan over the undulating foothills of the Batéké plateau, around and between alternating patches of forest and expanses of grass that look like golfing greens. It is a town in which one feels that one might live for many years without ever discerning its center.

Franceville's present importance has been assured by more than its proximity to the lucrative mines. Some of the most noteworthy institutions, such as the El Hadj Bongo Airport and the headquarters of CIRMF, were established in Franceville less for the convenience of its location than for the desire to add luster to the birthplace of its most famous native son, the president of Gabon himself. President Bongo came to power in 1967, when he was only thirty-three years old, on the death of Leon M'Ba, the first president of the independent republic. In 1968, Bongo established the Parti Démocratique Gabonais (PDG), Gabon's only legal political party. The president, who holds executive power and is chief of the armed forces, is elected to office for a term of seven years. In the last presidential election, held in 1979, Bongo, the sole candidate, was reelected by a gratifying 99.85 percent of the more than 700,000 votes cast, a total surpassing not only all expectations but also the number of registered voters. The other organs of government are a Council of Ministers, appointed by the president, and the unicameral National Assembly, with one hundred and twenty members, also elected by universal suffrage. All legislation is subject to presidential veto, and the president is also empowered to dissolve the Assembly.

The president is popularly said to be of Pygmy stock, a fact not overly cited and easily overlooked, as photographs are careful to conceal the fact that he is under five feet tall and wears platform shoes. Bongo announced his conversion to Islam in 1973; in 1975, Gabon became a full member of OPEC. The president's person is protected by a bodyguard of Moroccan troops and European mercenaries.

I had viewed my trip to Franceville as in some way obligatory but was less interested in the town than in getting to the Batéké plateau (the Bateké, the Batsangui, and the Mbedé tribes inhabit the Upper Ogooué), which Mary Kingsley had described but had not, of course, been able to see. "Two or three days' journey from Franceville going east, the nature of the country changes," she wrote, "to the clayey soil of the Ogowé basin and its richly wooded moist valleys succeeds a sandy, arid, hilly country, with here and there in the neighbourhood of a village a group of palm trees. This is the aspect of the country which forms the watershed between the Ogowé and the tributaries of the Upper Congo."

The plateau is sparsely inhabited by scattered villages that are reached by a few narrow, sandy trails. As the *taxi brousses* do not as a rule make this trip, getting to the plateau might have presented a problem had I not once again been fortunate enough to fall in with the Peace Corps. Brent Friedrich, the leader of the outing to Alonha, had given me a letter of introduction to a volunteer in Franceville, whom I found sitting with three other volunteers in the sandy compound outside Mariann's Bar, under the shelter of a Peace Corps–built cinder-block gazebo. In that twilight hour of a weekend payday, with Mariann's provisions a stone's throw away, nothing was a problem to those happy souls, and within minutes I was assured of a place to stay, dinner, and dancing that evening, and on the following morning, a trip with one of the volunteers, Jonathan Pitts, who was returning to his plateau village.

Jonathan was a silent, bearded redhead. With his childhood in Jordan, his adolescence on a Crow reservation, and his five years of construction work in the Louisiana bayous, he had accumulated a bewilderingly diverse range of life experiences. He had read Mary Kingsley's *Travels* and remembered one passage in particular: "She was spending the night in a village, but couldn't sleep, and so she snuck out of her hut and went to the river and canoed downstream to be away by herself. Has there been a moment for you as magical and peaceful as that?" I had to confess that there had not.

Jonathan's village, Onga, was some six hours away from Franceville, no more than twelve miles as the crow flies from

Gabon's eastern Congo border. The red laterite road that dipped and rose from the outskirts of Franceville seemed to have been brutally bulldozed through the forest, having a more than usual raw and makeshift appearance. After several hours, we emerged from a deep gully of forest onto the plateau. I had anticipated the savannah landscape of Lopé, but the plateau was a green and yellow scrubland, tufted with feathery clumps of high grass and twisted, silver-barked trees that resembled olive trees. All across the landscape, jaundice-colored termite mounds, in tiny Gothic outlines of towers and turrets, stood amid the grass like miniature castles on mountain crags. An occasional band of forest would break across the treacherously sandy road, often screening an isolated village behind.

Jonathan's village was in fact two Bateké villages, Onga and Djoué, which had been "regrouped." A long road of drifted white sand ran between young palms and houses built of termite mud and wattle. At the bottom of a steep hill behind the village, one reached the Djoué river, a winding, fast-running, lucid green stream overhung by the forest and festoons of purple flowers. A wooden footbridge led to the village plantations, which were backed by grassland and then the forest.

Onga initiated me into a world that is supposed to exist no longer; a European might find its counterpart in ancient pastoral poetry—a world of riverbanks and flower garlands, of goat bells and gentle hills. In the mornings, I followed a narrow trail along the hillslope to the river and swam or did laundry on an overturned pirogue. When Jonathan and I wandered down the sandy road to the other end of the village, people called out friendly greetings from their houses or came over to shake hands. The communal "clubhouse" was down this way, an unfinished one-room wattle hut with a large, smoldering log in the center of its sandy floor. Here one sat and smoked, sat and talked, or sat and stared through the imperfect walls at the world passing outside. Climbing up into the hills behind the village one had a hazy view across the plateau, with its small oasislike clusters of palm trees that mark a village. At night, we sat outside Jonathan's house while a big moon shone on the road of white sand. In the alleyways between the houses, people sat around their fires, their voices coming in murmuring undertones or sharp shouts of laughter. A band of ragged children came dancing down the shining road, stopping before Jonathan's house to plead for a special song on his tape recorder. One small boy of no more than five mischievously wrapped a *pagne* around him and began to imitate a woman dancing, looking coyly over his shoulder at his swinging backside.

If one looked hard beneath this surface appearance, the mirage of pastoral peace was disturbed. Long days of back-breaking work in the plantation fields, swollen bellies, lack of proper education and medical care—these realities were not immediately apparent to a visitor on the wing. The latter reality was that most dramatically revealed to me: a little boy, hardly more than a baby, who had passed a great many of the evenings of his short life on Jonathan's lap, was dragged before us one afternoon by the roaming troop of children. The baby's sister, a little girl herself, entrusted every day with her brother's care, hoisted the baby toward us and reported that he had been found drinking petrol out of a storage can. The baby raised round and worried eyes to the crowd of his alarmed but orderly playmates. An unhealthy-looking mustard-colored dribble was oozing from his mouth. The doctor at the next village, which several miles away, was known to have a stomach pump; there was no doctor or medical assistant in Onga. A hair-raising jeep ride followed, from one village to the next and even the next, where in each case we found that the doctor was "away." The baby's symptoms were unreadable; he had coughed and wheezed badly, then suddenly fallen into a profound sleep. Jonathan and I were by this time heading back empty-handed toward Onga and looked at each other worriedly—was this a sleep, or a coma? Miles from the village, we came across the baby's mother, who had been called from her plantation after our departure, half running, half striding through the plateau stubble under the hot afternoon sun, accompanied by a youth of fourteen, who was valiantly struggling to keep apace. Without a word, the mother entered the truck, took her baby from my lap, and folded herself around him while the young boy looked in anxiously through the window. The baby now opened one, then the other cautious eye, peering around him with feigned innocence.

"Oh!" the mother cried out and slapped him with relief.

That evening, the chief invited Jonathan and me to dinner at his house, where we were served antelope, minced manioc leaves, and manioc root. His conversation was largely about the progress of the school that Jonathan was building and about the worry of getting supplies to the village.

"Here, everything is free. One doesn't need money. But if you step outside the village— No! The prices are impossible." His wife, a tall bony woman, made only a brief, shy appearance before returning to her kitchen.

What would Mary Kingsley have done at Onga? Would she have inquired as to how the chief's wife had prepared the manioc? Investigated the nature of the spirits that almost certainly haunt the Djoué river? I had none of her inquiring, anthropological passion. Are Bateké women allowed to eat antelope? Do they rejoice or despair at the birth of twins? I would not know what to do with such knowledge.

Mary Kingsley was so thorough in her presentation of geographical, historical, and anthropological detail that she does not bear repeating. I can now confess, after the fact, to a desire to have made a unique contribution, a discovery all my own. I had thought that some startling revelation, some unforeseen truth, might await me when I came to the end of the line, far beyond the territory she had claimed—as if fresh ideas can be won only on literally untrammeled soil. In fact, I did very little inquiring at Onga but found myself being absorbed passively into its rhythm of life.

Toward the end of my visit, Jonathan offered me a choice of two routes back to Franceville: either by way of the Lekoni canyon (which Le Couteau had described) or by way of a Pygmy village off the same route by which we had come. The Pygmies are thought to be the original inhabitants of what is now Gabon.

There are but an estimated three thousand of these former possessors of the land, living in remote pockets of the forest in the northeast, central south, and extreme southwest, where they pursue their traditional life as hunters and gatherers. Pygmy forest lore is legendary among other tribes, as is Pygmy elusiveness, and it is extremely difficult for an "outsider" to make contact with Pygmies still living in the forest. My interest in the Pygmies, however, derived less from these compelling characteristics than from the following verses:

> . . . *the Trojans came on with clamour and shouting, like birds,*
> *as when the clamour of cranes goes up to the heavens,*
> *when the cranes flee the tempests and the rains unceasing*
> *and with clamour wing their way to the streams of Ocean,*
> *bringing to the Pygmy men bloodshed and death. . . .*

This passage from the *Iliad* of Homer has long intrigued me and refers to a mythological tradition regarding a battle between "pygmy men" and cranes. Our English word *pygmy* is in fact derived from the Greek *pygmē,* "fist," presumably referring to the people's "fistlike" size. Since this latter part of my journey was being shaped by no consideration other than my own personal interests, I had no hesitation when Jonathan gave me a choice of routes: we would return by way of the Pygmy village. At the back of my mind was the idea that I would find therein a white-haired Pygmy elder who would be able to corroborate Homer's verses by imparting to me the Pygmy version of this same myth.

The Pygmy village into which I intruded my uninvited presence was a shabby rectangular roadside clearing containing two rows of dilapidated bamboo and wooden huts. An old man dressed in rags greeted me with courtesy too great to inquire about my business. Other people, all of whom were far shorter than I, appeared in the doorways of their houses. There was little occasion to ask if anyone here knew his Pygmy myths, for it is the sad fate of these people to suffer a complete disassociation from their own traditions once they come to settle outside their forest home. So my dream, perhaps not unsurprisingly, remained unfulfilled.

Later, I read a description of the Lekoni canyon: protruding from a deep trench of forest, brown and white spikes of mountainous rock rise skyward like spires from the canyon floor, extending over many miles; it would have been a haunting sight. I should have kept my eyes on the reality, and not the myth, should have gone on and on to the edge of the canyon, should have walked to the Congo border. . . .

OVERLAND
TO THE REMBOUÉ

SUDDENLY, I was on my way back to Lambaréné. After traveling to Ndjolé by train, I caught a ride with a truck driver from Chad who—with his diabolical smile, curling pencil-line moustache, and snarling laugh—was an African embodiment of the vaudeville villain who ties maidens onto railway tracks. The back of his truck was empty, save for the wife of a companion who was sharing his cabin. The driver asked me with a sneer what I thought of Gabon, and then answered this question himself: "It would not be so bad if it weren't for the Gabonese."

"Oh ho! The Gabonese!" His companion rolled around the cabin in laughter. "The Gabonese! Please," he gasped, "say no more about the Gabonese!" In fact, he was himself from Gabon, an accident apparently nullified by his close association with the driver.

"I am Gabonese," he said, laughing, "but I am not as *they!*" The Gabonese could not run businesses, could not work, were lazy, could only drink. . . . He ticked off their characteristics on his fingers while the driver bared his white teeth in a laugh of theatrical evil: "Heh, heh, heh."

We were traveling swiftly along the forest road, passing infrequent villages and occasionally enveloping people on the roadside in our shadowing red cloud of dust. Two old women, bent almost parallel with the ground by their backloads of wood, waved their hands for us to stop, but we had sped past them before the driver relented and came to a halt.

"Hurry up, *mamans,*" his companion called out of the window. "Run, run! We do not all move so slowly!" The women caught up with us. They looked very small as they stood with their creased faces turned up toward the cabin. One of them asked the price of a ride.

"Oh! Listen to them!" The companion shook with glee. "Never mind, never mind, we shall arrange it later. Get in!"

"But we must know," the woman replied. She was worriedly fingering her money, which was knotted in a handkerchief she had drawn from her bosom.

"Do you hear them? Oh! Do you believe these old women? Three hundred francs!" he called out. "Do you want the ride or not?"

There was a wail of disbelief. "Three hundred francs! Monsieur, we are tired, we are old. It is not far—"

"Get in!" both men shouted, and the women scurried to obey, climbing up beside the lone wife in the truck's open back.

"If it was not far, they would not want a ride," said the companion, laughing.

"*Voilà!*" sneered the driver in agreement, "heh, heh, heh!"

We thundered along the road until the women banged on the cabin window for us to stop.

"Here? By this village of two houses? Why, twenty people in all the world know this place has a name," the companion mocked, peering at the few hut roofs that appeared above the high grass beyond the road. The women were waiting anxiously for their change.

"But I shall keep it all," the driver teased while his companion tossed his head in delighted laughter. "There! Take your money," he said as the women began to wail again. "There! There!" and he threw it out the window.

"Oh, these Gabonese," sighed his companion, when we were under way again. "They exhaust themselves on this little walk, and yet on Mother's Day, those old women will dance all night at the village *fête*. Do you have such women in your land?" he inquired, turning to me.

"Heh, heh, heh," the driver laughed through clenched white teeth.

·/·/·

I ARRIVED in Lambaréné toward the end of the ten-day "safety margin" in which I had promised Sister Carmen I would return, and found that my new room had been prepared for me a week before. There were several touching additions: an extra bath towel and flannel, a gold-rimmed water glass, and vase of flowers. Most tellingly, my new room was not across the courtyard but in the same wing where the Sisters lived.

While I was away, Mother Jacques Marie had left to take charge of the more populous and demanding mission at Port-Gentil, a transfer befitting her superior skills. The new *Mère* was to arrive in a few weeks' time—"a Dutchwoman, very large and very enthusiastic," Sister Carmen told me. Meanwhile, Sister Marie Amparo had come from Libreville to oversee the mission affairs. She was an older woman, worn, faded, and infinitely gentle.

"I came here to Lambaréné for the first time in 1950," she told me in her soft voice. "Before you were born. I myself was young then." On the second morning, she brought me a flower that looked like two blossoms of white tissue folded one inside the other.

"It is white now, but by evening it will have changed to the color of blood—*Le Dieu* has made it so," she said. I asked her the name of the flower.

"*Caprice. Caprice de la femme*—because a woman is so changeable."

•/•/•

AFTER SEEING the rapids, Mary Kingsley had left Talagouga and returned to the Kangwe Mission at Andèndé, where she stayed for several weeks, occupied for the most part, it seems, in inquiring after the customs of the Galoa tribe and in learning to canoe. It is impossible to tell from the *Travels* how many weeks she spent in the Lambaréné area on this second visit, as she gives no dates between her first arrival at Talagouga and her final departure from the Kangwe Mission on July 22, when she began her return to Libreville. For this trip, the obliging mission supplied her with a canoe, a Galoa interpreter, and a crew of four Adjoumba paddlers, who hailed from Arevooma, a village a few miles downstream from Andèndé, and where the party spent the first night of the return journey.

The usual way of getting back to Libreville from the interior, as would be expected, was by following the Ogooué downstream to Nazareth Bay and then heading up the coast. Kingsley, however, for reasons never clearly given in the *Travels,* quit the Ogooué and headed north through the forest to the Remboué river, by which she eventually arrived at the Gabon Estuary. Thus, instead of following the main channel of the Ogooué all the way from Lambaréné to the coast, she and her crew joined the Rèmbo Ouango ("Small River"), the Ogooué's lesser northern arm, and traveled northwest to Lake Nkonié, which they reached on the evening of their second day. The overland trek commenced on the third morning from the shores of Lake Nkonié: "We run our canoe into a bank of the dank dark-coloured water herb to the right," Kingsley wrote, "and disembark into a fitting introduction to the sort of country we shall have to deal with before we see the Rembwé—namely, up to our knees in black slime."

This overland journey is one of the great adventures of the *Travels.* It required three days of unbroken hiking through forest, rivers, swamp, mountainous terrain, and muddy gullies, encounters with elephants and gorillas, and near brushes with leopards.

On the outskirts of one of the more unsavory villages they stayed in, Kingsley fell into a fifteen-foot-deep game pit and claimed that she was protected from its lethal ebony spikes only by the cushioning of her thick woolen skirt—a reminder that she made this hike through equatorial forest weighed down by ankle-length Victorian clothing. Late in the night of the fifth day, the party at last stumbled into Akondjo, where Hatton and Cookson had a factory. Here Kingsley paid her men in trade goods and took a much-needed rest before continuing down the Remboué to the estuary and thence to Libreville.

The chapters describing this venture most resist paraphrase. They not only contain some of the most memorable characters and incidents of the *Travels* but are also distinguished by a striking new mood. Although Kingsley's familiar jocular style is very much in play, the narration is nonetheless pervaded by a succession of disquieting and sinister images that loom up between the humor and beauty of other passages and hint that this adventure was in its reality more frightening and unnerving than is directly conveyed.

A host of incidents speak of Kingsley's sense of vulnerability on this trip: her very departure from Lambaréné with a severe headache and the conviction that a bout of fever was in store for her, her initial misgivings about the Adjoumbas who were her crew and guides, and her disorientation throughout the entire trip. One of her guides accidentally fired his gun so close to Kingsley's head that it singed her hair. The landscape, which she usually describes in glowing terms, became threatening: the marshlands before the entrance to Lake Nkonié, for example, represented "a strange, wild, lonely bit of the world." The scenery is "savage." There was a gruesome burial site, from which streamed a busy train of ants; eerie ruins of an old trading station, deserted because, as one of her guides says, "No man live for that place now"; the foreboding entrance to Lake Nkonié: "Sign of human habitation at first there was none; and in spite of its beauty, there was something which I was almost going to say was repulsive. The men evidently felt the same as I did. Had any one told me that the air that lay on the lake was poison, or that in among its forests lay some path to regions of utter death, I should have said—'It looks like that.' "

The forest that Kingsley and her guides were traveling through was all Fang territory, and the Fang, it must be remembered, were the most feared of all the tribes, by Africans and Europeans alike, because they were aggressive, ruthless, intelligent—and cannibal. The descriptions of the villages that Kingsley encountered are replete with unpleasant, at times grisly detail, a choice example being an incident in a hut in Efoua, the village where she and her party passed their third night:

> Waking up again I noticed the smell in the hut was violent, from being shut up I suppose, and it had an unmistakably organic origin. Knocking the ash end off the smouldering bush-light that lay burning on the floor, I investigated, and tracked it to [one of several hanging] bags. . . . I then shook its contents out in my hat, for fear of losing anything of value. They were a human hand, three big toes, four eyes, two ears, and other portions of the human frame. The hand was fresh, the others only so so, and shrivelled.

(I have generally tried to avoid plundering Kingsley's *Travels,* which should be read in its entirety, except in cases where her words are essential for setting up my own experience; but I cannot refrain from drawing particular attention in passing to the Remboué river trip, by way of tribute to my favorite passage—and, I think, Kingsley's favorite journey. The description of this leg of her travels, and in particular of her magnificent and unforgettable companion, Obanjo, is too brilliant and too devastatingly funny to pass over in silence, and on the many occasions on which I have reread this passage, I have never failed to laugh out loud.)

At the time of her journey, the forest villages in the territory between the Ogooué and the Remboué were interconnected by such an extensive network of bush trails that, as Kingsley later noted, one could enter this tract of forest by "coming down the Ogowé and turning in at any place you may see fit." The first

European to make this journey overland was a French naval official, Lieutenant P. Serval, who in 1862 had made an extensive exploration of the lower Ogooué in the company of Dr. Griffon du Bellay (later a member of the first Brazza expedition). Serval made the Remboué overland journey in the opposite direction than Kingsley did, traveling from the estuary to the Ogooué, which he reached at a point somewhat beyond the Ngounié confluence. In July 1874, at the outset of his first expedition to the interior, Nassau debated whether to travel from Libreville to Lambaréné by land or by sea and river, and eventually decided in favor of the latter route, which he thought would be less expensive. Some months later, however, he did make the overland journey and found it so easy that it became his preferred route, largely because he could avoid the boat journeys that always made him seasick: "The journey was not difficult. There were swamps crossed by logs, and many streams across which I either waded or swam. There were dark ravines and steep ascents, until the top of the watersheds between the Ogowe and the Rémbwe was reached. . . . The path was narrow, but well-trodden." Thus did Nassau render the journey that took Mary Kingsley three full chapters—replete with haunting and unnerving detail—to describe. The fact that Nassau made this particular journey so often must also account for his noncommittal diary entry of July 30, 1895, noting Mary Kingsley's arrival back in Libreville at the end of her epic trip: "Letter came, from the Ainsleys, by hand of Miss Kingsley, who had walked overland from the Ogowe. Spent the morning in looking over the mail. . . ."

The most straightforward land route was the one Nassau had been in the habit of taking, which was also used by Reverend Good, whose trip Kingsley refers to: traveling by way of the Rèmbo Ouango to the northeastern shore of Lake Azingo, which lies in an almost direct line below Akondjo, the village on the Remboué for which Kingsley's party was specifically aiming. This was also the trade route used by the Africans, as Kingsley noted. The reason she did not go this way, she tells us, was because her crew had told her that it was blocked by the dangerous Fang—in fact the Fang were ubiquitous in this region.

The route that Kingsley did take was geographically the most difficult—indeed almost senseless. Lake Nkonié (Ncovi) not only lies farther west than Lake Azingo, and therefore to the west of all the trails leading directly to Akondjo and the Remboué, but also does not extend so far north; by using its shores as their starting point, Kingsley's party ensured themselves of a longer than necessary hike in marshy ground over a distance that could have been covered comfortably by boat, had they struck out from Azingo.

Immediately on her return to England in November 1895, Mary Kingsley was interviewed by a reporter for the *Times,* to whom she gave a summary of her adventures. In this interview, as in the *Travels,* she offered no explanation as to why she undertook the overland route, but an interesting fact is nonetheless revealed. According to the article, "Miss Kingsley returned to the Gaboon by way of the Rembwe, and when she informed the French authorities and traders of her travels, they were astonished that she had returned alive. Had they known of her intention beforehand, they would probably have prevented the journey."

This explains a point that has long puzzled me: namely, the apparent lack of advice on the part of the missionaries and traders at Lambaréné. While the overland route was not entirely novel, it was also certainly not normal, and it has struck me as highly uncharacteristic of the generally protective and helpful European community that they did not provide more complete information regarding the intended trip of their unescorted guest. As residents of the area, even if not personally well-traveled in the lake region where Kingsley ended up, they should have at least been abreast of its general tribal movements—Lake Azingo was, after all, only a day away from Lambaréné—and if the most direct route through Lake Azingo was indeed blocked by hostile Fang, it seemed strange that Kingsley had been given no inkling of this fact prior to her departure, let alone been *allowed* to go this way in the first place. If, however, it was the case that the French authorities at Libreville would not have granted her the necessary permission to make this trip had they known of her intentions, it is unlikely that the authorities at Lambaréné would have done so either. And if, in turn, Kingsley made her journey without the knowledge of the French authorities, it is almost certain that she did so without the knowledge of the French mission, who would have been unlikely to have sent her off on an expedition that had not been sanctioned by their superior authorities.

While Kingsley's ingenuous account to the *Times'* interviewer may explain one puzzling point, it also raises another question: when did she first broach her plan of traveling overland to her Adjoumba crew and guides? If she secretly discussed her plans with them before her departure—in itself extremely unlikely—it is odd that she confessed in her book that she "did not much care for these Ajumbas on starting." It is also difficult to imagine that she made a change of plans once they were under way, given her account that she had left Kangwe with "an awful headache, complicated by the conviction that I am in for a heavy bout of fever. . . . I lay among the luggage for about an hour, not taking much interest in the Rembwé or anything else, save my own headache; but this soon lifted, and I was able to take notice, just before we reached the Ajumbas' town. . . ."

Additional light is shed on the overland trip by yet another account of this expedition, which Kingsley gave in January 1896, before she had written the *Travels,* when she delivered the first of what were to be many public lectures, to the Royal Scottish Geographical Society, in Edinburgh. The lecture, published in the Society's journal, commenced with the statement that she had gone to West Africa to collect fish, and then went on to give a rough outline of her travels: "I started fishing in the Ogowé, pottering up that lovely river. . . . I then pottered down, and made my way to the Rembo Ongo into the Karkola river [the channel that leads from the Rèmbo Ouango to lakes Azingo and Nkonié]. Thence to Lake N'Covi, and then overland . . . to Ndorko, on the river Rembwe. From Ndorko I went up the river to Acondgo, and from there down to Glass, where, well knowing my wanderings through the Fan country would not meet with approval, I said I had done it from scientific motives. 'No, Miss Kingsley,' said my English friends, 'you fell into the hands of those Fans, and they took you touring about their country like a circus.' I admit there is some truth in the statement."

In conjunction with this confession, there is evidence within the text of the *Travels* itself that the itinerary chosen by Kingsley's Fang guides was tailored to suit their own trading interests. In M'fetta, a Fang village on Lake Nkonié to which her Adjoumba guides led her, Kingsley and her crew were joined by Kiva, a Fang friend of one of the Adjoumba boatmen, and two other fellow tribesmen. These characters set the "circus" in motion by telling Kingsley that the only way they knew to the Remboué was by way of Efoua (a village it is impossible to place on a map). In Efoua, as in every subsequent village they came to, unfinished personal business of some sort awaited one or the other of these Fang companions, the outstanding legal affairs of Kiva alone being eloquent testimony to a close involvement with the villages in question. Between Efoua and Egaja, the Fang clearly got out of hand and attempted to delay Kingsley further: "The Fans were in high feather," Kingsley wrote, "openly insolent to Ngouta [her interpreter, loaned by the Kangwe mission], and anxious for me to stay in this delightful locality, and go hunting with them and divers other choice spirits, whom they assured me we could easily get to join us at Efoua."

I am not entirely convinced that the conduct of her Adjoumba crew is to be held above suspicion either, and I feel there is the distinct possibility that, in spite of Kingsley's assertion early in her account of this adventure that she and her party were bound for the Rembwé, she may never in fact have planned the overland trip—through Azingo, or by any other route.

It is at least possible that Kingsley set off from Kangwe, accompanied by both the crew and the blessing of the mission staff, with the intention of making her trip by the more conventional route down the Ogooué river to Nazareth Bay (an adventurous choice in any case, as she had the option of taking the comfortable steamer that left Lambaréné for Libreville only days later), but that this plan was turned aside by her wily Adjoumba guides. Perhaps the Adjoumba persuaded her to break the journey by passing the night in their village, Arevooma, which lay on the Rèmbo Ouango—or perhaps they took advantage of her headache and the fact that she was lying in the boat "not taking much interest in the Rembwé or anything else," and simply went there of their own accord—and once in their village, suggested making the journey to the estuary overland. Kingsley would no doubt have heard of this overland route, and it would have been characteristic of her to take advantage of this "sightseeing" opportunity. At some point after their departure from Arevooma, however, the Adjoumba broke the news to her that they were going not by way of Azingo, as she would naturally have assumed, but by Nkonié, where their own trading interests lay. Once in Nkonié, as we have seen, the Fang implemented their own plans, to the cost of even the Adjoumba.

This hypothesis would answer the problematic questions I have referred to, as well as clarify certain additional points. It is interesting to note, for example, that the Adjoumba passenger who joined Kingsley's party in Arevooma had been waiting for some time specifically to go overland to the Remboué: "We have an addition to our crew this morning," Kingsley wrote, "—a man who wants to go and get work at John Holt's sub-factory away on the Rembwé. He has been waiting a long while at Arevooma, unable to get across, I am told, because the road is now stopped between Ayzingo and the Rembwé by 'those fearful Fans.' " In fact, if the Adjoumba were genuinely afraid of a Fang threat, it is more likely that they would have insisted on the conventional route of the Ogooué—Nassau's diary gives ample evidence that villages had no qualms about refusing to provide guides if they had misgivings about making a particular trip. The "Fang threat" may have been merely a ploy to ensure that the party went by way of Nkonié.

If Kingsley did in fact travel blind, then her journey must be considered all the more courageous. In addition to having to contend with the dangers inherent in this venture, she would have had to combat that most unnerving dimension of foreign

travel—a heightened sense of vulnerability, of which the striking mood of disquiet that interjects itself throughout her final,
much-edited account may be a residual hint.

•/•/•

I CAME TO GABON with the anticipation that I might have to face
two major difficulties in repeating Mary Kingsley's overland
journey: I was apprehensive about the logistical problems, such
as finding guides and porters; and I was worried that the forest
between Lake Nkonié and the Remboué might now be depleted
or even built over. It was therefore ironic that the sole difficulty
I had to contend with arose from the fact that the forest is if
anything denser now than when Kingsley made her trip; while
in Kingsley's time this region was riddled with villages and
interconnecting bush trails, there are today, as I belatedly discovered, no villages in the tract of land between the Ogooué and
the estuary, let alone between the Ogooué and Remboué rivers.
This is in part a result of government pressure to relocate villages
to sites where they are accessible to roads and supplies, and in
part because many villages disbanded as people drifted away to
the nearby towns for work, and when the villagers left, the vital
bush trails swiftly became overgrown.

I started making inquiries about a possible forest route as early
as Libreville, where, to my extreme delight, I came upon a map
that indicated an almost ruler-straight forest road running directly from a lumber chantier on the northeastern shore of Lake
Azingo to none other than a village called Akondjo, on the
Remboué river. My happiness at this discovery was almost immediately dashed by the forestry department, however, who
drew my attention to the fact that the map was more than
twenty years old. Nor were they able to tell me of other roads,
paths, or even trails in the region, and they assumed that this
area was by now completely overgrown.

The extensive inquiries I made in Lambaréné confirmed that
no road or trail existed, a fact that for some while caused me no
particular concern—I would obviously just have to muster up a
team of Africans to chop a path out of the forest for me. It was

with great surprise that I came to learn that Africans are no more willing to undertake a journey through dense and unbroken unknown forest than are Europeans, even when offered the guidance of a transient stranger equipped with the hazy directions given in a book published in 1897.

The demise of the comprehensive trade network that once existed among villages and tribes has ensured that the modern villager's knowledge of the nature of the forest is restricted to his immediate neighborhood. Trade is now localized in central markets or towns, in this case in Lambaréné, which can be reached by boat. The only occasion for going any distance into the forest today would be to take part in a hunting expedition, and even when these extend over several days, the hunters do not march in a straight line miles away from their home, but rather fan out in shallow forays into the bush. This state of affairs may or may not represent a regrettable loss of traditional skills—as I was of course selfishly inclined to believe at the time; the fact I had to face was, very simply, that if no path existed, there would be no guide, and if no guide, no overland journey to the Remboué.

I turned for advice to Jean, the boatman who had taken me to Samkita. Gravely considering the matter, he suggested that we first consult with the fishermen who knew the territory around the outlying lakes of Azingo and Nkonié. This practical suggestion was followed up by many hours passed on the beaches and in the inlets that ring Lambaréné island, where the fishermen unload their boats or look for possible passengers to ferry elsewhere, and where the women go to do their laundry and the children to splash and play. To sometimes interested, often amused audiences, I would make my plea for information about a way to the Remboué river, Jean meanwhile usually standing solemnly to one side, holding my copy of Mary Kingsley's *Travels,* which he showed around as a kind of emblem of authority. ("Is that your picture?" I was often asked of the photograph of Mary Kingsley on the cover.) Surprisingly, few people were familiar with Lake Nkonié (locally referred to as "Ncovi"), although Azingo was well known. Most people had not heard of a river leading to the estuary—whether called the Remboué or anything else—although, paradoxically, several had heard of Akondjo and knew it was on a river.

Gradually, however, I was able to assemble some useful facts: in recent memory there had been not only a trail but an actual bush road leading from an Elf oil depot on the shores of Azingo directly to Akondjo. No one, however, had personally seen the trail or, more disconcertingly, knew of anyone else who had. Akondjo was said to be deserted: on this point everyone was in agreement. But, it was also thought that if I *did* manage to get there, I might meet with hunters or fishermen who had come from farther upstream and who could give me a ride with them back to the estuary.

"It seems to me," said Jean, speaking with characteristic gravity, "that what we must do now is go to Nkonié," and we made plans to meet early the following morning. Back at the mission, Sister Marie Amparo made her usual gentle inquiry after my progress.

"Courage, Alexander," she said. "We pray for you every evening."

The next morning was so gray that it seemed to have robbed even the forest of its color. From under the Lambaréné bridge, a long ribbon of shrilling sparrows streamed into the air and then scattered in a black-flecked cloud like a handful of flung cinders. We passed Andèndé to our right, the forlorn church showing a dignified front from the distance of the beach, as if it still might await a loyal congregation. Farther downstream a village called Arévoma appeared on the right bank.

After half an hour we turned sharply into a channel that entered the Rèmbo Ouango from the north, its dark course occasionally broken with patches of white water that were easily avoided. Slowly the day brightened, the grayness that seemed to have been born of neither clouds nor mist simply dissolving into a hard blue sky. We passed alternately between forests of vine-hung trees and meadows of low-lying saw grass banked by hedges of tasseled papyrus. Then the land seemed to disintegrate altogether, and we found ourselves in a broad, picking our way through the channels and spongy isles of a marshy delta. A sudden profusion of red- and yellow-billed hornbills, herons and pelicans, crisscrossed our path from the maze of isles. Stationed on the stark branches of the dead trees that arose gauntly from the water, anhingas held their water-logged wings out to dry—sinister carryovers from an epoch when it had not yet been irrevocably determined that birds would fly. In and out we zigzagged, and then came to the entrance of Nkonié itself, which opened before us in a scalloped outline of curving bays and spits. Mary Kingsley's description of the lake's geography was exactly accurate: the entire lake is ringed with forest-covered hills, which on the northeast descend to the water in ridges, and which elsewhere rise behind a broad tract of level forest. But the whole seemed neither sinister nor repulsive, as she had seen it; in this light it had the aura of an exclusive choice lakeside property— the lines of forest too trim, the shoreline too beautifully sculpted, the whole too thoroughly landscaped, to have its possession left to chance.

"In the north and north-eastern part of the lake several exceedingly beautiful wooded islands show, with gray rocky beaches and dwarf cliffs," Mary Kingsley wrote, and I saw that Jean was steering toward the very one that if left to follow my own judgment I would have chosen as that to which Kingsley's Adjoumba crew had first brought her: "We . . . made our way towards the second island," she wrote. "When we got near enough to it to see details, a large village showed among the trees on its summit, and a steep dwarf cliff, overhung with trees and creeping plants came down to a small beach covered with large water-washed gray stones."

A pirogue painted with green and yellow stripes was lying upside down on the stony beach. We landed and, climbing a steep red path that tunneled through foliage up to the village, arrived on a sandy street that ran between wooden houses, where the benches outside almost every entranceway bespoke an easygoing sociability. Our presence was quickly discovered, and the villagers informally lined up for greetings: as usual, no one was so impolite as to ask my business before I had volunteered it.

Jean knew the chief, who had relatives in the village on the beach side of the Schweitzer Hospital, where he did his business and lived when away from his own "real" village, near Samkita. The chief was an old man, thin but agile, and with a mobile, expressive face that reminded me of Bing Crosby. He invited us into his house, which was airy and sparsely furnished with only a table and a few chairs. Old lace curtains were surviving in the windows, and the horn of an animal of some kind decorated one of the walls. We were joined by the elder men of the village, who took seats around the table or pulled up chairs they had brought with them and then sat with folded arms and expressionless faces, looking directly ahead. The chief had an excited, jerky way of speaking, and his words at times came out in a rapid stammer. He spoke in French and Fang, first welcoming us, and then telling us when he had last been to Lambaréné, the elders nodding in approval.

This civil scene was brutally interrupted by a terrible screaming, which seemed to have begun at one end of the village and to be steadily working its way toward us. A huge, shapeless girl, young for all her great size, with a thick, swollen-looking face disfigured by a scarlet birthmark, crashed through the doorway, jerking convulsively as if she were on the verge of a fit. For no apparent reason, she lurched toward me and positioned herself behind my chair, holding her twitching hands to either side of my head, as if she were restraining herself from strangling me only with great effort. A smile rippled among the solemn elders, and the chief touched his head by way of explanation of her mental condition and continued talking. Although trying hard to concentrate, I found myself somewhat distracted and was glad when Jean took over.

"We wish to go to the Remboué river, from Azingo—" he began, but the chief interrupted.

"Oh yes," he said, "I know the path. It leaves from Elf Gabon, and it comes out at Akondjo. I have done it: it took one day. We left early in the morning and we arrived at six o'clock. But now it is overgrown. It would take two days."

Jean hit the table with his fist, and for the first time ever I saw him smile. "I *knew* such *connaisseurs* existed! He is an older man— yes; one needs the *anciens.*"

Unperturbed by our excitement, the chief continued: "You need four or five men for the path. And you will have to carry your own food and water. I cannot say if there are piroguers at Akondjo. You must be prepared to walk back. When do you want to go?"

Before I could answer, another character entered the hut. It is typical of travel books written up until not so very long ago to make unabashed pronouncements concerning a "native's" phy- sique: a number of memoirs written by the wives of colonial officials, for example, comment admiringly on the "magnificent physiques of the male African," and the reader is embarrassed for the author's inadvertent revelation of more private thoughts. With full consciousness of all the implications, I state that I looked up to see standing in the doorway a young African man with a magnificent physique. He was wearing only a pair of cut-off army fatigue pants, the top buttons of which were un- done, and he was carrying a rifle that he appeared to be in the process of cleaning.

"And you will need guns," he said, entering the conversation. "If you are taking five men, four must be armed," and he made his way over to the wall behind the chief's chair and folded his arms across his massive chest.

"When do you want to go?" the chief repeated.

We arranged to set out in two days' time. The chief dictated a list of provisions to Jean and then stood up: "Good, it is arranged." The elders also rose, and we shook one another's hands. The magnificent man followed us to the door, stabbing the air with his finger in the direction of the departing chief.

"You will be safe. Once a chief has received you, no one can touch you. If you come to our island and the chief says 'Stay,' you can stay. If he says 'Go' . . ."—he jabbed the air more vehemently than ever—"then you GO!" The magnificent man told me that he had been in the navy and had served abroad.

"I was in Holland," he said. This was a surprise; I asked him in what town, but he just laughed.

"We were working on boats. We just worked, then we went to the bars nearby, then back to the boat to sleep—I don't know what village we were near."

I caught up with the chief and Jean, who were making their way down the cliff path to the boat. "Get in," said the magnificent man, who had followed us to the water. "I will give you a push." Easily lifting the pirogue's prow in one hand, he drew back his massive arm and sent us skimming backward over the surface of the lake. His job done, he turned back up the trail, leaving the chief to watch us alone from the beach.

By the time we passed through the marshland at the entrance to the lake and reentered the narrow river channel, the sun was sinking, appearing either directly behind us or to our right as we wound our way back toward the Rèmbo Ouango. In its late light, the upper foliage of the forest had become glistening and golden, and the clay banks above the river were reflected like burnished copper in water that was itself the color of a dark liqueur. On the outskirts of Lambaréné, we passed motorized pirogues overburdened with passengers and goods, heading back toward the lakes. The mission building appeared grandly in the distance on the high ground to our right; I had never before bothered to study it from this perspective and was now amazed to see the extent to which it was surrounded by the forest.

Through all the days I spent scurrying back and forth across the island and in and out of the lakes, life at the mission flowed on in unchanging serenity. I usually left in the morning before the Sisters had come out of their rooms to go to chapel, and when I returned in the late afternoon they were closing up their day in preparation for vespers. My new room had two doors; one opened onto the courtyard, the other onto a narrow verandah that looked over the mission walls to the Ogooué and, within the grounds, to the little white chapel. Here I would sit and watch the final light fade over the river and, later in the evening, watch the Sisters process to the chapel for their evening service, which in spite of the small number of participants was conducted with strict formality. Every evening, after the iron gates had been closed upon the world that lay beyond the dusty road, one of the Sisters took a turn at chiming the old mission bell, and then the four small white figures would file in silence down to the tiny chapel. A glow of light would appear through the door and windows; then there would follow a long pause while they prayed. Outside, the night would ring with insects and the patient grating call of frogs in the rushes. The thin song of four voices would break the silence of the chapel, and the Sisters would file out into the night, talkative now, and chatting; and always someone stopped by to visit me where I sat on the back verandah.

Their deep contentment to abide like this—here, in this one small mission on the edge of an out-of-the-way river in equatorial Africa—forever, if need be, contrasted poignantly, I felt, with my own nervous energy. Someone once said that exploration is the physical expression of an intellectual passion, and it is the traveler's conceit that there is much wisdom to be gained in the investigation of this wide world. Yet wrapped in the darkness of those matchless evenings, I knew that no knowledge I might ever amass would win me the naive wisdom possessed by the Sisters of the mission. Against my nature, I could not help wondering whether it would not be better to submit humbly to the miracle of existence than to be worn out by a continual prowling and pacing, peering and prying, into the nooks and crannies of the world.

On the evening of my return from Lake Nkonié, Sister Carmen met me excitedly at my room to tell me that there were two young men staying overnight, and that they had asked me to join them for dinner. "We thought you would be so happy to spend time with someone young," she said with kindly solicitude.

I found the new guests preparing their meal in the classroom that also served as the kitchen. They were French soldiers who were taking their vacation leave by traveling around Gabon. One of them was stationed in Libreville and therefore knew the country, and the other had come from the Congo to visit his friend. Both were lean, shaven-headed, and dressed in crumpled odds and ends of their uniforms. They attacked their freeze-dried food aggressively and talked rapidly of where they had been. They spoke of "the Africans" *(les noirs)* with a curious mixture of contempt and affection.

"But don't mistake me," said Stephanos, the soldier from Libreville, suddenly slowing his speech. "I could not live anywhere else. Once you've lived in Africa, you *can't* live anywhere else."

They had heard about my upcoming journey from the Sisters. Stephanos seemed unduly unhappy that I had found a guide. "This is a guide you can trust? How do you know? Oh—your boatman? And who is *he?*" He also wanted specific information about where I was staying in Libreville and when I expected to arrive there. Finally he pressed on me a bottle of water-purifying tablets. I thanked him but said I had some of my own.

He dismissed this. "These are French," he said and slapped the bottle into my hand.

The next day I went shopping for the provisions I had been instructed to buy. They were:

> 10 loaves of bread
> 10 tins of sardines
> 5 packages of cigarettes
> 2 heads of tobacco leaf
> 10 boxes of matches
> 5 liters of *vin rouge*

The men to be selected by the chief were supposed to bring their own guns and ammunition. The Hotel Ogooué Palace up the road had kindly undertaken to drop off my largest bag at their associated Hotel Dialogue in Libreville, which meant that I could travel light. My leave-taking of the Sisters, made in the evening, was extremely mournful. Their apprehension about the trip showed undisguisedly on their faces.

"And you return after you reach the estuary?" Sister Carmen inquired, and I had to explain that this was not in fact my plan.

Jean and I departed the next morning at the break of another gray day, whose dismal pall was never entirely burned away. The ride in the boat was cold, the river the color of a swamp. The marshland before Nkonié had been deserted by all except the anhingas, whose sodden feathers kept them shivering on their barren perches. This time I felt that the scene before us as we entered the lake was as Mary Kingsley had seen it: in the bright sunshine of two days before, it had been the lake that dominated in a landscape that invited participation—one wanted to plan picnics in its sculpted coves, to sail and swim in its blue waters; but with the light banished, the lake, drained now of all recognizable color, sank into insignificance, and it was the distant forest that held one's attention. Devoid of any welcoming glow, it had withdrawn into itself, presenting a front so inscrutable, so hopelessly alien, that for a human to enter into it seemed presumptuous and unthinkable. The whole world seemed to hold its breath while we floated like a twig on a wide world of water toward the island.

We found the chief sitting in his house, and from the moment we entered we knew something was wrong. He was sitting very stiffly in his chair, with one shoulder hunched up and his head held to one side. His wife was with him, a sturdy woman some years younger than her husband, and it was she who spoke to Jean.

"It is his heart," said Jean, translating.

"This has happened before," said the chief, now speaking for himself in his rapid-fire manner and evidently striving to brush this off as a matter of no importance. "A few days' pain—then gone."

It was evident that playing guide on a two-day hike was out of the question. I asked him if he wanted to go to the Schweitzer

Hospital, but he waved me aside, speaking energetically in Fang.

"He says he will take us to another *connaisseur,* in Azingo, and that there he can also get his medicine," said Jean. This sounded confusing; was there a clinic in Azingo? Jean translated my question to the chief.

"He says that we shall see the *connaisseur,* and he will get his medicine," Jean unhelpfully translated back. The chief's wife had disappeared to another house and returned with a raincoat and hat for her husband.

"I am well, I am well," he kept laughing. With his brimmed hat worn almost jauntily on one side of his tilted head, he reminded me more than ever of Bing Crosby. We found the magnificent man, still unclad and still holding his gun and cleaning rag, waiting outside the chief's house.

"He can't go," he told us angrily. "The chief is an old man."

•/•/•

"I HAVE SEEN many lakes in many countries," wrote Trader Horn, "but should anyone ask me which is the most beautiful I should answer Azingo." Azingo was vast, like a sea, its northern shore lost to view on a blurred horizon. Its contours could not be taken in at a glance as could Nkonié's, and its beauty thus depended on no particular set of features so much as an unaccountable atmosphere, a mood of self-contained peace, which prevailed over the uninspiring grayness of the flat day. An archipelago of tiny islands was embraced within these protective shores, each with its own village and character, so that a traveler could wander Odysseus-like over this brineless deep from miniature realm to realm.

We had first to obtain more petrol, as we would now have to take the chief back to his Nkonié village before returning to Azingo, an extra trip on which Jean had not been banking, and our first port of call was an island near the entrance to the lake. The low sandy cliff that arose from the island's insignificant beach appeared to have been barricaded by a mesh of something gray and twisted, which from a distance I took to be barbed wire, but which on coming closer I realized were the snarled roots of enormous upturned trees. We moored the boat to a sunken log and then scrambled up the cliff face, where I saw that many upturned trees lay sprawled full length along the ground. Old and dead, they had evidently been lying there for some while, no apparent effort having been made to clear them out of the way, although they took up an inconvenient amount of the island's small area. Rather, the villagers had adapted their lives to accommodate the trees, by sitting among the fallen branches and hanging their washing on the exposed roots. This gave the village a random, slovenly appearance; to enter it was like walking into a house and finding that tables and chairs that had been accidentally overturned years before were now being used as beds and bookcases. Most of the village seemed to be assembled among the branches when we arrived, and we were welcomed by a modest crowd.

Jean went off to see about petrol, the chief seated himself on one of the branches, and I was conducted to a more decorous seat, one of several sawn-off stumps some way apart from the fallen trees. Before I could claim this place, however, I was accosted by a man of abnormally large size, a true giant, who crashed heavily to his knees in front of me and began to kowtow by my feet. At length he rose, stiffly and clumsily, and with a gesture of deference so theatrical it could have been mocking, bowed and indicated the way to the stump. A little boy solemnly handed me a can of Orangina, which he said his mother had sent. The giant settled himself on a stump opposite me, from which vantage point he commenced to scrutinize me with an unaccountable look of increasing suspicion. I anticipated him and explained the purpose of my visit, giving him the benefit of my full spiel: that more than ninety years ago an Englishwoman had written a book about her travels in Gabon—a book that was still famous in her country—and that I was now making the same journey as this woman, in order to see what had changed and what had remained the same since she had written. As so often, I had Kingsley's book in hand, having found that people were usually interested in seeing its photographs. The giant turned the book over and looked at me more suspiciously than ever. Finally he spoke.

"What I want to know," he said loudly, and with the dramatic slowness of one who knows that what he says will be a *dénouement,* "what I want to know is, *if* you *already* made this trip ninety years ago, *why* are you doing it *again?"* And he looked around in triumph, as having unmasked me. My subsequent explanation carried little weight.

"Where are you from?" he next asked, regarding me very closely. I told him, and he asked if that country was in France. I said no.

"Then why are you speaking *French?"* he said in a menacing whisper, intimating that I had completely given my game away. When, however, I retorted that I had learned French in the same way that he had, his manner changed. It was a difficult language, he sighed. Did I too find it difficult? I considered and said it depended on whom I was talking with.

The giant leaned across his stump. "I will tell you what I find most difficult," he confided. "My problem with French is that my mouth cannot say the words."

Shortly thereafter, to my immense relief, Jean came to collect me, and after loading the boat with petrol and dried fish, we set out again. The grayness of the day had not lifted, but had brightened. The lake surface was extremely calm; one somehow felt that Azingo always harbored its waters from the harsher elements of the outside world.

The new *connaisseur*'s island also arose in a low blond cliff from shallow beach, but even before disembarking, one knew that this village would have an entirely different character. We beached the boat and walked up the cliff path, where the sound of voices and laughter could be heard coming from the village above us. An assembly was gathered in a well-swept compound and under the surrounding trees that looked out over the lake's gray-blue water from the cliff edge. The gathering was commanded—dominated—by a strapping, handsome, six-foot-tall woman of indeterminate age, who was dressed in a long blue traditional dress, the skirt of which was stretched tight across her confidently wide-spread legs. A baseball cap with the word *Captain* embroidered across its peak sat rakishly on her almost shaven head. This was Chief Josephine, and even without knowing that women could in fact be chiefs, one would have chosen her as the only possible candidate for this office. People were still drifting in from the other end of the island, and she greeted the newcomers with teasing warmth, playfully swatting at one old man and grabbing a youth around the neck and holding him headlocked in the crook of her arm. The island rang with her laughter.

Our small embassy was greeted with no apparent surprise, and we were immediately included in the assembly, two young men racing off to get additional chairs at the wave of Josephine's hand. The old chief from Nkonié sank into his chair, nodding at the many people who seemed to know him. Jean told me that someone had gone to get the *connaisseur,* who turned up minutes later. His shock of white hair indicated that he was old, but he looked otherwise remarkably fit. He was smoking a pipe and eyeing me thoughtfully.

Our old chief now held the floor and began to explain excitedly why we had come, repeatedly tapping his thin chest toward the end of his speech. He was answered by the *connaisseur,* who from his first appearance had aroused my misgivings. He struck me as a blusterer. Speaking in French, he explained for some long while that he was the only individual in all the lakes who knew the trail. He had a refrain, which he interjected after every few sentences: "The road is closed, it is I *(c'est moi)* who will open it."

We began the negotiations. "First he will say a price, then we will say one lower," Jean explained, which sounded straightforward enough. I had sensed that Jean also did not care for our prospective guide. The *connaisseur*'s opening suggestion of roughly ten thousand dollars was met by shrieks of laughter from his audience. The *connaisseur* had no sense of humor and stamped his foot for order. "I am the *connaisseur* of this route; the road is closed, and it is I who will open it."

By painful degrees, the price was at last lowered to roughly one hundred and seventy dollars, which was still exorbitant but, as was now clear, was the *connaisseur*'s bottom line. Someone went to Josephine's house for a cup of wine, and I was told to drink one sip and hand the cup to the *connaisseur,* who spat wine in three directions and then took a long swallow, after which everyone applauded. It was agreed that we would take four men in all.

Jean turned to me. "Madame," he said, drawing himself up very straight, "I would like to be one of those men. I would like to finish my commission."

The only remaining detail to be fixed was the date of our departure; as we had our supplies with us, I was ready to go at once, but the *connaisseur* said that he could not leave for three days; he was responsible for conducting a festival on another of Azingo's islands for a relative who had died a year ago. "There will be dancing for two days, and it is I *(c'est moi)* who will conduct it."

As it was now late in the day, it was agreed that we would spend the night in Josephine's village and return to Lambaréné the following morning: I had succeeded in persuading the old chief to go to the Schweitzer Hospital—or at least, I believed at the time that I had succeeded. In the meanwhile, the chief said, he would get some medicine here. Most of the people had dispersed, while we remained sitting under the trees. An old woman dressed in a drab brown *pagne* and headscarf and a man who had been in the assembly came over to greet the old chief, saying that they had brought his medicine. The chief stood up and matter-of-factly took off his shirt before going over to the nearest hut, where he reached above his head with both hands and grasped one of the cross beams of the overhanging roof. Stretched between the ground and cross beam, with his thin chest exposed, he was approached by the man from the assembly, who suddenly darted forward and cut a square around the old chief's heart, working so rapidly that I never saw the knife blade, but only the thin lines of welling blood. The old woman then took something out of a leaf-package and rubbed it into the wounds while the old chief sharply drew in his breath between his teeth, which he had clenched in a frozen grin. The medicine, I learned on inquiring afterward, was a mixture of chewed tobacco and lime.

"Ahh." The old chief smiled with satisfaction and proclaimed himself to be much better. "I can feel it getting strong," he said, thumping his chest again and again.

As the evening drew on, Josephine invited me into her home, which was made up of a complex of several houses; the largest contained her well-appointed living and dining area, a small house immediately behind was used exclusively as a bedroom, and two small huts contained the kitchen and bathroom. Chief Josephine's prosperity was evident in every well-scoured, well-furbished inch of her property. Her ample furniture was all in good condition, and the main house boasted an enormous sideboard stocked with glistening china and glass. The bathroom, in which a large clay urn had been filled for my shower, was also the repository of Chief Josephine's stockpile of petrol drums. She had her own boat, and she told me that when she got tired of her island, she could go to Lambaréné; and when she got tired of Lambaréné, she could return to her island. The bedroom was virtually filled by a large platform bed with an extremely deep mattress, which had been made up for me with well-washed white sheets and lace-edged pillowcases. Chief Josephine, like the other women in the village, did her own washing on the river rocks, and her own ironing with her heavy old-fashioned iron, which she filled with embers from the fire. It was also she who had prepared the delicious dinner that was served to me that evening, a rich fish stew with French bread, which I ate at her low, lap-level table in the light of two oil lamps. I was concerned that I had ousted her from her bedroom, but Josephine only laughed and told me that she would sleep with her sister, who lived down the way. She had never had a husband, although she had several children.

"I have not needed one," she said. She had become chief on her father's death, and her eldest son would in turn inherit the title from her. The village was justifiably proud of their chief. On numerous occasions, someone would nudge me and say, "Our chief is a woman," in a tone of marked respect.

Also visiting the village was a relative of a relative of Josephine, a young man who had come from Corisco Island, a small Spanish-speaking island off the coast of north Gabon and southern Guinea. He and another young man joined me toward the end of my meal, inquiring for the most part about the difficulties of learning English. The Corisco Islander, however, grew quieter and quieter, and I became aware with some discomfort that he was staring at my head. Finally, he could restrain himself no longer and reached out to stroke my hair, dropping his hand as if he had received an electric shock when his friend sitting opposite angrily growled words of reproach in Fang.

"We are going," said the friend, clearly feeling that matters were getting out of hand.

Outside, the lake was lost in darkness. Lanterns and cooking fires glowed all along the main sandy road in a constellation of friendly light. A few people could be seen sitting in their doorways smoking and talking, but most of the village had retired to their houses early in the evening. I washed with the pitcher of lake water and then turned in. Josephine's mosquito curtain was made of a muslin sheet, not netting, which enveloped her great bed like tapestries, through which the lantern shone in a mellow haze.

I slept deeply without once waking until dawn, when the whole village seemed to awake as one; somewhere down the line of houses, I imagined, Chief Josephine had yawned and stretched her great limbs, and her movements had reverberated through the thin walls of the closely adjacent houses, waking the next household, who woke the next, and so on down the street in a wave of stirring humanity. The morning was a blue mist when I came outside, water and sky not yet disposed into their separate spheres. A table had been placed beside the chairs under the trees that overlooked the lake. Josephine came out with a thermos of coffee and loaves of bread, and having seen to breakfast she went down to the lake, balancing a bale of laundry on her head. Later, her cheerful, hearty singing resounded from the beach.

We left Josephine's island with a pledge from the *connaisseur* that we would start for Akondjo four days hence. Having returned to Nkonié to pick up the old chief's wife, we set out again for Lambaréné. When we reached the familiar stretch of river by Andèndé, it had become a billowing day, the water steel-blue and feathered by the wind, the sky bulging like a spinnaker (it has always surprised me that Mary Kingsley nowhere dwells on Lambaréné's beauty). Jean dropped me off at the reedy beach below the mission and then crossed over to the Schweitzer Hospital with the chief and his wife.

At the mission, I was warmly welcomed by the Sisters on my unexpected return: I think now that at the bottom of my heart I had known all along that the final good-bye had yet to be said.

Sister Carmen came to the door of my old room that evening.

"Tonight we dine together," she said excitedly. There was almost an air of triumph in the festive meal. The Sisters commiserated with me on my setback but said repeatedly that they were relieved I had not made the walk through the forest.

"But I am still going to do it," I reminded them; and to my extreme annoyance I could tell from the unconcerned air with which they received this repeated protestation that they simply did not believe me.

·/·/·

JEAN AND I had arranged to meet as usual at the beach below the main road, but on the morning of our departure he turned up at the mission looking gray and strained. His daughter had become seriously ill with malaria, and he had taken her from his village near Samkita to the Schweitzer Hospital the day before: "Madame, I don't know what to do. I feel I must be with my child, but I don't want you to go alone into the forest with that *connaisseur*—if it had been *our* chief there would be no problem." He offered to take me to Nkonié and leave me there, but he was not happy with this option.

Neither was I, but I did not see that I had any alternative but to proceed as planned. We set out in Jean's boat to get petrol at the floating station that lay offshore from the market. While the boat was being filled, I went ashore to make a few purchases and unexpectedly ran into the Corisco Islander. Pleasantly, I told him that I would soon be joining him again in Azingo. He looked uncomfortable.

"You are really coming today?" he asked, and I replied—somewhat sharply—that this had been the agreement. He paused.

"Ah, I do not think you will find the *connaisseur* there," he said at length. The *connaisseur* had not returned from the island where he had gone to be master of ceremonies of the dance: it was not known when he would be back.

"I do not think he will be going *en brousse* when he returns; there will have been much drinking."

I beckoned for Jean to come over, and he nodded slowly and self-righteously when he heard the developments. "Truly, fifty thousand francs is too much money to have asked. I said I did not trust him." He told me flatly that I should not go—advice that was not contravened by the Corisco Islander. And wearily, I agreed.

There were now two options open to me: I could go directly to Kango, a town on the estuary from where I could rely on getting a ride *up* the Remboué as far as Akondjo, thereby at least being assured of making the river journey, albeit in the opposite direction; or I could persist in trying to reach the Remboué from this side, cutting into it from somewhere along the main road that led to Kango. According to my map, this latter option was entirely possible: from a large roadside village called Four Place, a forest road led directly to a chantier called Sainte-Croix, which was situated on the shores of the upper Remboué. Getting to Four Place would be unproblematic—and surely once there, I could somehow get a ride to the chantier and the river.

This time my farewell to the Sisters had the pain of finality. They received the news of my change of plans with the unsurprised acceptance of those who had all along expected their prayers to be answered. Jean insisted on waiting until he had seen me safely off in a vehicle of his choosing. Once I was in the taxi, he loudly demanded a piece of paper and pencil, and when the driver good-naturedly obliged, he ostentatiously wrote down the taxi's license number. My last sight of Jean was of him standing in the dust of the departing taxi van, straight-backed and gallant as ever.

The old chief, Jean had told me before I left, had never gone to the Schweitzer Hospital but had used the money I had given him for his treatment to buy tobacco and groceries; he believed that he had been cured and, in any case, did not trust European medicine. As for the wily *connaisseur* of Lake Azingo, had he ever intended to make the trek? Did he in fact know the route? Ultimately, I suspect that Kingsley and I learned the same lesson, namely that it is one's choice of guides that determines one's itinerary. I made many plans that came to nought; Mary Kingsley's overland trek may never have been planned—but at least it had happened.

·/·/·

WHEN I ARRIVED at Four Place, a village meeting was in the process of settling a difficult divorce case: a wife who had gone off with another man had returned to her husband, who for his part now wanted a divorce. At issue was the bridal fee that the husband had paid his wife's family some years ago, in this case one hundred and fifty thousand CFA francs, or approximately five hundred dollars. The man maintained that the fee should be returned, as it was his wife's infidelity that had forced the divorce; the woman's relatives claimed that the man had no right to reimbursement, as the divorce was solely of his choosing. The villagers were congregated in the shade of an open shelter that stood close to the road, a little in front of the chief's house. Each disputing side was allowed to give their account of the case and to make their demands for satisfaction: it was the chief's job to determine an equitable settlement that, however disgruntled either party might be, he could be assured would be respected. When I arrived, the chief momentarily suspended the meeting so as to escort me personally to his house while the assembly turned as a body on their rows of benches to stare after us. The chief was stout, bald, and dressed in a gray safari suit. He exuded patriarchal power. From the moment of my arrival he treated me like an errant teenage daughter.

"Don't go wandering around the village. You stay here until I return," he ordered, after he had led me into his very large, dark, and almost furnitureless house. The interior walls were made of plywood panels, the floor of cement. Two posters, of the pope and President Bongo, were its only decoration. A table and a few chairs stood by the front window, and an extremely uncomfortable, unpadded sofa with a slatted wooden back like a garden bench was pushed up against one wall. It was in the latter that the chief placed me before hurrying back to his meeting. The chief's wife entered and, having greeted me, wordlessly set about working her way through an immense pile of ironing, using a flatiron that had to be continually refilled with embers from a fire outside.

The first of what was to be an unending stream of adolescent boys made his appearance, walking confidently into the chief's gloomy house as if it were his own, and eventually settling himself on the arm of the bench. A little boy with a crippled leg lurched through the doorway and remained for some time leaning against the wall and staring into the street. A knot of very dusty babies rolled in from one of the other rooms and continued to roll and fight together on the floor. The chief's wife ironed on, the pile of impossibly smooth linen rising higher and higher as she carefully folded each finished article with hands that were stretched to a size out of all proportion to her thin body. More youths came in, each perching or sitting on some part of the bench. Of course, they wanted to talk about America.

"If, for example, a young man wanted to study biology, for example, to become, for example, a doctor, let us say—could he go to the U.S.A. and work, for example, while going to school?"

"Where can one learn English if one does not live in Libreville? Are there books that tell you how to speak English?"

"I have a book a Peace Corps volunteer gave to me; if I get it will you read it?"

Strutting back and forth in yellow satin trousers, sometimes with a blaring radio, sometimes with a newspaper, always with something calculated to gain attention, was a youth who asked questions of a very different type.

"Is it true that in America white women sleep with *les noirs*? If I go there, could I sleep with a white woman?" he asked with a smirk. I replied that there was always that possibility, when he grew up. The chief's wife had finished her ironing and had begun to sweep the floor when the chief returned from his meeting.

"Oh ho! *Les garçons!*" he exclaimed, regarding the crowded bench from the doorway and flashing a look of unconcealed suspicion at me. "Out, out, everybody out," he shouted. "I am getting my eldest son to *promenade* with you around the town," he told me, wagging a finger in my face. "You are NOT walking here and there on your own." In the meantime, a group of men had gathered outside to discuss the problem of getting to the Remboué.

Yes, they said, a forest chantier lay on the Remboué as my map had indicated, and it was possible to get there from Four Place. *But,* it would be difficult to find a local boat to take me from there to Akondjo. *However,* the chantier was managed by a European man who had his own motorboat. *But,* the European man was unfortunately on holiday in Port-Gentil. *However,* he had left a manager, who would certainly take me (because I was also European—this was the implicit premise) to Akondjo, if I supplied the petrol. *But,* no bush taxi would make the trip to the chantier in the first place, on account of the fearful condition of the forest road and of its being so out of the way; and no one in the village had a car. The only chance of getting there would be to catch a ride with one of the lumber trucks that evidently regularly passed by the village in the early morning on their way into the forest. This the chief thought he could arrange.

So far, then, so good. And once at Akondjo—would I find anyone there to take me to the estuary? No, there was no one there. Really, *no one* at Akondjo at all? "No one," the crowd shook their heads in unison.

"But you could perhaps get a ride with hunters who go there," said the chief. I was confused: there were then *some* people there, who even, it seemed, had boats?

"Yes," said the crowd, nodding their heads in unison. Gradually I realized there had been a confusion of terminology. I had asked if there would be anyone *(quelqu'un)* at Akondjo; the answer was no, there could only be Africans.

Pierre, the chief's eldest son, normally worked in Port-Gentil but had been forced to take a "vacation" from his employment for the duration of the economic crisis. He suggested we take a walk down the length of the village, which extended for a couple of miles on either side of the main road. Once beyond the area where the chief lived, the village street dipped and the houses, interspersed with banana trees, stood on considerably lower ground. The houses were built of flimsy-looking two-by-fours with corrugated iron roofs, and through their open doors one could see their few articles of furniture—the rickety chairs and tables covered with oilcloth, standing on cement or beaten-dirt floors. Four Place, like so many villages, was a regroupment of what had once been the distinct settlements of two different tribes. No, said Pierre, there was no tension between them, but they kept their distance out of respect for their different traditions. The Fang had a house for Bwiti initiates, for example, which the Myené took care to avoid.

Everyone we passed, on the road or at a distance, came out of their way to greet us and to shake my hand. We met with one of Pierre's sisters by another father, as she was on her way home. She was nineteen, pregnant, and had a two-year-old baby on her back. Women here marry from age fifteen on, Pierre said, adding that they had to marry young because their childbearing years were over by the time they were in their mid-twenties (research conducted by CIRMF suggests that the prevalence of sexually transmitted diseases is responsible for this widespread early infertility). Yes, he said serenely, the women had a hard time; they did much work. They worked from when they were little girls and were sent out to gather panniers of wood until "the age when they were tired." I asked Pierre what work the average village man did. He considered.

"In the dry season, they clear the land for the plantations [which are worked year-round by the women] and of course it is they who build the houses." Houses have to be rebuilt roughly every five to ten years, "depending on how well they were made." No, the men did not work as hard as the women, he allowed. "But it is our way."

An old woman was calling to us from her doorway. "Are you going to walk past me without a greeting? Are you not going to introduce me to your guest?" As we turned off the road and down the steep bank that sloped toward her house, Pierre cautioned me, "She has been drinking, but we must be social in the village." We walked on a bit more before he added, again, "It is our way."

The old woman, tall, gaunt, and dressed in dark rags of no identifiable color, cackled with delight when we entered her bare and filthy home. "I will get some beer," she said and disappeared into a side room. The woman's granddaughter slouched in with her own baby and sat quietly in a corner, watching us. The grandmother entered and handed us each a bottle.

"Drink, drink!" she urged heartily. She had brought a bottle for herself and, suddenly lifting her skirt, she pretended to thrust it between her legs, cackling raucously. "She is old," said Pierre mildly. The granddaughter, apparently out of boredom, had begun to pinch and slap her child, and was soon joined in this activity by her grandmother. A crowd of children who had been drawn to the doorway as irresistibly as splinters of iron to a magnet stood in a watchful throng exactly on the threshold. Outside it was growing dusky, and through the doorway above the darkening silhouettes of the children, I could see the red and yellow streaks of a violent sunset. The two women had at last succeeded in making the baby cry and were now convulsed with laughter. Pierre suggested that we continue with our walk as far as his home, where he lived with his mother, and then return to the chief.

In the compound before his house, a young boy was brandishing a machete among a crowd of fighting children while a tiny boy dressed in a shirt but no trousers circled wide-eyed around them. Gibbering to itself in the doorway was a pet monkey that had been tied to a post with a piece of dusty rope. Pierre's mother was not to be seen: *"La vache,"* said Pierre softly as we turned away.

Occasionally the headlights of a truck rounding a curve projected alarming yellow wedges of light and veering shadows across the huts and bamboo trees, before swinging back in alignment with the road. The chief, Pierre was telling me as we walked back in near total darkness while the trucks roared by, had many children in the village by many different mothers. The chief was also the shopkeeper and bartender of Four Place's main shop and bar. It was in the latter capacity that we found him serving on our return.

"Where have you been?" shouted the chief over the noise, springing out from behind the counter as we walked in. I said I had been walking with Pierre. "Why did you keep her out after dark?" he next demanded, turning upon his son. The same group of young men who had kept me company earlier now emerged from the shadows of the dark bar, which seemed to be crowded with most of the village's male population. Music was blaring, and it was difficult to hear anything that was being said. The circle around me was suddenly beaten aside by the chief, who almost grabbed me by the scruff of my neck and marched me to the back of the room behind the counter where he stood.

"Bring a chair, bring a chair!" he bellowed and wiped the heavy perspiration from his face with a handkerchief.

"But she is lonely," protested one of the young men, after the chief had seated me at his elbow. "Look! You are making her unhappy!"

"Lonely? I want her to be lonely," stormed the chief. Pierre had come forward to say that his mother would be happy to give me dinner. The chief turned on me.

"Absolutely *no!* NO! You eat, you sleep here, under MY roof," he thundered. Shortly afterward, he abruptly closed up shop, brutally killing the music, slamming the cooler shut, and flicking off the few feeble lights that had kept the room from utter darkness. Deaf to the protests and shouts of surprise from his disappointed clients, he grimly escorted me outside.

"We are going to have dinner," he informed me.

The chief's wife had quietly prepared a feast. Dishes of meat, spicy fish, cooked plaintains, tubercules, banana "bread," and manioc completely covered the table by the window, where the chief and I now took our seats. The rest of the family sat around the wooden sofa and waited for us to finish our meal, as they would eat whatever was left over.

The chief seemed to relax now that he had me safely in his sight and within the walls of his own home. "And what does your husband think of you taking this trip?" he asked with fatherly concern. "Is he not angry that you are so far away for several months?"

Countering the barrage of questions I had earlier met with from the youths, I had found it easier to lie and say yes, I was married. I now paid for my dishonesty by being forced to fabricate careful answers to specific questions in order to maintain this fiction: my husband was a businessman (safe and respectable) and while of course we missed each other (traditional family values) he was immensely proud that I was doing this project (independence in a woman is not subversive).

"Are you not worried that he is seeing another woman while you are away?" asked the chief, who had remained unmoved by this portrait of my marriage. The extended family members on the sofa looked suddenly alert at this interesting turn in the conversation. I was not worried at all, I replied in the complacent manner of a well-settled matron. I trusted my husband, as he trusted me. Unwittingly, I had floundered onto precisely the point that most troubled the chief.

"And how can your husband trust you?" he demanded, in a

tone of voice that was inoffensive only because it was so clearly paternal, "when here you are, far from your home, traveling alone and away from your husband's eyes?" I replied somewhat priggishly that my husband trusted me because he knew me.

"But . . . but . . . excuse me, but do you not find it hard to go so long without a man? I mean—well, when one is hungry, one eats; when one is thirsty, one drinks . . ."

After dinner, the chief's wife conducted me by the light of a kerosene lantern to their bedroom, where she had prepared a bath for me. A white sheet had been spread on the cement floor under a large metal tub of lukewarm water. I washed by the light of the lantern that she left on an overturned box and shortly afterward went to bed in the bedroom next door, from which two of the children had been evacuated. The chief bade me good night, and his final words filled me with hope for the morrow.

"We shall start off tomorrow for the lumberyard at seven o'clock."

Two days later, from my now customary place on the wooden sofa, I was conducting what had become an ongoing English lesson for the youth of Four Place. One of the young men had brought the book the Peace Corps worker had given him. The book's opening dialogue was about a brother and a sister who were going to Holloway Home for the holidays, where they would learn riding and tennis. I had slept fairly well on my first night, in spite of the racket made by the very large rats that circled the roof beams continuously and at top speed, and had woken up early so as to be ready for departure at seven. At noon, the chief suggested that I plan on leaving the following morning, explaining that no trucks would be going to the lumberyard that day. On the same day, I had received additional information concerning the boat that, according to the plan, was supposed to take me to Akondjo: a man in the village who was a friend of the watchman who guarded the boat of his European employer in his absence said that he knew from his friend that the master had taken the motor of his boat with him to go fishing in Port-Gentil. *But* he thought there might be ordinary pirogues at the lumberyard.

The chief, who had been present when I received this new information, must have seen my face brighten at the expectation of another traditional pirogue ride. "Absolutely NO! No paddles. And *I* myself will go with you to make sure."

During most of the two days in which the truck did not appear, the divorce case outside dragged on and on. Within the house, the chief's wife continued to wash and iron and sweep, the children to roll on the floor, the young man to ask questions about America and the West. Did I know Michael Jackson? How much was a fare to the U.S.A.? Why did I have no children?

In the late morning of the second day, when the chief's house was relatively quiet, a woman came and stood in the doorway to cry in silence, wiping her face from time to time with the back of her worn hands. The chief's wife came and without a word put an arm around her, and the two of them were joined by another woman from the street, who wiped the crying woman's eyes with her own stretched-out hands, and chucked her under the chin until she smiled.

Another woman, with deep folds in her face as well as a general look of weariness, stopped by the house and spoke with one of the youths who sat glued to the sofa.

"That was my mother," he said when she had left. This surprised me because she had looked unusually old by village standards to be the mother of a sixteen-year-old boy, and I took the liberty of asking the son how old she was.

"Thirty-one," he replied—exactly my age.

Usually the young men had disappeared by the time the chief returned from overseeing the meeting, or from managing his shop, but on the afternoon of the third day he surprised them by appearing unexpectedly in the doorway.

"NO! NO *garçons* in this house. Out, OUT!" he raged and descended upon them, wielding his fly whisk. "OUT! They are like flies around the honey pot! OUT!" he cried, swatting his whisk in all directions until he had cleared the room. I began to explain that we had been practicing English, but the words died in my throat. The chief had closed both doors in the room and was energetically barricading the windows. He left without a word, and I sat motionless on the sofa, almost in the dark, until he reappeared propelling before him a young woman, who had obviously been dragged without warning from her own house and was still smoothing her dress and adjusting her wig of chic modern curls.

"Converse with her!" barked the chief to the woman, seating her on a stool opposite me.

"How do you do?" asked the woman, recovering herself as the chief stormed outside again, closing the door behind him.

The woman had been chosen as a chaperone both for her respectability and for the fact that she was young and "modern." Like Pierre, she had worked in Port-Gentil, as an assistant in a clothes boutique, until given temporary leave of absence for the duration of *la crise.* She commiserated with me about my predicament.

"It is not your fault. In the days of your woman, it was easy. You turned up in a village and if you were white—well. You organized what you wanted."

Once again, I wearily took stock of my situation. Once again, there were many important questions for which I despaired of ever obtaining answers. Did lumber trucks *still* go regularly to the lumberyard—even when the manager was on holiday and even in the ongoing *crise?* If I did manage to get there and found only paddle canoes, could I count on finding a boatman willing to undergo the long trip to Akondjo—from where he would, of course, have to paddle back again against the current? Would I in fact find anyone with boats at Akondjo?

And there were other, more pressing questions: how much longer could I continue to take advantage of the chief's hospitality? How long continue to eat his food, displace his children from their bedroom, and generally disrupt his household's life? Suddenly, I felt the need of friendly advice and I abruptly asked my companion what she would do in my position.

She was silent for a while. "I do not think this truck that you say is coming will be here so soon," she said cautiously. "Sometimes people say things will happen because they wish to be polite and they do not wish to disappoint you," she continued more boldly, and then added, echoing Pierre, "It is their way."

I excused myself and went outside to find the chief, who was occupied in breaking up a fight that had arisen in his shop. When order had been restored, he joined me outside in his dusty road-side yard. I told him that I was concerned that the truck might not come for a long time, and thought it better to go to the estuary by road.

"And go *up* the Remboué to Akondjo?" he suggested with an alacrity that betrayed that this was an option he had long men-tally rehearsed. He took a handkerchief from the breast pocket of his safari suit and mopped his brow. "I think that would be the best decision," he said with evident relief.

A small boy was commissioned to wait by the roadside so as to flag down a passing car or truck. I had packed and was waiting on what I had come to think of as my sofa, surrounded for the last time by my young companions. There was a cry from the road, and the little boy came running in to tell me that I had a ride.

"They are Europeans," the chief told me outside, nodding at the car with great approval.

·/·/·

KANGO LIES only forty-odd miles from Four Place by road, located toward the extreme eastern tail of the Gabon Estuary. There are more convenient places from which to enter the Remboué—the small town of Donguila, for example, off of which Mary Kingsley's boat had moored on the night it reached the estuary, is situated across the bay, almost directly opposite the river's mouth. Kango, however, was the only place with petrol, its position just off the important Bifoun-Libreville road ensuring that it is usually kept in supply.

Kango had the soft humid air and clear bright colors of a Caribbean town. At the bottom of the main street lay the blue estuary waters, and green banana trees and palms flashed and rattled continuously in the wind blown in from the bay. The main road that led from the Libreville turnoff to the waterfront was in the process of being repaved, and even the newly poured black tar seemed to shine and glisten with striking brightness. Here too was a sight unique in Africa: the workmen laying the road were European, not African. This was due less to the usual shortage of Gabonese labor than to the fact that when French companies garner particularly attractive contracts from the Gabonese government, they are able to provide lucrative work for their own employees.

At one time, some ambitious entrepreneur must have seen Kango in the same Caribbean light that I had and dreamed of building a prosperous resort nestled in this protected niche of the bay. At least, that is what I had to assume when I first set eyes on the luxurious but completely vacant hotel that was perched on heights overlooking the estuary waters and encircled by its own park land. When I arrived, the hotel's only other guests were checking out, an elderly couple equipped with telescopes and binoculars who had come for a weekend of bird watching. The hotel manager was an almost annoyingly efficient Austrian who spoke clipped but impeccable English. He took such professional pride in being able to anticipate one's every wish and whim that it was virtually impossible for me to speak a sentence without his finishing it for me. He moved restlessly through his establishment, tidying papers, pinching dead leaves off plants, straightening tables, and aligning silverware. Pulsing through his every gesture was the frustration of all who are doomed not to shine in use. His wife, who was from Martinique, seemed more placid and less discontent. Their previous hotel posting had been on the Ivory Coast.

"Oh, it was much better, very different," said the proprietor, who was too well trained to vent his frustration on a guest but masked it under a tight, professional smile. "On the Ivory Coast there was life, there were things to do!"

Getting to Akondjo was to be no problem. The hotel owned its own boat and employed its own boatman, in anticipation, no doubt, of a busy trade in organized outings and tours of the estuary, of popular excursions to the river channels and mangrove forests. Pierre, the piroguer, was small and round, with open honest eyes and an earnest face. I met him at the hotel's private dock, where he carefully outlined the program of our outing to Akondjo on the following day.

"We cannot leave today, because it is too late. It is a full day's trip. We shall leave tomorrow early in the morning; you may choose a time, but it is better to leave early. We shall have to stop first in the town for petrol; you may sit in the boat, or by the shop while you wait—it will not take long, and you do not have to be concerned with the petrol—that is for me to do. Then we shall depart. It is a journey of about four hours in each direction." Pierre must have had considerable prior experience with catering to Europeans, I thought, perhaps in the heady days before *la crise*. Why can't we go now? How long does it take? I thought you said we were going directly from the hotel? Am I supposed to hang around the station while you get petrol?— How many impatient questions lay behind this careful, almost anxious exposition of our upcoming trip?

From the balcony outside my room, I watched a spectacular sunset, as if the heavens—like everything else at Kango—were pulling out all stops to prove that they knew what was called for in a fashionable resort at this hour: after the light had been appropriately lowered, a bank of clouds properly compiled in shades of light and darkness was marshaled across the sky that moments before had been absolutely clear. From behind this variegated screen, the sun beamed itself with all its might before retiring gracefully below the horizon line of forest and then water.

We set out early the next morning and proceeded exactly according to Pierre's plan. The shops that lined the road leading to the petrol station were already bustling: there was throughout Kango a marked degree of alertness and activity, and one wondered if the invigorating wind that blew in from the estuary had not swept away with it the dust and torpor that usually characterizes a small town of this kind. Many of the men going up and down the steps of their shops and houses were dressed in shorts and white undershirts, as if they had not waited to dress themselves completely before getting on with their day. The "station" where we bought our petrol was a concrete shop with a storeroom of drums, kept under lock and key by a brawny woman in a flowing turquoise caftan and turban. Pierre did his errands quickly, being careful to give me an advance explanation of each.

At eight o'clock we pulled away from Kango's waterfront. The overcast sky was the color of mottled alabaster and shed a strange opaque gray light, and from erratic cloud breaks, long shafts of sunlight broke through to spotlight random patches of the forest. Ahead of us the windblown water was choppy and silver. The forest that enfolded the estuary was here reduced to surprising insignificance, and did not tower above the water on strategic cliffs or stand grandly back on its own intervening beach, but rose somewhat feebly directly from the water, reduced, for all its many dark acres, to only a shallow shadow line between the agitated, vital salt waves of the estuary and the looming sky.

The entrance to the Remboué was wide and rough, but gradually the estuary waves gave way to the smoother water of the river, which from here until Akondjo would pass between mangrove forests that claimed its either shore. The roots of the mangrove trees lay above the black ooze of mud along the banks in splayed stilts and confused coils and whorls, like rolls of stored chicken wire. Long vines descended from the upper branches of the forest into the water, dangling loose like sheets from a yardarm or, if they had somehow become anchored in the river, stretched taut like a lyre or bow string.

The true color of the river lurking beneath the deep green reflection of the mangrove foliage appeared to be dun yellow. Strewn across its almost oily-looking surface, swaths of yellow mango pollen formed bold calligraphic patterns. The occasionally interspersed patches of equatorial forest appeared to have been crammed with as much variety of green and texture as their meager allotments would allow, as if to present a showcase of what "real" forest could look like: ferns, raffia, long-stemmed palms and other trees, exploded from their bland surroundings in astonishing bouquets. The mangrove forest manifested none of the rich variety of equatorial forest, having nothing to display save its unremarkable foliage of dull, leathery leaves. And yet the mangroves were not tedious: there were breaks between the trees, intriguing avenues which appeared to open onto clear areas behind the swamp, and one always had the impression that a radically different terrain might lie behind, just out of view, that once past the tangle of roots one might stumble on a hidden park or meadow. Nonetheless, it was difficult to imagine this forest harboring wildlife—the scanty foliage and lack of undergrowth of any kind among the tangled coils of roots that looked like brush or deadwood did not strike one as a habitat providing protection or sustenance for anything other than snails. Occasionally, when passing close to shore, one caught a warm whiff of the decaying vegetation that festers in the swamp's black mud and water. The very few villages one saw were usually glimpsed down corridors in the forest, where the river had cut a lateral channel into the swamp. On the firmer ground of the right bank, abandoned chantiers sat in the wide, bald clearings they had despoiled; in a few deserted villages, the remaining huts were slipping quietly into the oblivion of high grass and foliage that had overgrown their clearings.

It had been a long while since we had passed any inhabited village or any sign of humanity when we finally came to Akondjo, another overgrown clearing, opposite a bend in the river. I wondered how I would have felt if I had arrived on these muddy shores at twilight after a two-day hike, confronted with my first sight of the mangrove forest wall on the facing shore.

Pierre pointed ahead to indicate that he was going to land on the black, muddy rim of the clearing. The boat ground to a stop with its bow in a patch of long-stemmed reeds. We disembarked, taking long strides to avoid the black morass of mud. A thicket of close-pressed raffia and palm lay to our right; standing out from the blur of overgrowth were red and yellow hibiscus, a "cultivated" shrub that thrives suspiciously well in places that humans have deserted.

Pierre was looking around with an air of eager anticipation. "There is a big mango tree past the palms—you can see the tops of its yellow flowers. And I can show you where the houses and paths were."

Had Pierre once played tour guide in Akondjo? I asked him how he knew the area so well.

"Madame! This used to be my home!" A sheet of rusted corrugated iron lay flatly on the ground besides some stumps. "This was my uncle's house. It was a big house—my uncle was a wealthy man. A path led here—you can see—to the plantations." We walked single file through the grass that at times stood above our heads. "Under this mango tree, my mother was born. That is what I was told. Of course it would not have been so big." Pierre looked up into its dark glossy leaves. "I too can remember this tree from when I was a child." We went farther inland toward the forest that ringed the clearing, arriving at a wide area where the grass was low and hedged by dark foliage: a place surely to hold feasts, to dance. . . .

Pierre stood with his hands on his hips and looked around. "It is not so overgrown as I would have thought. Perhaps the elephants keep the grass away," he said. There were elephant droppings all about the clearing and even near the place where we had landed. "Yes, they come at night. You can hear them tearing, tearing the trees," he said, stretching his short arm in front of him to represent an elephant's trunk. "They knock down the trees, they damage our houses, they spoil the plantations. . . ." Yes, there had once been a road through the forest to Lambaréné, he nodded when I asked. A bush trail had led from the village to a nearby chantier, where the road began. The road had been big enough for trucks to use, and it had come out near Lake Azingo. Once people used to go to Azingo for food and supplies; now, of course, they went to Kango.

"I took the road with my mother when I was a boy," he said. The chantier had been abandoned in 1970, and the chantier road had not been used since then and was closed over. "No one knows the route now; it would be very hard," he said. Why, I asked, had the people left Akondjo?

"Because of the elephants. They destroyed things and people were afraid." He looked around. "But it would be a nice place to live."

We made our way back to the boat along the trail we had

partly cleared. The scene ahead of me—the green water through the rushes and the mangrove forest on the other shore—was as I would have seen it if I had walked here out of the forest. Perhaps, I thought, it would not have seemed so dismal as I had at first imagined. One could see now from the ripples in the water that the river current was very swift beyond the shore where we had landed, and its surface strewn with bubbles, which perhaps at twilight, when the light softened, would have become gold. The long-stemmed reeds, I noticed, were capped with dry, yellow-white blossoms, like narcissi that have just begun to fade. It may be that more birds would come this way at evening. A boat might have appeared at dusk and offered me a ride.

Above all I might have seen the mangrove forest in the darkness, as had Mary Kingsley when she sailed downstream on the final leg of her arduous journey, homeward bound.

"Indeed, much as I have enjoyed life in Africa, I do not think I ever enjoyed it to the full as I did on those nights dropping down the Rembwé," she had written. "The great, black, winding river with a pathway in its midst of frosted silver where the moonlight struck it: on each side the ink-black mangrove walls, and above them the band of star and moonlit heavens that the walls of mangrove allowed one to see. . . ."

Near the mouth of the river we passed lumbering fishing boats that were painted yellow and red, or black and green, like old-fashioned gypsy wagons. A few boats had been moored within channels in the mangrove swamp, where the men perched on platforms to coil their nets and clean their fish against the backdrop of great, naked mangrove roots that rose above their heads. When we reached the estuary, the sun seemed to bear down on the marbled clouds that had deadlocked the sky all day and thus succeeded in penetrating them at last. A muted, diffused light was spread over the blue-gray waves.

In the middle of the estuary a large boat was anchored while its crew hauled in their nets. Pierre watched them, then turned resignedly to face ahead. His thoughts were easy to read: The trip had gone well, but Europeans can be so unpredictable! The

Madame may get angry if I use her petrol to buy my fish. Better to stay quiet. I called back to him from the bow of the boat to ask if he didn't think we should stop to buy something for dinner, and his face brightened with pleasure: truly, there was no knowing these Europeans!

The boatmen were Nigerians, far from home in their thick sailor jerseys and gum boots. The bottom of the boat shimmered with thrashing silver-scaled sardines and a larger fish that had the long snout and tiny teeth of a pike. Crab and jellyfish were brusquely prized and disentangled from the heavy nets. With wide grins, the fishermen helped Pierre carefully choose his fish and then waved to us as we pulled away and left them. The hotel manager had been insistent that we return before dark, and we arrived only just on schedule; the shore and forest fringe had already melted into the dusk when we docked at the bottom of the hotel's sloping garden.

•/•/•

THROUGHOUT my travel in Gabon, I had hoped that somewhere I might come across someone who had heard of Mary Kingsley through stories that had been passed down by his or her ancestors. Oral traditions are tenacious, and Kingsley had made her trip not so very long ago; it was not impossible that somewhere a great-grandchild of one of her boatmen or porters might have heard of this unusual white woman traveling alone several generations ago. But individuals, villages, and whole tribes shift and scatter; the same factors that had caused the disappearance of the interior forest trails have also ensured that people today do not necessarily live in the villages of their ancestors. Nonetheless, if traditions of Kingsley survived anywhere, Akondjo would have been one of the most likely places; it had at least continued to exist into the last decade.

No, said Pierre, he had never heard of the woman who had made this trip. But, he exclaimed, with sudden inspiration, he could direct me to the oldest person who had once lived in Akondjo. The man's name was André, and I would find him in Libreville.

"I will draw you a map to find him," he said. He did, and it looked like this:

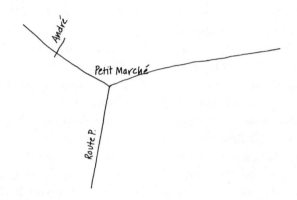

Back in Libreville, in the late afternoon, I stood at the intersection of Route P. and the busy marketplace and started to walk. The streets were narrow and in poor repair, and a backlog of cars and trucks was laboring to get by. The shop stalls and booths I passed made an intricate maze of alleys and side streets of their own.

Knowing that I had to begin somewhere, I randomly stopped a man in the confusion of the crowd and told him that I was looking for André.

"Straight ahead," the man replied and kept on walking. Encouraged, I asked again, and was again directed ahead. The third person did not give directions but pointed to a young man standing in a nearby doorway, telling me that he would know.

"André?" asked the man in the doorway. André from Akondjo, I replied. The man called over his shoulder to someone inside, and then said that he would take me. We turned off the main street to the right, following a quiet, narrow bystreet that eventually led us to a bar.

"André!" called my guide. "There is someone to see you."

André was the bartender. Life in Libreville must have suited him well, for in spite of his white hair, he did not seem so very old. He eyed me suspiciously. "I'm not answering any questions," he said, before I could speak. "Who are you? I have done nothing wrong."

I explained that I had come from Akondjo, and he looked more relaxed. His wife came out of the shadows of a back room to stand defiantly and protectively at his shoulder, and a few other people wandered in. Gradually André began to unwind. Akondjo had been too quiet, he said. It had become difficult to get supplies, to move about. Life was better here. And the elephants had been very bad.

But as for my burning question:

"No, I never heard a story about this woman. I think if someone had known her, they would have remembered. There were not many white people at that time." His wife spoke up: "It has to be that someone remembers. Anyone who went into the forest with this woman would tell his children. No, it has to be that someone knows."

·/·/·

IT HAS TO BE that there is a path from Lake Azingo to Akondjo; and it has to be that someone knows the way. It has to be that in all Gabon there is someone who has heard of Mary Kingsley. But it has to remain for someone else to find him.

HOMEWARD BOUND

AFTER MY WEEKS of travel on narrow forest roads and waterways, Libreville seemed an impossibly hectic complex of sturdy, soaring buildings, stocked with all that one might need or covet. The sea lying immediately beyond the main highway implied sudden access to the rest of the world.

At Baraka, nothing had changed within the Pastor's household, but the situation in Deborah's apartment below was very different than when I had departed. Deborah had left her gift shop and was employed as a secretary in a French firm. Her tiny apartment was being measured for curtains, and there was a new raffia carpet on the living room's cement floor. She no longer appeared to be in a blazing hurry to get to Israel.

"Perhaps in one year, in two . . . first, I shall save some money."

Christine, the lumbering, good-natured girl who lived next door, had moved in with Deborah, for whom she worked not so much as a servant but as a drudge. She had been given the small spare room next to Deborah and Jean-Louis's bedroom—or, more accurately, she had been given the floor of the spare room, which was now completely bare except for a mat that served as her bed and a neat bundle of clothes in one corner, which represented her wardrobe. The girl's duties were to cook, shop, clean, wash, iron, and look after Jean-Louis. She also served as a convenient object at which Deborah could hurl high-pitched abuse.

"You fool! Do you hear nothing? Does anything happen in that big head of yours? Is it true that I told you to buy bread?"

Christine stood hugely awkward with her big hands dangling at her side. "Madame," she replied, hardly protesting, "you did not leave me any money."

"I'm asking you about bread, not money!" Deborah screamed. "She is not right in the head," she exploded, turning to where I stood transfixed. "Go, go! Here's the money. You dolt, you fool. . . ." Her features, which had been trained to steely composure throughout her more vulnerable years, were now permanently demented. Ordinarily, when making someone's acquaintance, one operates on the assumption that the individual in question is in possession of his senses, but it now occurred to me that Deborah might in fact be just a little mad.

The Pastor had been saving several questions to ask me on my return. *"Sic semper tyrannis*—can you tell me what it means?" he inquired, reading from the scrap of paper on which he had written the phrase. " 'Thus always to tyrants,' " he repeated after I had translated. "Ah, it is good, very good," he said with satisfaction.

I was mildly curious where he had come by this. "It is what John Wilkes Booth said when he shot Lincoln," said the Pastor offhandedly and moved on to other topics.

The long grass in the Baraka cemetery behind the church had been cut, and I was able to enter it and roam around. The gray and broken tombstones were often sunk in turf, but it was possible to make out many names familiar from Nassau's autobiography: Mrs. Griswold, Reverend Bushnell, Mr. Ford, Mrs. Walker.

"We had the grass cut for President Reagan's daughter's visit," said the Pastor, and explained that Miss Reagan had been in Libreville for a few days on a diplomatic tour—in what official capacity, I was not clear. "She saw the church, but she did not go into the cemetery—she was too tired. Perhaps too she was afraid she would fall into a hole; it wouldn't do to have the daughter of the leader of the most powerful nation on earth fall into a hole," said the Pastor with just a hint of irony. "She gave me this," he continued and opened a small case containing some cuff links enameled with the American flag, and a fifty-dollar bill. "She didn't say what this was for," he said, unfolding the latter. "I suppose it is for the church. *I* shall use it for the church. How much would this be in African francs?"

·/·/·

IT WAS TIME to book my return flight. In the Air Gabon office where I went to make my reservation I watched as an impassive airline agent pushed random keys on a new computer whose screen was permanently lit with the sign INVALID COMMAND. At first alarmed that I might not get my flight, then merely annoyed, and finally, as the day was hot and languid, lulled into a kind of hypnotized stupor, I settled down to watch the invariably flashing screen with passive fascination. Half an hour at least had passed before the agent looked up to inform me that it was not possible to make advance reservations. Aroused, I asked her why not.

"We cannot tell how many people will come to the airport on the day of the flight—perhaps there will be only ten people, perhaps there will be hundreds. It would not be fair to promise you anything."

·/·/·

I HAD ONE last journey to make. On her return to Libreville, Mary Kingsley had paid a call on Dr. Nassau at Baraka and learned from him about the possibility of adding to her collection of fish.

"In one of these talks [about Fetish] the doctor mentioned that there were lakes in the centre of the Island of Corisco," she wrote, "and that in those lakes were quantities of fish, which fish were always and only fished by the resident ladies, at duly appointed seasons. Needless to say, I felt it a solemn duty to go and investigate personally. . . ."

Nassau loaned Kingsley the mission sailboat and a crew, and on the morning of August 6, she set out for Corisco Island. The journey must have seemed straightforward enough; Corisco Island lies only forty miles north of Libreville—with good weather, only a day's sail away—and there was even a Presbyterian Mission on the island where she was able to stay. But her expedition came to nothing; she remained for several days on the parched and not overly friendly island, waiting with evident mounting anger for the people to take her to the lakes and fish. Both turned out to be a disappointment, and with some disgust, she had cut her losses and turned back to the Gaboon. Tossed by rough seas and then becalmed, she and her crew took three days to make this miserable return journey, first touching the mainland at Cape Estarias, on the northwest tip of the Gaboon estuary's northern shore. Here Kingsley was received by a "very comely-looking brown young lady" whose name was Agnes, a subtrader for John Holt and Co., who spoke fluent trade English. She remained only a day, staying at Agnes's house, and paying a visit to the Catholic Mission, "the only representative of white men here," which consisted of a small residence and a church. She left the Cape the day after her arrival, having only a short run back to Hatton and Cookson's wharf in Libreville.

It would have been virtually impossible to replicate this journey in any meaningful way, for by far the most eventful part had taken place at sea, and I was fairly confident that my chances of persuading, say, local fishermen to take me on a day trip to the island were remote. In any case, Corisco Island now belongs to Equatorial Guinea (Spanish Guinea at the time of Kingsley's visit) and was therefore outside the province of my predetermined territory. But Cape Estarias, where Kingsley had landed, was in Gabon.

Cape Estarias is now a holiday resort with a hotel and weekend bungalows, chiefly used by Europeans who live in Libreville. I had a companion for this trip, whom I had met by chance during my first week in Libreville. David was a member of a small group of Israelis who had come to Gabon to set up a lumber company. He was brisk and optimistic, his colleagues variously cynical or bored; the youngest and most restless of the group had been able to tell me exactly how many days he had been in the country, and exactly how many remained until his leave of duty. On my return to Libreville, I discovered that he had after all not waited until his leave, but had quit and gone home.

There was of course no public transport to the Cape, and I was grateful when David offered to take me in his car. By land, the Cape is only twenty miles from Libreville, reached by a badly paved, quiet forest road. The first buildings one encounters are the neat, aggressively positioned houses of the Department of Water and Forests, which mount a proprietary guard over the whole territory that lies behind. The road took us as far as the Mini Hotel, which was empty and positioned in a clearing to look over the water. The hotel manager was watering plants in the garden, watched from under a copse of trees by a spindly-legged boy whose face wore a peculiar, dreamy smile. When he heard that we were looking for the Catholic church, the manager beckoned to the boy, who came skipping over to us. Looking him intently in the face, the manager made a series of rapid and dramatic gestures that included the sign of the cross. The smiling boy nodded and opened his mouth to emit the high-pitched chirping sound of a bird.

"He cannot speak or hear," the manager explained. "But I have told him to take you to the church." Still wearing the smile of his private world, the boy led us onto the road that ran past the hotel through the high, untidy tufts of wheaten grass that covered the sandy topsoil like shabby, depilated savannah. Judging only by the almost white, windy sky, one would have imagined it to be a blustery winter day, but in fact the air was balmy. A few dry bushes and stunted trees stood here and there against the bleached horizon. Farther along, the boy, twittering excitedly, led us off the road toward some huts, where there was a bar, but no church. I surmised that lines of communication had somehow been tangled and could not help reflecting how delighted Nassau would have been that the Catholic sign of the cross had been so interpreted.

Guided by the people in the bar, we eventually found the church; but it was not at all what I was looking for, having been recently built on a sandy lot spiked with new grass shoots and nowhere near the sea, as was the church that Kingsley had visited. Returning to the bar, I inquired whether the church we had just seen had replaced an older one, and was told that it had not. There was, however, *another* church that *was* old, one man ventured, but it was some distance from here, and he gave us directions to the road that led toward the beach.

Returning to the turnoff near the Department of Water and Forests, David and I drove cautiously on a surface so eroded by craters and trenches that we risked overturning the car. The road dipped and rose sharply, the juncture between downslope and incline at times forming a treacherous V, and eventually it seemed safer to park and continue on foot. Through the trees, we soon saw that we were parallel with the coast where the sea, like the sky over the tufted grassland, appeared wintery and wild. Silver okoumé logs that must have been blown from the port at Owendo littered the beach, which was deserted. Farther along, the road narrowed considerably and then came to a dead end before some attractive beach bungalows, set in lawns of coarse grass.

In one of the gardens, a group of young men were just finishing their barbecue, an impressive assemblage of sporting equipment—boats, motorbikes, fishing gear—piled by their two jeeps. The men themselves, dressed in jogging shorts and sneakers, were extremely friendly; the church, they were sure, was straight ahead, although none of them had ever seen it. We continued on past the other bungalows until their cropped lawns gave way to a wilderness of high, broad-bladed grass, in the midst of which stood the lonely church.

"The church has a concrete floor and wooden benches," Mary Kingsley had written, "the white walls relieved by a frieze of framed prints of a religious character, a pretty altar with its array of bright brass candlesticks, and above it the tinted and gilt figure of the Virgin and Child. Every part of the place is sweet and clean, giving evidence of the loving care with which it is tended."

On the grubby white walls of the building before me, the eventual successor of Kingsley's church, the word *Maria* had been painted in pink letters over the doorway, to one side of which was a crude and defaced religious image, to the other a painted map of Africa. Inside, blackened walls and charred roof beams gave evidence that the church had only narrowly escaped complete destruction by fire. The graffiti that covered the walls and the remains of two iron camp beds indicated that the building had been used most recently as an army barracks.

I had embarked on this abbreviated version of Kingsley's trip with the awareness that the most I could expect was to see the same scenery as had Kingsley, but that I would have no approximation of her experience. Still, this was my last trip within Gabon—in two days' time, I would be back in Europe—and I now realized that I had after all looked forward to some kind of emotional climax. Standing in the entrance of the blackened church, I tried to imagine Mary Kingsley climbing up to the verandah, being offered wine and bread by the friendly, isolated priests—but try as I did I could make no connection; there was nothing evocative on this scorched and desecrated site, where even the view of the sea and western horizon was obscured by the overgrowth of grass. Then too, my own sense of having come to journey's end was undercut by the knowledge that at the same point in her travels, Kingsley still had ahead of her the ascent of Mount Cameroon and a twelve-week boat trip up the west coast back to England.

Slowly, David and I made our way back to the holidaymakers, who kindly offered us a lift in one of their jeeps to where we had parked the car. This was, effectively, the end of my travels.

·/·/·

AT THE LIBREVILLE airport, all departing passengers were summarily searched before being allowed to enter the departure lounge, which resembled a detention room with windows. Virtually all the people around me were French, on their way home on leave or returning for good. While we sat in obedient silence, waiting for further instructions to embark, a French soldier entered the lounge and made a slow study of the passengers. To my alarm, he made his way across the room to me and asked my name; and when I told him, he handed me a square of folded paper. Nervously, and aware that all eyes were on me, I opened it and read:

Dear Caroline,
The Pastor told me I had missed you. But I have come to say goodbye—I shall be looking for you from the balcony.
Stephanos.

Once cleared for boarding, we walked out of the lounge directly onto the tarmac. Looking behind me up at the departure balcony, I caught sight of Stephanos, one of the two vacationing soldiers I had met at Lambaréné, and a group of his friends. He waved, smiled, and shrugged his shoulders, and waved again. Less than six hours after takeoff, the plane touched down in Marseilles.

·/·/·

MARY KINGSLEY left the Gaboon on September 4, making port calls and brief excursions in Cameroon, Calabar, Sierra Leone, and the Canary Islands before arriving in Liverpool on November 30, 1895. On December 2, the *Times* reported that Miss Kingsley had "furnished to a representative of Reuters' Agency a few particulars of her travels." Reports of Kingsley's homecoming had preceded her, and the "Reuters' representative" had been on hand to meet her at the harbor as she disembarked.

The same Monday edition of the *Times* also contained advertisements of Victorian Government Inscribed Stocks, news from the colonies, a review of a concert given at the Crystal Palace, and notices of the departure of an Ashanti expedition, the meeting of the North Borneo club dinner, and the projected demolition of an almshouse. There was also an eye-catching advertise-ment for "THE INCANDESCENT GAS LAMPS proved by experience and the severest tests to be the finest artificial light in the world." In short, it is here in the cramped columns of the *Times* that one is made inescapably aware that Kingsley was a woman of a spe-cific, bygone era, a fact that one can overlook while reading the *Travels* themselves. This is largely the result of Kingsley's vivid, personal style and modernly appealing sense of humor, but also because Kingsley encounters little that is "dateable" in European terms in the course of her travels—jungles and rivers are timeless and for the most part must still be traversed on foot and by boat. Only rarely does her choice of words or a specific reference jar the reader back to an awareness of her belonging to a different era: Kingsley's mention of her long, protective skirts is one such example, as is her description of a crowd of running people "legging it like lamplighters."

This essential insulation from a sense of specific time had persisted throughout my actual retracing of Kingsley's route. Clearly I had been aware of important differences between our journeys, but this had never overwhelmed the sense of stepping back into "time past" that so often—at least for a visitor from the West—characterizes travel in Africa. Traditionally, African life is based on a cyclical, not linear, view of human history, and it is therefore not the progression of generations that defines the rhythm of life, but rather the preservation of an ancestral way of doing things. It is to this end that the same methods of preparing food and building houses are retained over the genera-tions, as is the use of the same rituals to mark and celebrate life's important transitions—the dancing of the same dances, the sing-ing of the same songs, the telling of the same stories. Disrupted as the traditional way of life as a whole now is, there are none-theless many striking surviving elements, and the western trav-eler will find that it is easy to confuse the present he experiences with a more distant past. Only on my own return did the circum-stances of Kingsley's homecoming have their full import: she had disembarked after a lengthy Atlantic crossing of some weeks' duration. She and her luggage would have been taken to her London address on Addison Road by a horse-drawn hansom cab. The streets would have been lit with gas lights. The men would have been wearing top hats and long frock coats, the women long skirts, shawls, and bonnets.

The *Times* article, following a preliminary statement that Miss Kingsley had made her second trip to Africa "chiefly for the purpose of collecting piscatorial specimens and of studying the 'fetish' customs of the natives," gives what is essentially a summary of what was to be the *Travels,* highlighting, as would be expected, Kingsley's adventures on the rapids, the overland journey to the Remboué in the company of cannibal Fang, and outside of Gabon, her ascent of Mount Cameroon. It is not difficult to tell from the events that are emphasized (and distorted) which features of her trip had the most public appeal—namely, overturned canoes, cannibal guides, unexplored lakes, gorillas, and cannibal "larders" containing human body parts. The article concludes by noting that Miss Kingsley's "diaries were regularly kept and ought to enable her to furnish a valuable and most interesting volume."

Kingsley began work on the *Travels* only weeks after her return to England, and she submitted the final chapters in November of the following year. The writing of what was to be a seven-hundred-page volume demanding much varied research was, one would have thought, enough to monopolize her energy, and yet this was not the only task that she undertook during this period. Africa and African affairs were much-discussed topics in the London press of Kingsley's day, the majority opinion being, to quote the author of an article published in the *Spectator* and largely prompted by the reports of Kingsley's travels, that "it is in Africa that the lowest depth of evil barbarism is reached." Goaded by such articles, written for the most part by people who had never set foot on the African continent, Kingsley had sprung to its defense and consequently found herself drawn into the ongoing public dialogue. These polemics served to increase her reputation, or notoriety as the case might be, and she became sought after as a public speaker, a role in which she proved to be very popular. Finally, all the while that she was adhering to a hectic schedule of lecturing and writing about her own travels, she was also making substantial progress in the preparation of a memorial volume of her father's writings.

Travels in West Africa, published in January 1897 by Macmillan and Company, was an immediate best-selling success. The reception of the *Travels,* in the words of Stephen Gwynn, Kingsley's only biographer who had known her, "altered the whole shape of her existence. It made her a public personage and a champion of causes—certainly not for her happiness." The requests for public speaking engagements increased, as did the flood of invitations to the salons and dinner parties of those whom Kingsley termed "the haut politique." In popular, social, and political circles, she became "the" African authority, and her opinion was sought on topics ranging from polygamy to the Crown Colony system in West Africa. She was pressed to write other books and produced in 1899 *West African Studies,* an extensive study of African law and religion, and also in 1899 *The Story of West Africa,* a chatty but informative volume in the popular Story of the Empire Series. Her publicity and fame, while gratifying, was not, as her biographer noted and as will be seen, for her happiness. Nonetheless, this whirl of social, literary, and public obligations shaped her life until her departure on March 10, 1900, for South Africa, on what was to be her final journey.

Everything one needs to know about Kingsley's life for the purpose of understanding the *Travels* is to be found in the preface to the book itself; one does not, however, undertake to retrace someone else's journey without the expectation of coming to know that person a little better than before one started. Ironically, however, one's greatest insight into Kingsley's character comes, as does the appreciation of the time lapsed since she made her journey, not from the events that took place in Africa, but from what happened once she had come home.

"It was in 1893 that, for the first time in my life, I found myself in possession of five or six months which were not heavily forestalled, and feeling like a boy with a new half-crown, I lay about in my mind, as Mr. Bunyan would say, as to what to do with them." These are the sunny first words of the *Travels,* in which Kingsley informs the reader of the impulse that originally made her decide to embark upon a journey to the tropics. On May 12, 1899, however, in a letter to Major Matthew Nathan, the one man with whom she seems to have fallen in (unreciprocated) love, she gave a very different account: "My life has been a comic one," she wrote. "Dead tired and feeling no one had need of me anymore when my Mother and Father died within six weeks of each other in '92 and my brother went off to the East, I went down to West Africa to die."

Extended travel in countries very different from one's own demands an ongoing suspension of one's personality. There is often no scope or no point, for example, in asserting preferences in matters as basic as food, shelter, and the company one keeps, and it is often even beyond one's powers to direct one's own itinerary. In such circumstances, a sustained attempt to cling to the same habits, the same outlook, the same tastes cultivated at home is to risk being driven slowly mad: it is a truth at least as old as Homer's *Odyssey* that the resourceful traveler is the one who can adapt to whatever is thrown his way. In this respect, Kingsley's instinctive yearning for an exotic journey was most fortuitous; her travels not only took her physically far away from the associations that would have caused her the most pain, but they also allowed her a period in which to lose her personality and to savor briefly what she tells us is her idea of heaven— the loss of "all sense of human individuality, all memory of human life, with its grief and worry and doubt" in the contemplation of sky and sea from the deck of a slow-going liner.

This state of abeyance, of course, ended with her journey, and Kingsley's return to her London flat entailed the resumption of her old identity. It may be that the task of writing up her travels allowed her to retain the magic of Africa a while longer, as has been suggested by at least one biographer. I find it more likely, however, that Kingsley regarded the book as simply another "odd job" that it was her duty to complete. One must not forget that she came from a literary family, and a family with a penchant for travel narrative. Her uncle Charles Kingsley's *At Last; a Christmas in the Indies,* was a description of a seven-week tour of the West Indies; her other uncle, Henry, had published a re-working of famous travel stories entitled *Tales of Old Travel;* her cousin Rose (breezily referred to by Kingsley in the *Travels* as "my cousin Rose Kingsley, who had successfully ridden through Mexico when Mexico was having a rather worse revolution than usual") had written of travels in North America and Mexico in her book *South by West;* and of course George Kingsley, Mary Kingsley's father, had published several travel articles and was the coauthor of *South Sea Bubbles,* an almost unreadably dull ac-count of his adventures in the South Pacific. Within this context, it might have seemed to Kingsley that the writing of her travels was the logical and proper "next task," perhaps even a family duty.

It may also be significant that her father had had wider, unful-filled literary pretensions, as is evident from extracts of his let-ters printed in the biographical preface to *Notes on Sport and Travel,* the collection of his surviving travel accounts that Kingsley ed-ited. "I feel very much inclined to make a venture in the every-day life of the time of Charles II," he had written to Daniel Macmillan in 1857. "With such a command of books of every sort and description as I have at the Bridgewater Library, I can-not help thinking that I might work up a tolerable *piece d'essai.'* "Why the deuce didn't I write a novel?" he wrote to another correspondent. "Faith! I know not." Mary Kingsley noted fur-ther that her father "had thoughts of extracting bits of early song and poetry, quaint stories, and quaint conceits out of the larger books, and welding them together into a pleasing and more popular book." Fortunately, to judge by the tedious articles that he did bring to light, none of the larger projects he threatened materialized. Nonetheless, her father's unfulfilled literary dreams may have provided Kingsley with an additional incen-tive for writing up her own travels, offering her yet another opportunity to meld her life and work with his.

Kingsley's own literary aspirations had been formed years before she embarked upon the journey that was to result in the *Travels.* Immediately on her return from the West Coast of Africa in January 1894, she began work on a piece entitled *The Bights of Benin,* and later in the same year approached her father's publisher, George Macmillan, about the possibility of having it published. She submitted as much as two hundred typescript pages to Macmillan before deciding to scrap the project, as her subsequent studies in history, commerce, and anthropology made her wish to write something less superficial than a personal travel account. In November 1895, toward the end of her second, famous journey, she wrote to Macmillan from the Canary Islands, this time indicating her interest in publishing an account of her most recent travels—and shrewdly informing him that she had already received offers from rival publishing houses.

The forging of a literary work from one's own experience necessarily entails that the whole truth be to some degree curtailed. "The amount of expurgation my journals have required has been awful," Kingsley wrote to her friend Lady MacDonald in 1896 while she was in the midst of writing the *Travels.* ". . . For example, I have had to entirely eliminate a lovely scene in the Ogowé, when I and the captain of a vessel had to take to the saloon table because a Bishop with a long red beard and voluminous white flannel petticoats was rolling about the floor in close but warful embrace with the Governor of the Ogowé. . . ." We know that she did not include half as much as she could have written about Nassau, or indeed about most of her time in Libreville. Further incidents omitted in the *Travels* were revealed in her public lectures: an account of a trading expedition made to a Fang village is given, for example, in an article published in *The Cheltenham Ladies' College Magazine* of autumn 1898, and it seems that this excursion was made in the course of either her stay at Talagouga or her adventure on the rapids. And, of course, the fact that she was led astray by the Fang on the overland trip to the Remboué also came to light only in a lecture.

The motives for excluding these particular incidents were various. The bishop story was omitted because it was too scandalous to print; her friendship with Nassau in Libreville was perhaps played down, as I suggested earlier, because Kingsley was sensitive to the mission politics in which he was then embroiled; the trading excursion might have been excluded for literary reasons, as it would have seriously detracted from the dramatic rhythm of the self-contained adventure on the rapids; for an audience for the most part unfamiliar with the peculiar trials of African travel the Fang duplicity would have represented an unnecessary embarrassment. If these and other omitted incidents had been included, the *Travels* would, obviously, have been a very different book—and, more to the point, the Kingsley literary character might have taken a very different shape. This is especially the case when one considers that the whole of her first extended journey, during which she was initiated into African travel, ultimately passed unrecorded, so that the Mary Kingsley one first meets in the *Travels* is already an old Africa hand.

The newspaper articles written immediately after Kingsley's return indicate the kind of direction her narrative was expected to take, and the kind of role that she was expected to play: "Yes! anything seems possible in Africa," the *Daily Telegraph* reported on December 3, a few days after her arrival, "yet almost more wonderful than the hidden marvels of that Dark Continent are the qualities of heart and mind which could carry a lonely English lady through such experiences as Miss Kingsley has 'manfully' borne. It is a curious and a novel feature of the modern emancipation of woman—this passion on the part of the sex to emulate the most daring achievements of masculine explorers." The possibility of exploiting the fact that in the eyes of the general public her femininity made her journey somehow more sensational was one that Kingsley had already met with and resisted some years before. In a letter to George Macmillan written in December 1894 concerning the projected account of her first travels, she had suggested that its publication be anonymous: "Of course I would rather not publish under my own name and I really cannot draw the trail of the petticoats over the Coast of all places, neither can I have a picture of myself in trousers or any other little excitement of this sort added. I went out there as a naturalist not as a sort of circus. But if you would like my name, will it not be sufficient to put M. H. Kingsley?"

Kingsley's refusal to capitalize on her lady-explorer role arose from at least several discernible reasons. As someone who was always acutely conscious of being an "outsider," she may have feared that being cast as a New Woman would have placed her even further beyond the pale. She was in any case violently antifeminist, as both the *Travels* and her correspondence attest ("shrieking androgyns" was her term for the suffragettes). One may observe that her denial of the equality of the sexes assured her among other things of the impossibility that her own travel exploits could surpass those of her hero-father.

All these considerations—the selective editing of personal experiences and a vehement resistance to being typecast as an intrepid lady explorer—eventually combined with her naturally vivid style and sense of humor to create the Kingsley character of the *Travels*. As a narrator of matters of fact she is sober, thorough, and conscientious; as a narrator of personal adventures—or, to use Nassau's distinction, of "personal incidents"—she is self-deprecating, ironic, bantering, and above all comical. The "Calamity Jane" character whom Kingsley invented allowed her to convey, uncompromisingly, the excitement and even daring of her adventures while making it clear that she did not presume to be taken altogether seriously.

Kingsley's literary character, then, reflected herself insofar as qualities peculiarly her own combined to create a specific fiction that could not have been generated by any other author. But the character was not Mary Kingsley, and to see how great was the discrepancy between fiction and fact, one must turn to her letters and the descriptions of her given by her contemporaries. "I am really a very melancholy person inside," she wrote to her friend Dennis Kemp, a Wesleyan missionary. "But I don't show that part of myself. I feel I have no right to anyone's sympathy. . . ."

A glimpse of Kingsley as she could appear to others is given in a cruelly snide social piece: "Poor Mary Kingsley! . . . never shall I forget the disconsolateness of her appearance at the *Entente Cordiale soirée* given last year in honour of the 'divine Sarah' [Bernhardt]," its author sniped. "If ever a fish looked out of water it was the Rev. Charles Kingsley's niece upon that occasion . . . everyone seemed in the highest spirits, except Mary Kingsley. Holding aloof from the animated groups around, grave as a judge, for an hour or more she paced up and down, her antiquated *coiffure* and dress rendering her all the more conspicuous."

Memorial tributes printed after her death showed her characteristic reticence and unaffected manner in a kinder light: "She possessed that rarest trait," read one, "a deep interest in her friends. 'And what of yourself?' she asked, turning her large quiet eyes towards me, and making me feel that she cared to know."

The public lecture circuit must have been especially difficult for someone of Kingsley's temperament, for surely her success as a public speaker depended to some extent on her enacting on the lecture stage the character she had created. To this end, she was undoubtedly *not* helped by the fact that she possessed one particular trait commented on by many of the tribute writers: "This woman, who could read Sanskrit, who had all the 'ologies' at her finger-ends, and who could produce a well-written book," one of the anonymous tributes ran, "this woman could never master the mysteries of the letters *H* and *R*. She talked like a Cockney to the day of her death."

Even an inveterate storyteller can tire of public speaking. "Why relate this story again, since yesterday in your house I told it to you . . . ?" asks the hero of the world's earliest travel narrative, Odysseus, of his captive audience. "It is hateful to me to tell it again, when it has been well told." In her written work, Kingsley judiciously selected and edited her material so as to form a narrative of her choosing; now, in the public retelling, she brought bits and pieces of the omitted material to light. The narrative line changes; the itinerary is seen to be different from that given in the book; new motives are revealed. One can only wonder whether these "revelations" helped Kingsley sustain her literary character, or whether they threatened to undermine it.

The strain of the lecture tour was great, the physical demands of having to travel across the country from lecture hall to lecture hall alone being fatiguing; and the references in Kingsley's letters to her headaches, bouts of ill health, and low spirits are evidence that she was overtaxed with her new duties. Her reasons for enduring the hectic pace were clear, though: every pound earned, she told her lecture agent, meant five miles in West Africa.

Toward the end of a lecture she gave in February 1900 to the Imperial Institute, Kingsley thanked her audience as follows: "Up to to-night you have been very kind and tolerant to me about my West African discourses, and I humbly beg to thank you all most sincerely on this, the last night I shall, in all human probability, have the honour of speaking to London." She had laid plans to depart for Africa again in only a few weeks. Even in cold print, the passionate conclusion of this farewell speech is thrilling: "Goodbye," she said, "and fare you well, for I am homeward bound."

On March 10, Kingsley departed from Southampton on her final African journey—her immediate destination this time being not the West Coast but South Africa, where the Boer War had broken out in October of the preceding year. On arriving in Cape Town, she reported to the British medical headquarters and asked if there was any need of her service. Her offer was accepted, and she was sent south to Simonstown, where an emergency makeshift hospital had been established for the nursing of Boer prisoners of war. She served at the military hospital for two months, under appalling conditions, nursing typhoid patients as well as the wounded before falling fatally ill herself. On June 3, 1900, she died of enteric fever. On June 4, she was buried at sea, as she had requested, and given full military honors. The Mary Kingsley Society of West Africa, later the African Society, was founded in memory of her and of her work.

The subsequent legend held that Kingsley had gone to South Africa specifically to nurse wounded soldiers. Other accounts were that she was going as a correspondent to cover the war. "Her object in going to South Africa was 'simply to be of use, and to get rid of a little money, with which those books' had endowed her," one of her tribute writers claimed. According to her biographer Stephen Gwynn, she "provided herself with a theoretical reason for going to South Africa—to collect fresh water fishes from the Orange River for Dr. Günther. How this was to be accomplished in the midst of war is not easy to see. . . ." More probable is the account she apparently gave her friends, that her eventual destination was her beloved west coast, but that she would "look in" on South Africa. The matter was perhaps put most succinctly, however, by that good lady Miss Isabella Nassau, who on hearing of Kingsley's departure from England had written to her brother, Robert Nassau, then on leave in the United States: "You will not I suppose see Miss Kingsley as I see that she is going to South Africa for study and adventure." Whatever her motives, a return trip to Africa had been long planned: the *Times* interview held virtually at the moment of her disembarkation had reported that Miss Kingsley "intends to return to West Africa again in a few months to explore other parts."

Mary Kingsley would have been a remarkable woman had she never gone to West Africa. Her heroic and lonely struggle to obtain knowledge at all costs, evidently begun while she was only a child, was one she unflaggingly persisted in throughout her brief life. Every fact, every insight she possessed was a hard-won, solitary gain. Her accomplishments were very great; but her potential may have been greater, and one can only deeply and indignantly regret that she was never given any of the formal training that could have so facilitated her trial-and-error method of learning—if not greater wisdom, she would have surely gained a measure of self-confidence and thereby, perhaps, a greater capacity for happiness. As it was, her abiding loneliness was revealed with unbearable eloquence in her deathbed request to the doctor and nurse in attendance that she be left alone to die.

"I doubt," she once wrote, "whether if an energetic individual were to go round with a dust-pan and broom and sweep the universe for me that sufficient could be got together to be called a personality." It is tragic that she never comprehended or acknowledged that hers was a personality singular to an extraordinary degree. For me, she was a delightful companion, if at times an intimidating guide, and I would have given much to have shared with her the deck of an Ogooué river steamer. Our accounts of our experiences differ widely; nonetheless, if you go there you will find things as we have said.

ACKNOWLEDGMENTS

My first debt of gratitude is to all those people, mentioned by name or not, whom I met in the course of my travels.

I would like to thank my mother, Elizabeth Kirby, my sister, Joanna, and my friend Jan Mitchell for their encouragement.

But my greatest debt is to my friend and mentor, Laura Slatkin, whose selfless dedication to other people's projects is legendary among her friends.

SELECT BIBLIOGRAPHY

WORKS BY MARY KINGSLEY

Travels in West Africa, Congo-Française, Corisco and Cameroons. London, 1897.
West African Studies. London, 1899.
The Story of West Africa. The Story of the Empire Series. London, 1899.
Notes on Sport and Travel. By George Kingsley, edited and introduced by Mary Kingsley. London, 1900.
Other lectures and letters referred to in this book are:
"Travels on the Western Coast of Equatorial Africa." *The Scottish Geographical Magazine,* March 1896.
"A Lecture on West Africa." *Cheltenham Ladies' College Magazine,* Autumn 1898.
"West Africa from an Ethnographical Point of View." *Imperial Institute Journal,* April 1900. (Reprinted as "Imperialism in West Africa," in *West African Studies,* 2d ed., 1901.)
The *Spectator* article that aroused Kingsley's anger appeared in the issue of December 7, 1895. (See "The Negro Future," *Spectator,* December 28, 1895, for Kingsley's rebuttal.)
Kingsley's letters are scattered throughout different collections around the world. The major collections are in the Bodleian Library, Oxford; the British Library, London; the National Library of Ireland; the Rhodes House Library, Oxford; the Royal Commonwealth Society; the South African Library. The letters cited in this book are:

to George Macmillan, August 23, 1894; British Library
to George Macmillan, December 18, 1894; British Library
to George Macmillan, November 21, 1895; British Library
to Lady MacDonald, date not given (but sometime after June 1896),
cited by Stephen Gwynn (see below), pp. 130ff
to Matthew Nathan, March 12, 1899; Bodleian Library
to Dennis Kemp, May 1897, included in Kemp's memorial "The Late
Miss M. H. Kingsley," *London Quarterly Review,* July 1900, p. 142

BIOGRAPHIES OF KINGSLEY

Stephen Gwynn. *The Life of Mary Kingsley.* London, 1932.
The most recent biography, by Katherine Frank, is particularly useful for
its citation of Kingsley's correspondence and its bibliography of Kingsley's numerous articles: *A Voyager Out.* Boston, 1986.

GABON

Richard West. *Brazza of the Congo.* London, 1972. A particularly readable
history of the French Congo, approached through the work and personalities of its most important explorers.
David K. Patterson. *The Northern Gabon Coast to 1875.* Oxford, 1975. Although narrow in scope, this scholarly account of the intricacies of
French, Mpongwé, and Orungu politics and European and African trade
up until the time when the European traders penetrated to the interior
is an excellent way of getting a feel for the complexities of the imperial
process. Its bibliography is a useful source of important primary documents (as is West's, above).
Rémy Mylène. *Le Gabon Aujourd'hui.* 3d ed. Paris, 1985. A general history-
cum-guidebook that offers practical (if optimistic) information as regards
traveling in Gabon. An earlier edition, published in 1977, has been
translated into English by M. Huet and M. Marenthier under the title
Gabon Today.
Charles and Alice Darlington. *African Betrayal.* New York, 1967. Charles
Darlington was the first U.S. Ambassador to Gabon. This book is a highly
personal account but contains interesting information about the strong
French role in modern Gabonese politics.
Abbé André Raponda Walker. "Les Tribus du Gabon." *Bulletin de la société
des recherches congolaises,* 4 (1924). Abbé Walker was the Gabonese son of
Hatton and Cookson's pioneer manager, Robert Bruce Walker. This work
is still the most thorough general treatment of Gabon's many tribes to
date.
James W. Fernandez. *Bwiti: An Ethnography of the Religious Imagination in Africa.*
Princeton, 1982. (This is the primary source for the information regard-
ing Bwiti initiation rites, described in Chapter Six.)

EARLY EXPLORERS AND TRAVELERS

Paul B. du Chaillu. *Explorations and Adventures in Equatorial Africa.* New York, 1861. *A Journey to Ashango-Land.* New York, 1867. The biography referred to in Chapter Three is that of Michel Vaucaire, *Paul du Chaillu: Gorilla Hunter.* New York, 1930. (David Patterson, "Paul du Chaillu and the Exploration of Gabon, 1855–65," *The International Journal of African Historical Studies,* 7, no. 4 (1974): 647–667, is the work of the "modern historian" cited in Chapter Three.)

Richard F. Burton. *Two Trips to Gorilla Land and the Cataracts of the Nile.* vol. 1. London, 1876. (Burton was a personal hero of Mary Kingsley's, and the man she felt her father most resembled.)

Brazza's expedition reports and associated documents have been prepared in an annotated three-volume edition by Henri Brunschwig. Most pertinent to Gabon specifically is Volume 1, *Brazza Explorateur: L'Ogooué 1875–1879.* Paris, 1966. A more vivid account of the expedition is given in Brazza's long article "Voyages dans l'ouest Africain," *Tour du Monde* 54 (1887): 289–304; 305–320; 321–336; and 56 (1888) 1–16; 17–32; 33–48; 49–64 (the first installment of which is referred to in Chapter Five).

Also to be included among these first-person travel accounts is *Trader Horn.* Ethelreda Lewis, ed. London, 1927.

WORKS BY ROBERT HAMILL NASSAU

Crowned in Palm Land. Philadelphia, 1874. The biography of Nassau's first wife, Mary Cloyd Latta Nassau.

Fetishism in West Africa. New York, 1904.

My Ogowe. New York, 1914.

The Path She Trod. Philadelphia, 1909. The life of his second wife, Mary Brunette Foster Nassau.

Citations of Nassau's unpublished manuscript autobiography and diaries are made with the kind permission of Speer Library, Princeton Theological Seminary.

The letters from Nassau to his sister (and the one letter referred to in Chapter Eight, from Isabella Nassau to her brother) are quoted with the kind permission of the Burke Library, Union Theological Seminary in the City of New York, and are from the Robert Hamill Nassau Papers in their collection.

The description of Anyentyuwa is from Nassau's unpublished typescript *Two Women: the Lives of 2 Native African Women,* and is used with the permission of the Langston Hughes Memorial Library, Lincoln University, Pennsylvania.

ALBERT SCHWEITZER

The material relating to Schweitzer is largely taken from his own works. Works of his referred to in this book are:

African Notebook. Mrs. C. E. B. Russell, trans. New York, 1939.
On the Edge of the Primeval Forest. C. T. Campion, trans. London, 1922.
Out of My Life and Thought. C. T. Campion, trans. London, 1933.
The Psychiatric Study of Jesus. Charles R. Joy, trans. Boston, 1948.
The Quest for the Historical Jesus. New York, 1948.

For a look at Schweitzer from a point of view other than his own, see Gerald McKnight, *Verdict on Schweitzer: The Man Behind the Legend at Lambaréné* (New York, 1964).

OTHER RELEVANT MISSION MATERIAL

E. C. Parsons' *A Life for Africa* (New York, 1897) is the biography of Reverend Good. Robert H. Milligan's *The Jungle Folk of Africa* (New York, 1908) gives other details of Reverend Good's story.

By way of comparison with Nassau's work, Reverend Joseph Reading's *The Ogowe Band* (Philadelphia, 1890) is more typical of the missionary travel genre. It is particularly interesting for its descriptions of early Libreville (referred to in Chapter One), Glass, and Baraka.

The official Mission Board correspondence referred to is part of material contained in the archives of the Department of History, Presbyterian Church, U.S.A., in Philadelphia, and is used with their kind permission. Nassau's letter to Dr. Lowrie and the letters of Reverend Gault and Dr. Laffin are found in the Records of the Board of Missions, Secretaries' Files, African Mission 1835–1910 (vol. 9, no. 138, vol. 20, no. 97, and vol. 21, no. 7, respectively), on microfilm in Butler Library, Columbia University.

For those *truly* interested in missionary history, see the American Board of Commissioners for Foreign Missions, *Report,* published annually in Boston from 1843 until 1870, at which time the ABCFM Gaboon stations were transferred to the Presbyterian Church in the United States, Board of Foreign Missions. Their annual reports were published in New York until 1893, when the Société Évangelique du Paris took over the Ogooué stations.

For the parallel history of the Catholic Missions in Gabon, see Père J. B. Piolet, "Missions d'Afrique," in *Les Missions catholiques françaises au XIX siècle,* vol. v (Paris, 1902).

A NOTE ABOUT THE AUTHOR

Caroline Alexander is completing her doctorate in Classics
at Columbia University in New York. A Rhodes Scholar at
Oxford, she was lecturer in Classics at the University of
Malawi for three years, and has also lived in Europe and
the Caribbean. Her work has appeared in *The New Yorker.*

A NOTE ON THE TYPE

The text of this book was set by CRT in Compano, a film version of Palatino, a typeface designed by the noted German typographer Hermann Zapf. Named after Giovanbattista Palatino, a writing master of Renaissance Italy, Palatino was the first of Zapf's typefaces to be introduced in America. The first designs for the face were made in 1948, and the fonts for the complete face were issued between 1950 and 1952. Like all Zapf-designed typefaces, Palatino is beautifully balanced and exceedingly readable.

Composed, printed, and bound by
The Haddon Craftsmen, Inc.,
Scranton, Pennsylvania